Educating America

Educating America

How Ralph W. Tyler Taught America to Teach

MORRIS FINDER

FOREWORD BY HENRY LOUIS GATES, JR.

Westport, Connecticut
London

Library of Congress Cataloging-in-Publication Data

Finder, Morris, 1917–
    Educating America : how Ralph W. Tyler taught America to teach / Morris Finder ;
    foreword by Henry Louis Gates, Jr.
        p. cm.
    Includes bibliographical references and index.
    ISBN 0–275–98197–5 (alk. paper)
        1. Tyler, Ralph Winfred, 1902– 2. Educators—United States—Biography.
    3. Education—United States—History—20th century. I. Title.
    LA2317.T95F56 2004
    370′.92—dc22   2004049564
    [B]

British Library Cataloguing in Publication Data is available.

Library of Congress Catalog Card Number: 2004049564
ISBN: 0–275–98197–5

First published in 2004

Praeger Publishers, 88 Post Road West, Westport, CT 06881
An imprint of Greenwood Publishing Group, Inc.
www.praeger.com

Printed in the United States of America

The paper used in this book complies with the
Permanent Paper Standard issued by the National
Information Standards Organization (Z39.48–1984).

10 9 8 7 6 5 4 3 2 1

Contents

Foreword

"I think I may say, that of all the men we meet with, nine parts out of ten are what they are, good or evil, useful or not, by their education," wrote John Locke in a 1693 treatise on the subject. Four centuries later, Locke's belief in the paramount importance of education is widespread, even if we find ourselves a little less confident than he was about its basic principles, and a great deal less sanguine about its transformative powers. One reason that the educational system is such a battleground is that it has, in no small part, been entrusted with the very reproduction of our society. The question of what we want our schools to do has become bound up with another question: What sort of people do we want our children to be? Aims such as these are open to dispute—and in the realm of education, whatever can be disputed *will* be disputed.

This is why the Enlightenment dream of an entirely instrumental conception of pedagogy has proven so alluring, and so elusive. The dream, we might say, is of a *Consumer Reports* model of evaluation: Does this washing machine or that microwave do what it is supposed to do? Asking and answering such questions is a wonderfully straightforward business; to know what such machines *are* is to know what such machines are *for*. By contrast, a school is not a machine built with some purely instrumental purpose; an instructor's particular aims are never pregiven, fixed, and beyond revision. If you teach, and if you take your teaching seriously, you have to reflect not just upon what you are teaching but upon what you hope to achieve by doing so. That means attending not only to the *what* but to the *why*.

Ralph W. Tyler (1902–94) became one of the most important figures in twentieth-century education by pursuing the logic of this seemingly simple idea. You cannot evaluate something unless you know what it is meant to do. This much would appear self-evident—if a visitor from Mars evaluated a watch by its taste, or a candy bar by its ability to tell time, we would agree that the creature did not understand the purpose of these objects. All too often, however, attempts to measure educational achievement proceed with Martian-like obliviousness. Teaching lends itself to a variety of objectives; it is a complex human practice in the service of other complex human practices. Educational objectives may vary, legitimately, from classroom to classroom and place to place. Yet, as Tyler toured the classrooms of America he regularly found that teaching was being evaluated without any reflection on its purpose. Means were detached from ends. He found himself repeating the so-called Tyler Rationale: You cannot properly teach or assess teaching until you have determined what your objectives are.

To determine those objectives calls for reflection. How nice it would be if they came with the classroom assignment or fell into your lap like the instructions that accompany some Milton Bradley board game; but that is not how it works. Not only do they require deliberation but they should, ideally, be responsive to the particular needs of the students in question. This is what makes teaching hard, and what makes it matter. There have been countless attempts to industrialize public education—to bring some version of Frederick Winslow Taylor's "scientific management" to the classroom. That these attempts have met with failure is the inevitable consequence of the complex and variable nature of pedagogical ends. Education cannot be Taylorized—but it can usefully be Tylerized.

This book just might help with that. In *Educating America,* Morris Finder provides a briskly illuminating examination of the achievements of Ralph Tyler, who, though one of the most influential educators of the twentieth century, is surprisingly little known. An advisor to seven presidents of the United States, Tyler was a founding member and the first president of the National Academy of Education, dean of the University of Chicago's Division of Social Sciences under Robert Maynard Hutchins, and the first director of Stanford's Center for Advanced Study in the Behavioral Sciences. In the thirties, he oversaw a groundbreaking and in-depth evaluation of American high schools, with results that ultimately changed the way colleges admitted applicants. He wrote one of the most widely used guides to planning school curricula, one that moved students and teachers away from deadening routine. He devised a national program, now legally mandated, by which the success of the public education system could be assessed—and he did so, Finder shows, amid political battles and controversies. His role in shaping this country's educational policies in the twentieth century was unrivaled; his brilliantly original approach to curriculum design and evaluation made him one of the most important figures in American education.

These days, there is a great deal of talk about national standards, about assessing school performance by means of nationwide tests. Because it was Ralph Tyler who first devised such a program of nationwide educational assessment, you might assume that the current enthusiasm for national standards and testing represent the ascendance of his thought. In fact, his was a more demanding creed—not for him the putative panacea of "competition" or the one-size-fits-all certitudes of the psychometricians. But if you want insight into what is right and what is wrong about the current debate over standards, you would be well advised to start with the redoubtable Ralph Tyler.

First, though, cast aside your prejudices. Americans have grown accustomed to a debate that invokes two caricatured visions of education—one focusing on the transfer of rote knowledge and the other on the development of "critical" skills. On the one side is a glowering Thomas Gradgrind, on the other a flock of wood sprites with flowers in their hair. We are asked, even now, to choose between "curriculum-based" and "child-centered" models of education. Under such banners do neo-traditional approaches joust with the legatees of progressive pedagogy. Tyler, who despised cliché above all, cannot be assimilated to either of these strains. He was well trained in statistical techniques, and, unlike some child-centered sentimentalists, adopted a rigorously empirical approach toward education. Intuitions and anecdotal experience were to be ratified by sound empirical evidence. At the same time, he shared the democratizing impulse of the progressives, and he never lost sight of what made education vital—the welfare of the individual student.

In the course of a lifetime that spanned most of the twentieth century, Tyler witnessed sweeping changes in the character of American public education, beginning with the democratization of its enrollment, as a far greater percentage of American youth came to complete the full K-through-12 system. He thought that education could and should be a dynamic experience; in part because of his own efforts, he saw it become far more so than it once had been. Even as he watched educational crazes come and go—the new math, values clarification, creative spelling, and on and on—he never lost sight of the fundamentals or surrendered to shrill polemics. His vision of education was fundamentally democratic—it was not faddishly populist.

He was a man who helped shape his age, yet who could be stubbornly out of step with it. As Finder stresses, Tyler's views, buttressed by empirical evidence, often ran up against received wisdom—and sometimes even prevailed. Tyler doubted the merit of "tracking," grouping by ability in schools; he argued that smaller classes are not necessarily better. He cast a skeptical eye, as I mentioned, upon the proposed cure-all of competition, whether in the classroom or between schools, which he believed shifted focus on learning to winning. He was an opponent of the "bell curve" premise of standardized tests: Why, he demanded, would the curve you got when you charted random errors be appropriate to a purposeful activity like education?

To be sure, many of his views were guided by ethical, rather than strictly empirical, concerns. For Tyler, the value of liberal democracy—and, in particular, the ideal of moral individualism—underlay his distrust of much standardized testing. Many testers, he noted, were pleased to find a correlation of, say, 0.6 between SAT scores and first-year college grades; such predictive value, however imperfect, seemed to vindicate its worth in the admissions process. Tyler saw things differently; in his opinion, the reliance upon such crude statistical process raised questions of ethical responsibility. In a totalitarian regime where the people serve the state, he argued, such a system does its work; it provides institutions of higher learning with a crude but serviceable sorting mechanism. But liberal democracies are predicated upon moral individualism, the principle of equal concern toward persons, not statistical composites. Why content ourselves with a statistical method that generates aggregate predictions, this masterly statistician asked, when we could learn more about the individual in question and make a fairer decision? These were not merely instrumental question, as far as Tyler was concerned; they were, irreducibly, political ones.

I said that Tyler could be stubbornly out of step. It was among his most appealing traits. Perhaps I should explain that I came to hear of Ralph Tyler because of my interest in the social anthropologist Allison Davis, who was the first African-American to be given a regular status professorship at a mainstream university. When Davis's appointment at the University of Chicago was proposed, in 1942, it met with a strong current of resistance. What secured the appointment was the vigorous perseverance of the head of the university's education department—Ralph Tyler. Often, when Tyler was out of step with the times, his peers would just have to hurry to catch up.

Nor was Davis the only beneficiary of his eye for talent. Indeed, like the master pedagogue he was, Tyler could count among his accomplishments the careers that he fostered or launched. Among them, as Finder relates in a fascinating final chapter, were those of such luminaries as Daniel Boorstin, David Riesman, James Michener, and Bruno Bettelheim. (There is a remarkable revelation here, an episode told for the first time, of how Tyler helped secure Bettelheim's release from a Nazi concentration camp.)

We can add Morris Finder's own career to the list. A professor emeritus of education at the State University of New York at Albany and the author of *A Structural View of English* and *Reason and Art in Teaching Secondary School English*, Finder was a student and longtime friend of Tyler's. He devoted many years to interviewing and corresponding with Tyler and benefited from access to Tyler's personal archives. He is, in short, uniquely qualified to have written this, the only book on the work of Ralph Tyler.

Like the Tyler Rationale itself, Morris Finder's account is deceptively modest; the author has carefully defined his objective—to describe and appraise Tyler's achievements, especially in connection to his two most ambitious projects, the Eight-Year Study and the National Assessment of Educational Progress. Best of all, he has executed the task with clarity and brevity, two qualities Tyler held in the highest esteem. Tyler was fortunate to have such a meticulous and clear-eyed expositor, and we are fortunate to have such a meticulous and clear-eyed exposition.

Henry Louis Gates, Jr.
Cambridge, Massachusetts

Acknowledgments

In April 1986, Ralph W. Tyler visited the State University of New York at Albany as a consultant. I was then on SUNY's faculty, and I was his host during his visit; I had known Tyler since my days as a graduate student at the University of Chicago during the early 1950s. When Tyler had completed his 1986 consultancy in Albany, I proposed to him that I write an account of his career. He readily agreed but suggested that, because of his difficulty in hearing—he was then eighty-four and going deaf—our long-distance communication be conducted by mail. In the years that followed, until his death in 1994, we met in various cities throughout the United States—Boston, Chicago, San Francisco, Washington, D.C., New York City, Amherst (Massachusetts), and Milpitas and Palo Alto (California).

My main source in the writing of *Educating America* is a collection of 376 letters Tyler wrote me between 1986 and 1992. I am deeply grateful to him for the time and help in making himself and his sources accessible to me. The collection will constitute part of the Ralph W. Tyler Papers at the Regenstein Library, a division of the University of Chicago libraries. I received further assistance from Ralph Tyler's son, daughters, and their families: Ralph W. Tyler, Jr., Ann Tyler Fathy, Helen Tyler Parisi, and Helen's husband, Dominic Parisi. I am grateful as well to the State University of New York at Albany for awarding me a grant from its Faculty Research Award Program.

I am indebted to Malca Chall, who conducted and wrote an extensive oral history of Tyler about his career; to the late Helen Kolodziey, who produced a bibliography of Tyler's writings, more than seven hundred items; to Patricia Albjerg Graham, whose criticism and analysis of an earlier version improved the present one; to the late Paul B. Diederich of the

Educational Testing Service, who knew Tyler well, having participated in the Eight-Year Study; and to the writer and editor Joseph Epstein. Others informed me about aspects of Tyler's career, including James Michener, David Riesman, Francis Keppel, John Gardner, John Stalnaker, Thelma Gwinn Thurstone, and Frank Stanton. Sophie Bloom, the widow of Benjamin Bloom, gave me many facts about her late husband's career. With respect to the background of the Spencer Foundation, I am thankful to the Foundation's Judith Klippenstein. For all his help, generosity, and encouragement, I'll always be grateful to Henry Louis (Skip) Gates, Jr., W.E.B. Du Bois Professor of the Humanities at Harvard University.

I am especially indebted to Professor John I. Goodlad, who wrote his Ph.D. dissertation at the University of Chicago under Tyler's guidance. Goodlad is one of the most distinguished of American educators—professor of education at the University of Washington and president of the Institute for Educational Inquiry. He continues to be active beyond the usual age of retirement. When I was a graduate student at the University of Chicago, I was his student, and he later served as a member of my dissertation committee. Since then I have consulted Professor Goodlad on various matters, always with enlightening results.

In a sense, *Educating America* is a family enterprise. It has been vastly improved by the editorial oversight of our son Joseph, a novelist and a contributor of political commentaries and reviews to the *New York Times.* Our daughter Lisa, a librarian at New York City's Hunter College, has identified and located several hard-to-find sources; she also updated Helen Kolodziey's bibliography. Our son Henry, the editorial director of *The New Yorker,* has been generous with his counsel. As to rights to cite and quote, I have consulted our daughter Susan, a lawyer. For clarification of some of Ralph Tyler's illnesses, I have consulted our son Jonathan, a physician.

Finally, I am exceedingly grateful to Natalie, my wife of more than half a century, a former teacher in the Chicago elementary schools, a teacher of English in the Chicago City Junior Colleges, and an educator of prospective and practicing teachers at the College of St. Rose in Albany, New York. For the book in your hand, she did much to keep things on track: identifying sources, supplying footnotes, and in general letting me know where I had gone astray.

Ralph W. Tyler:
A Chronology

1902   Born, April 22, Chicago

1921   A.B., Doane College

1921–22   High School Teacher, Pierre, S.D.

1922–26   Faculty Member, University of Nebraska

1923   A.M., University of Nebraska

1927   Ph.D., University of Chicago

1927–29   Faculty Member, University of North Carolina

1929–38   Faculty Member, Ohio State University

1934   Published *Constructing Achievement Tests*

1934–42   Director of Evaluation, Eight-Year Study

1938–49   Chairman, Department of Education, University of Chicago

1939–45   Director, Cooperative Study in General Education

1942   Published (with E. R. Smith) *Appraising and Recording Student Progress*

1943–53   Director, Examinations Staff, U.S. Armed Forces Institute

1948–53   Dean, Division of Social Sciences, University of Chicago

1949   Published *Basic Principles of Curriculum and Instruction*

1953–67   Founding Director, Center for Advanced Study in the Behavioral Sciences, Stanford, California

1961   Published *Social Forces Influencing American Education*

1964–68   Chairman, Exploratory Committee on Assessing the Progress
            of Education (became the NAEP)

1965–69   President, National Academy of Education

1967–70   Chairman, Research Advisory Council of the U.S. Office of
            Education

1969   Published *Educational Evaluation: New Roles, New Means*

1969   President, System Development Foundation, San Francisco

1971–72   Acting President, Social Science Research Council

1975–78   Vice President, Center for the Study of Democratic Institu-
            tions

1976   Published *Perspectives on American Education*

1994   Died, February 18, San Diego

PART I

All Schooling Is Local

CHAPTER 1

Introduction

One day in February 1938, while I was in a Walgreens drugstore on the South Side of Chicago waiting for the soda jerk to prepare my chocolate malted, I noticed a copy of *Time* magazine in the magazine rack and began leafing through it. In the "Education" section I read a brief article announcing that "Ralph Winfred Tyler, 35 . . . who smokes cigars incessantly and races trains in his automobile . . . a professor of education and crack testman at Ohio State University" was to become the head of the University of Chicago's education department the following autumn.[1] That small item has remained in my mind ever since; it was a revelation to read about an educator portrayed not in the usual way—prim, meek, and desiccated—but as lively and colorful.

Ralph Tyler later went on to become head of the University of Chicago's education department (1938–49), dean of its Division of Social Sciences (1948–53), founding president of the National Academy of Education (1965–69), and founding director of the first social sciences think tank, the Center for Advanced Study in the Behavioral Sciences, in Stanford, California (1953–67). In addition to his seven-hundred-some publications and countless talks, Tyler's influence was felt, in particular, in three projects of historic significance:

- The Eight-Year Study, an innovative nationwide experiment begun in the early 1930s. Until then, the American high school curriculum had been intended mainly to prepare students to enter college. The Eight-Year Study was designed to develop and assess a broader kind of curriculum, one suited not only to the college bound but to those planning to enter the workplace after high school—suddenly a major percentage of the nation's high school students, with the shortage of jobs caused by the Depression.

- A course syllabus on the principles of education that continues to be sold worldwide more than fifty years after its first publication in 1949. *Basic Principles of Curriculum and Instruction* had a profound impact and has remained in use largely because it states in plain words what the principles of education are and how they work.
- The National Assessment of Educational Progress (NAEP), the first project designed to appraise the results of the nation's schooling, using a uniform system of assessment. It has come to be known as "the nation's report card." At the request of President John F. Kennedy's commissioner of education, Francis Keppel, Tyler was instrumental in designing, and campaigning for public acceptance of, the NAEP, which still provides Congress and the public with their main source of information about the performance of America's schools. Administration of the NAEP is now an obligation of the federal government.

In January 1950, as a graduate student at the University of Chicago, I enrolled in a course taught by Ralph Tyler. It met in the evening, once a week, not on the university campus but in downtown Chicago, to accommodate the area's teachers and other practicing and prospective educators.

No longer head of the education department, Tyler was then dean of Chicago's social sciences division. Robert Maynard Hutchins, the renowned president, later chancellor, of the university, who had recruited Tyler from Ohio State University, had appointed him dean. It was, to be sure, a remarkable appointment. Many in academia and the public have always held departments and schools of education in low esteem, and on a scale of snootiness, Hutchins and most of Chicago's faculty ranked high. It seemed remarkable that Hutchins, a strong proponent of faculty self-governance, could get away with appointing a member of the education department to administer such an illustrious division, the members of which included Milton Friedman, Hans Morgenthau, Leo Strauss, and Friedrich Hayek. Clearly Tyler's success as head of the education department for ten years and his national distinction as an educator outweighed his lowly education-department origins.

Tyler entered the room for the first class meeting that January evening looking like a conservative businessman or professional—he wore a dark blue suit, white starched shirt, tasteful unobtrusive tie, and polished black shoes. He was forty-seven then, a sturdy five feet seven, and weighed about 135 pounds. His head was large and bald; alert, light-blue eyes shone beneath thick lenses. Unlike many in the professoriat, he affected no tweedy airs. Exuding small-town friendliness, he might have been a successful country doctor. His manner was warm, self-assured, and approachable. He was a midwesterner and proudly so; his speech, like Harry Truman's, was plain and straightforward.

Tyler's class sessions consisted mainly of discussions about problems that arise unavoidably in teaching: ends, means, and assessment. I had heard that Tyler was a dull teacher, but no one I knew would have agreed with that opinion. If he once had been less than inspiring, apparently his national distinction as an educator and his status at a great university had enlivened his teaching. He encouraged discussion and questions, and he consistently gave incisive replies, usually with concrete reference to current and past practices, interspersing humor, sometimes ribald. It was clear that his knowledge of educational matters, historical and current, was encyclopedic.

For all his involvement, then and in the decades to come, in the more theoretical aspects of testing and evaluation and in propagating his highly original notions of how to reform and even revolutionize pedagogy, Tyler's chief interest was in the individual teacher, the classroom, the one-on-one experience of teaching. While holding multiple positions, he invariably made himself available to calls from the schools, where by his own estimate he spent about ten hours a week.[2] He was convinced, and argued all his life, that the problems and the solutions always begin in the classroom, that the problems of local schools were paramount. Just as the late Thomas P. ("Tip") O'Neill used to insist that "all politics is local," Tyler believed that all public *schooling* is local.

Through his intensive hands-on involvement in hundreds of classrooms, Tyler came to realize that there could never be such a thing as a truly uniform, national approach to education. Schools throughout the country inevitably serve their local communities, which vary widely. Therefore, he regarded the federal pressure for nationwide tests, standards, and curricula as unsuited to the very different communities across the country and doomed to failure.

Very early on, Tyler came to the realization that perhaps the single best way to help professionals improve was by means of what he called a "workshop," a seminar or gathering of teachers in order to solve problems or increase understanding. As commonplace as the notion of the workshop is today, it was a breakthrough when Tyler came up with it in the summer of 1936, at Ohio State University, as part of the Eight-Year Study. (It is a little known fact that Tyler coined the term "workshop," in this sense.) Before then, the prevailing method of instructing teachers had been "teachers' institutes," which were nothing more than occasions for teachers to sit passively, listen, and presumably become enlightened and inspired. Tyler, however, was more interested in having teachers learn how to improve their knowledge and skills—which he knew could not be accomplished in a lecture format.

In fact, one could not simply issue an edict to a teacher and hope to change his or her ways. He believed that one of the basic principles of human organizations is that professionals who consider themselves adequate do what they think best, and you cannot tell them what to do and expect them to change their activities. They may, if they are afraid of power, report that they are doing what authority demands—but they will not actually do what is demanded. A teacher will always teach the way he or she has found effective. Pronouncements from Washington, proclamations from armchair experts, and even directives from the principal's office may influence what teachers *claim* they do—but not what they really do.

In the decades since the first Tyler workshop, Ralph Tyler's achievements have remained unmatched. Very few other figures were as influential as Tyler in democratizing high school education; certainly no one did more to devise effective ways to evaluate the progress of the nation's schools. It is no wonder that governments, foundations, and seven presidents of the United States sought his counsel.[3] Yet outside his profession, his name has remained all but unknown.

CHAPTER 2

The Making of an Educator

In the early 1890s, Tyler's father, William Augustus Tyler, began his practice as a physician in Cozad, Nebraska, where he had been raised. By 1898, his income had reached what was then the princely sum of five thousand dollars a year, at which point his parents, worried about what they regarded as the corrupting power of money and convinced that prosperity would tempt them all to become less God-fearing, argued that William must give up his medical career and become a minister.[1]

William Augustus Tyler had concluded himself from his medical practice that the body heals itself and that what patients needed most was someone to "work with their spirits"—spiritual counsel, not medical treatment.[2] In 1900 he gave up his practice to prepare for the ministry. He moved his family to Chicago, where he enrolled in the Garrett Biblical Institute, associated with Northwestern University. At the time, he and his wife had two sons, Tracy, age five, and Harry, two. Ralph was born in Chicago on April 22, 1902, while his father was in divinity school.

Two years after Ralph's birth, his father was ordained as a Methodist clergyman. That year the family returned to Nebraska, where another son, Keith, was born in 1905. The Reverend Tyler became minister of the Methodist church in Table Rock. Soon, however, William Tyler left Methodism, unwilling to follow church policy, which dictated that ministers must serve wherever they are appointed. Reverend Tyler wanted to raise his family in a community where a college or university was located, valuing the cultural and educational advantages of such towns. At his wife's suggestion he became a Congregationalist, probably the church of her Pilgrim forebears; in any case, Congregationalists, unlike Methodists, run their own congregations. After serving as a minister in several small Nebraska towns, he ended his career as superintendent of the state's

Congregational churches. He retired to a Congregationalist retirement home for clergy and missionaries in Claremont, California, where in 1950, at the age of eighty-three, he suffered a fatal heart attack while going door to door urging residents to vote against Congressman Richard Nixon in Nixon's race against Helen Gahagan Douglas. According to Ralph Tyler, his father's strongly held belief that human service was far more important than financial gain had a marked influence on the course of his career.[3]

Money was in short supply when Ralph Tyler was growing up, but that was no deterrent to him. He began high school in Crete, Nebraska, in 1914, when he was twelve. He completed the four-year course in three years while working seven days a week, nine hours a day, in a creamery, first as a can washer and later as a taster and grader of cream. Following his graduation, he enrolled in Doane College, a small Congregational institution also in Crete, and majored in science. Throughout his college years he supported himself as a telegrapher for the Burlington Railroad, working seven days a week, eight hours a day. He graduated with honors in 1921 and continued with the Burlington Railroad, planning to save money for medical school.

When his father became superintendent of Nebraska's Congregational churches, Tyler moved with his family from Crete to Lincoln, the state capital. There, in the summer of 1921, at his parents' Independence Day party, he met a Mr. Haskins, the principal of the Pierre, South Dakota, high school, who also happened to be the son of one of his father's classmates in the theological seminary. Mr. Haskins, learning that Ralph had been a science major, told him that his high school had been without a science teacher since the war and suggested that Tyler teach in Pierre for two or three years to save money for medical school. The pay was less than that of a telegrapher, but the principal suggested that Ralph could make up the difference by supervising Pierre's swimming pool during the summer. Tyler, seeing that he was needed, accepted the offer.

On the following August 31st, Ralph married Flora Volz, whom he had met at Doane College. Flora and Ralph had two daughters and a son: Helen, born in 1922; Ralph, Jr., born in 1924; and Ann, born in 1932. The marriage was to end in divorce after twenty-one years.[4]

Now teaching at the high school in Pierre, Tyler found that his students came from a variety of backgrounds: some were native Americans, some the children of cow punchers, others the children of local tradesmen or state officials and civil servants.[5] (One of his students was Ernest Lawrence, builder of the first cyclotron, later a Nobel laureate in physics, whose father was state superintendent of public instruction.)[6]

An inexperienced teacher will often become discouraged teaching such a diverse group. Tyler instead was engaged by the challenge. He gave up plans for medical school and decided to learn more about the problem of teaching such different students in one classroom, and about the challenges of education generally. In the summer of 1922, after his first year of teaching, he enrolled as a master's degree student in education at the University of Nebraska, planning to return to Pierre the following autumn.

The head of the Department of Secondary Education at Nebraska was Professor Herbert Brownell, a friend of the Tyler family. Sixteen years earlier, the Tyler and Brownell families had been next-door neighbors in Peru, Nebraska, where the Reverend Tyler was minister of the Congregational church and Professor Brownell was on the faculty of the Peru Normal School. Ralph Tyler had also been a classmate of Professor Brownell's son Samuel, in Nebraska's first kindergarten, at the Peru Normal School. (Samuel Brownell went on to become President Dwight D. Eisenhower's first commissioner of education and later superintendent of the Detroit schools; his brother, Herbert, Jr., would become Eisenhower's attorney general and chairman of the Republican National Committee.)

Professor Brownell, taking notice of Tyler's ability, asked him to remain at Nebraska after the summer and teach a course in physics to war veterans who lacked the background needed to succeed in the physics curriculum. He also asked him to teach two courses in the high school of the University of Nebraska, adding that Tyler could get his master's degree at the same time.

Tyler accepted the offer, and he never returned to Pierre. By the following year, Tyler had his master's degree; he continued teaching at the University of Nebraska's high school and supervising student teachers of science. In the spring of 1926, Professor Brownell urged Tyler to seek a doctorate at the University of Chicago. Brownell, whose son Sam would be working toward his doctorate at Yale, offered to lend Ralph the funds to do so. The University of Chicago was the right place for Tyler, Brownell advised, because the head of education there was Charles Hubbard Judd, whom Brownell considered to be outstanding in applying scientific principles to problems of schooling. In Brownell's view, Tyler was by nature a scientist and would find Judd a compatible guide. Judd was nationally distinguished as a psychologist and a former president of the American Psychological Association. (*Time* magazine would later refer to Judd as "perhaps the first U.S. educational statesman.")[7]

Brownell's influence on Tyler went far beyond even his perceptive guidance and financial support. He imparted to Tyler his belief that there should be a system in teaching. Brownell was an advocate of the pedagogical ideas of the German philosopher and educator Johann Friedrich

Herbart, who proposed that teaching be conceived as a time-ordered series of formal steps.[8] Tyler, however, came to his own understanding of Herbartianism—that the abilities learners are to acquire determine the sequence of teaching as well as its nature and the testing appropriate to it.

In September 1926, with a two-thousand-dollar loan from Brownell, Tyler, accompanied by his wife and their two children, moved to Chicago to begin his doctoral work. Remarkably, he obtained his Ph.D. in only a year. He emerged from his graduate-school year with some clear ideas about the work that lay ahead, his views strongly influenced by several faculty members.

Charles Hubbard Judd, for example, held that education is an empirical science and impressed upon Tyler the importance of understanding education firsthand from the schools rather than from books or armchair speculation. Books, in Judd's view, must follow direct school experience.[9] John Dewey had been the first head of Chicago's education department, but Judd, ever the experimentalist, never hired a philosopher of education. He warned that many in and around schools—which are, after all, concerned with the well-being of children—were prone to soft-headed emotionalism. Practices and policies must derive from facts and tested principles, he insisted, rather than from speculation and fashionable notions about current practices.

Judd, on the basis of his observations, had concluded that learners can generalize—that, for instance, a little practice in adding seven and five, six and three, and so forth, can be followed by teaching the *process* of addition, leading to general competence in adding. Throughout his career, Tyler was to follow Judd's theory of generalization.

Another Chicago faculty member who influenced Tyler was George Sylvester Counts, a professor of educational sociology and a social activist.[10] In a 1927 article, Counts argued that an effective curriculum has to incorporate subject matter, in the sense of scholarship.[11] Throughout his career, Tyler regarded scholarship as the best available source for learning about the world, in contrast to newspaper opinions, hearsay, or received tradition. Under Counts's direction Tyler studied the experience of immigrant Poles in Chicago and their emergence from an isolated enclave to positions of power in Chicago politics.

In order to supplement the funds that Brownell had loaned him, Tyler found work as a statistician for a project in Chicago called the Commonwealth Teacher Training Study, directed by Werrett Wallace Charters. Charters, who embraced a notion popular in those days called "social efficiency," called himself a "curriculum engineer."[12] The author of a book entitled *Curriculum Construction* (1923) and later the founding editor

of the *Journal of Higher Education,* Charters had received a Ph.D. at
Chicago in 1904 under John Dewey.

The Commonwealth Teacher Training Study was an attempt to develop
a curriculum for preparing teachers by finding out from teachers on the
job, as well as principals and others, the various tasks that teachers do—
or ought to do—and the personal characteristics and attitudes that teachers ought to possess. The study was designed to be a kind of "scientific
curriculum construction," derived from earlier notions about "social efficiency" and the belief that the chief duty of schools is to prepare learners to be working adults.[13] The curriculum of higher and vocational
education, according to this view, should inculcate the skills and desired
personal traits of, say, practicing teachers, librarians, veterinarians, secre-
taries, and so on.

Charters had undertaken a similar study in 1920 at Stephens College,
a private women's college in Columbia, Missouri. Asked by the college
to design a new curriculum, Charters had begun with the assumption that
being a woman is in itself an occupation. He approached his research in
a scientific manner, asking the women he and his staff surveyed what they
did during a single week. His staff took the ninety-five thousand replies
and classified them into 7,300 groups, and then into such categories as
food, clothing, and health—which became the content of the curriculum
he proposed.[14]

At Chicago, however, Charters's scientific method was received with
scorn. Judd, among others, ridiculed Charters's approach, contending that
Charters was uncritically following the atomistic specificity of Edward L.
Thorndike and thereby disregarding the main point of education—
generalized learning. Instead of resenting the criticism, Charters asked his
critics for evidence in support of their arguments. Then, convinced that
the criticism was valid, Charters modified his procedures, seeking to reduce the specificities into fewer statements of wider generalizability.

Charters, of course, had run up against the age-old controversy over
whether it is the duty of schools to tailor their curriculum to what people
actually do for a living. It is, for instance, part of today's popular wisdom
that since computers are everywhere, schools must as a matter of course
teach "computer literacy." In 1897, John Dewey had dismissed the con-
tention that the job of schools is direct preparation for adulthood. He
argued that in a technically advanced society no one can predict the social, economic, or industrial conditions of the next twenty years. It is
impossible, he wrote, to prepare children for a future that no one knows
about. The best preparation for children, Dewey concluded, is to help
them become intelligent about their present-day concerns and interests.
(Dewey also believed that to prepare children for future employment was

hardly motivational.)[15] Obviously, with his "curriculum engineering," Charters had broken with John Dewey, his mentor.

As a statistician for the project, Tyler had to analyze and classify vast numbers of cards, each containing a suggested task or trait.[16] Years later, having successfully directed such large-scale enterprises as conceiving and initiating the assessment of the nation's schools, Tyler credited Charters with teaching him clear, systematic procedures for leading large projects and, in particular, the importance of expressing the goals clearly, engaging the entire group in the project, eliciting suggestions as well as criticisms, and accepting inputs likely to move the project forward. When Charters died in 1952, Tyler wrote a tribute to him, an article entitled "The Leader of Major Educational Projects."[17]

Charters's influence on Tyler was felt in another, smaller way as well. Charters saw Tyler's "tense interactions with colleagues" as a manifestation of stress in Tyler's personal life—at twenty-five, Tyler was simultaneously engaged in graduate work and in the Charters project, and had a young and growing family. He suggested that Tyler take up cigar smoking to relieve tension.[18] From then on, at professional meetings and after giving presentations, Tyler would light up a small Antony and Cleopatra cigar, a habit he gave up only when, in 1966, he developed a cancerous spot (fortunately small and curable) in his throat.

Galvanized by a range of influences—from Judd's empiricism to Dewey's stress on democracy and motivation in learning—Tyler left Chicago. Originally, because he was on leave from the University of Nebraska, he had planned to return to Nebraska to work with a proposed Bureau of Educational Research, which the state legislature had planned to finance. But now Nebraska was suffering a farm depression, and the legislature was unable to provide the funds. University salaries had been cut, and Tyler, with two children to support, would have had to return to his old salary, $1,400 a year.[19]

One of Tyler's classmates at Chicago, Arnold King, had been on leave from the University of North Carolina at Chapel Hill. The dean there had asked him to try, while in Chicago, to recruit someone who understood testing. King suggested Tyler. In 1927, UNC offered Tyler the position of associate professor of education and assistant director of its Bureau of Educational Research, at a handsome annual salary of $3,500.[20]

At Chapel Hill he spent much of his time driving through swamp and mountain regions of North Carolina, teaching extension classes, developing a state testing program, and assisting teachers with their problems. Rather than giving fast solutions, he preferred to provide ways for the teachers to discover solutions on their own. From these efforts he and a colleague, Douglas Waples, wrote *Research Methods and Teacher's Problems: A Manual for Systematic Studies of Classroom Procedure* (published by Macmillan in 1930).

In 1929, Tyler returned to Chicago to teach for the summer term. W. W. Charters, still at Chicago, was planning to take a position as head of the Bureau of Educational Research at Ohio State University, and he needed someone to administer the bureau's Division of Accomplishment Testing. Knowing Tyler's background in statistics and mathematics, Charters asked him to move to OSU, an invitation Tyler promptly accepted.[21]

Tyler had always taken on at least two jobs at once, but soon the pressure caught up with him. While he was at Columbus in 1930, he developed a stomach ulcer; his weight dropped from 135 to 124 pounds. He and his physician assumed that the ulcer had resulted from tension, as was commonly believed. Tyler's physician told him, "You won't have long to live if you keep up your worrying and tension."[22] Tyler tried to modulate his response to stress, to teach himself not to worry, but in short order he took on yet another task—what turned out to be one of the greatest educational experiments ever attempted.

CHAPTER 3

Democratizing High Schools and College Admissions

During the Depression of the 1930s, the nation's high schools filled with millions of teenagers who, in more prosperous times, would have dropped out of school and gladly gone to work. These "nonacademic" students found high school frustrating and disappointing, even stultifying. The curriculum seemed remote from their concerns. It was widely felt among educators that these disgruntled students would create havoc throughout the nation's high schools.

Most public high schools in those days were formal, stuffy, and rigid places designed for the college bound. In those classrooms substantive discussions occurred between teacher and class or between teacher and individual learner, rarely among the students themselves. Because of college entrance requirements, school administrations feared it would be unsound to make any changes that might turn schools into more pleasant places in which to teach and learn. The unspoken assumption on the part of parents and teachers had long been that schools were, after all, different from businesses, professions, or churches. They were *supposed* to be disagreeable. The curriculum should be demanding, and the students should be highly disciplined. This was the way it was supposed to be.

Until World War I, even elementary schools operated under these assumptions. After the war, however, American society became more liberated, with a "new freedom" in manners and morals expressed in bobbed hair, shorter skirts, and more open communication and relationships between the sexes. Responding to these social changes, and influenced by such works as John Dewey's *The School and Society* (1899) and *Interest and Effort in Education* (1913), a new generation of progressive leaders in education—including Carleton Washburne, Ella Flagg Young, Alice

Keliher, and Helen Parkhurst—wrought changes in the elementary schools. Suddenly grade schools became more informal, democratic, and humane places, their curricula far more suited to the interests of the students.

But the emancipation stopped at the high school door. Daunted by the serious business of preparing students for college, the high schools maintained their austere ways. The rigid atmosphere seemed particularly oppressive to nonacademically inclined students who had—compounding the problem—just graduated from the newly reformed elementary schools.

In 1932, the Progressive Education Association (PEA)—an organization founded thirteen years earlier with the aim of "the freest and fullest development of the individual, based upon the scientific study of his physical, mental, spiritual, and social characteristics and needs"—launched a nationwide experiment.[1] Its goal was to adapt curricula to the students then entering the high schools, and then to appraise the results. This experiment was called the "Thirty-Schools Study," or, more commonly, the "Eight-Year Study."

Each of thirty or so high schools enrolled in the study (there were a few dropouts and late entries) was to plan its own curriculum, one that would be uniquely suited to its learners and its community. These schools, dispersed throughout the nation, served a wide variety of communities and learners. They included both public schools and a progressive strain of private schools. (One participant, for instance, was New York's private, and progressive, Dalton School; such traditional places as Exeter and Groton were generally satisfied with their programs and chose not to participate in the study.)[2]

In order to free them to innovate, the thirty high schools were released from state requirements having to do with providing the conventional college-entrance curricula. With a few exceptions, their students took no college-entrance examinations. Instead, the schools would submit evaluative records to the colleges. Every major accredited college in the nation, except Fordham, agreed to those conditions.

At the end of the first year, however, a problem of evaluation arose. A member of the study's directing committee, William S. Learned of the Carnegie Corporation, was enthusiastic about using the General Culture Test, which had been developed by the Cooperative Test Service of the Pennsylvania Study of School and College Relations. Learned, an author of that test, insisted that the schools use it to assess the results of the study. But the participating high school principals rebelled, contending that this test did not correspond to what their schools were teaching and so could hardly be a reasonable measure of their success. They threatened to pull their schools out of the study, which would effectively have ended it.

The crisis worsened when the Carnegie Foundation, at Learned's urging, decided to stop underwriting the evaluative phase of the project. At the annual meeting of the study's participants during the summer of 1934 at the Princeton Inn, a member of the directing committee—Boyd Henry Bode, a professor of the philosophy of education at Ohio State University—announced that a young colleague of his named Ralph Tyler, who had an office across the hall from him, had some new ideas about evaluation. He suggested bringing Tyler in to discuss the problem. Tyler, who was teaching for the summer at Chapel Hill, came up to Princeton, where he was questioned for hours by the assembled study participants.[3] At the end of the day, persuaded by his ideas, they asked Tyler to become research director of the study's evaluation staff. The evaluation phase was still unfunded—the Carnegie Foundation's board refused to reconsider—so the president of Carnegie, Frederic Paul Keppel, persuaded the General Education Fund of the Rockefeller Foundation to step in.

Tyler's commonsense assumption was that what the students were supposed to learn had to determine what happened in the classroom and thus how the results should be evaluated. This clear-headed approach quickly influenced the entire project. What a school ought to teach and what a student ought to learn, Tyler argued, determine and legitimize all aspects of teaching and testing. This simple, forceful logic—the plainest of commonsense it seems to us now, but alien thinking in those days—came to be known later as "the Tyler Rationale."

The Tyler Rationale infused much of the thinking about the Eight-Year Study, especially when it came to the vexed question of standardized testing. The graduates of the Thirty Schools, admitted to college without the presumptive benefit of conventional college-entrance courses and tests, did at least as well in college as those who had been subjected to standardized tests. This was an important revelation.

As Tyler explained later, standardized tests had become widely accepted not because they were effective predictors of performance but for different reasons entirely. During World War I, the U.S. Army had hired psychologists to develop tests for classifying recruits—specifically, for predicting success in such army training programs as schools for officer candidates, for the signal corps, for cooks and bakers, and so on. The psychologists developed two instruments: the Army Alpha Test for the literate and the Army Beta Test for the illiterate. "Their relatively modest success in prediction," he wrote, "led to the development of psychometrics, by psychologists, not educators."[4]

After the war, these psychometricians took jobs in colleges and universities, where they taught the techniques they had acquired during their army service. Those now employed in schools and departments of education propagated these approaches as methods both of research and of testing.

But even before the heyday of psychometrics, the College Entrance Examination Board, which was founded in 1900, had served as a gatekeeper for Ivy League colleges. The CEEB guided the writing of the examinations, which were based on particular texts and expected competencies that were incorporated in the curricula of such private schools as Groton and Exeter but were not necessarily familiar in the public high schools. Exclusive private secondary schools across the nation taught this CEEB curriculum, and as a result, children of the wealthy received a significant boost over the CEEB hurdle. This gatekeeping served to stifle creative teachers, who were compelled to teach the college entrance material on the logic that their students would be at a disadvantage if they did not.

The CEEB, which thus favored old-line private schools, also tended to skew the student bodies of the Ivy League colleges. The majority of Harvard undergraduates, for instance, came from the northeastern states.[5] James Bryant Conant, who became the president of Harvard in 1933, wanted Harvard to become more of a national institution and less a creature of the Eastern Establishment. Conant learned from the Eight-Year Study that the college-entrance tests and courses were dispensable, even irrelevant. After all, as Ralph Tyler's evaluation program had shown, success in college could be ably predicted by assessing the student's competence in reading, writing, and just one high school subject. Tyler had also found that mathematics ability correlated with success only in engineering and technical institutions.[6]

So Conant persuaded the CEEB, which had sponsored the Scholastic Aptitude Test since 1926, to reformulate its college-admissions examination to make the conditions for passing it independent of any particular curriculum.[7] Today's SAT, now produced and administered by the Educational Testing Service, is the result of Conant's, and thus Tyler's, influence, and a consequence of the Eight-Year Study.

The study also gave Tyler a great deal of experience with various schools nationwide, providing a background, and much raw material, that served him in the years to come. With his earlier experiences at Nebraska, North Carolina, and Ohio State and his continuing involvement with a large number of very different schools, he had become still further informed about the realities of administering schools and of teaching and learning in their classrooms.

The Eight-Year Study was in full swing when in 1938 Robert Maynard Hutchins, the president of the University of Chicago, recruited Tyler to head the university's department of education. In order to induce Tyler to move, Hutchins had to provide for Tyler's Eight-Year Study evaluation staff. In fact, Tyler started at Chicago with no fewer than three positions: administering the education department, serving as a university examiner, and directing the evaluation staff of the study.[8]

The ambitious undertaking ended in 1941. The five volumes of the study's report were not published until 1942, by which time the nation was at war, and as a result the study got far less attention than it might have had in peacetime. Still, its effects were significant and lasting.

CHAPTER 4

The Tyler Rationale

One of Tyler's most enduring achievements was a book—a booklet, really—that he dictated over the course of a few weekends in the late 1940s.[1] It was a modest course syllabus with the unimaginative title *Basic Principles of Curriculum and Instruction*. At first, as a typewritten, stapled-together set of pages, it was sold in the University of Chicago's bookstores. But demand for the booklet among educators began to grow nationally, then internationally; the University of Chicago Press published it in 1949 as a small-format, eighty-three-page paperback. It has remained in print ever since;[2] it has been translated into at least eight languages, with bootleg copies in an unknown number of other languages, including Afghani Persian.[3] No other publication of its kind matches its brevity, clarity, comprehensiveness, or longevity.

The elegantly simple logic behind both his syllabus and the classes he taught was the Tyler Rationale—that what a school ought to teach and what a student ought to learn determine and legitimize all aspects of teaching and testing. Tyler had found that this elementary insight was lacking in most schools, colleges, and universities he had visited. Most teachers and professors, he concluded, were preoccupied with their immediate tasks and scarcely aware, if at all, of what they wanted students to acquire. A professor of history might be immersed in his lectures on the rise of the English middle class; a second-grade teacher might see her teaching as "covering" the Scott-Foresman second-grade reader; a teacher of high school science might be intent on getting his students to dissect frogs or participate in experiments on magnetism. Yet none of them had a clear idea of what abilities their students were to gain, or why.

In Tyler's view, endeavors like these become instruments of education only when subject matter and what the student is to gain from it become explicit, and thereby determine what is to be taught and tested. There is no topic, no Shakespeare play, no discourse of John Milton that is by itself educational; subject matter itself cannot be an educational aim. *Macbeth* is content, whereas "Explain the reasons for Macbeth's downfall" at least partially specifies what the student is to gain from the study of that play, and thereby of other plays as well.

The preoccupation of educators with content alone distracts them from thinking through what abilities, exactly, their students are supposed to acquire. This everyday confusion, this dwelling on means without ends, wastes enormous material and human resources, for as Tyler often observed, bad teaching costs school districts and colleges the same as good. What *appears* to be good teaching may result in no learning worth having.

Truly gifted teachers, moreover, may not be aware of why they do what they do. Tyler's *Basic Principles* helps to draw the curtain aside, to make the process explicit, so that the gifts of the talented few may become accessible to all. It can also guide the teacher out of stultifying routine toward fresh ways of teaching new or unfamiliar subject matter. Teaching, Tyler contends, requires unceasing adaptation to new sets of individuals or groups. Teachers who consider themselves burned out tend to be those who regard their work as bureaucratic routine rather than as a continuing, lively inquiry into adapting schooling to learners.

Basic Principles was in many ways a codification of all that Tyler had learned during his work on the Eight-Year Study, which was at once a great laboratory experiment and a massive harvest of data. But in fact he arrived at his rationale while on the OSU faculty in the early thirties. As he later recalled, several teachers of botany and zoology in the College of Agriculture were having problems with testing and asked for his help. He began by asking the teachers to examine their botany or zoology textbooks to see what in the books might actually increase their students' understanding of farming, which was the main reason the students were there. The teachers decided that their students ought to understand Mendel's laws, photosynthesis, energy, and the like, and then apply their theoretical learning to various problems of plant growth and animal husbandry. Thus, bearing in mind the specific achievements they were seeking, the teachers realized that their tests should call upon the learners to demonstrate the extent to which they had acquired those abilities.[4]

One of the greatest enemies of good teaching, Tyler insisted, was unthinking adherence, even enslavement, to routine. About 80 percent of teachers, he had found, followed without question the established routines of their schools. Only 20 percent attempted to understand the principles underlying their work.[5] The forces that compelled the majority of teachers simply to go along with the way things had always been done were considerable. Teachers, like professionals of all sorts, find it easier and more pleasant to fit in and not rock the boat. They find themselves praised by their principals and fellow teachers for being good team players and easy to get along with. The social constraints are powerful. However, despite forces that encourage conformity to the status quo, Tyler believed, any teacher with a sensible, if unconventional, plan to improve achievement would find that administrators and parents welcomed and supported such an attempt at forward motion.

Basic Principles, by making explicit the fundamentals of teaching and testing, serves also as a guide for analyzing or constructing curricula, educational practices and malpractices, proposals from Washington or anywhere else, and the educational concerns of students, parents, and the public. It is a commonsense approach that offers liberation from the usual recall-of-details manner of testing and that clarifies the rational grounds of teaching. By encouraging teachers to think through and make clear what learning their students are to acquire, it helps them teach so as to impart that learning, and to write test items that enable anyone to see the extent to which the teaching has been successful.

Tyler's little eighty-three-page book, and the objectives-based model of evaluation that it put forward, had a profound and lasting influence, not just on the narrow field of curriculum theorizing but on American education in general, even on teaching the world over. As transformative as his ideas were, though, Tyler maintained a certain no-nonsense modesty about his work. He insisted that he was not doctrinaire, that when he went into the schools he simply found out what the teachers or administrators thought their problems were and then exercised his common sense. He regarded himself as a pragmatist, one who derives principles from practice.

"I do not agree that my syllabus is an outline of the principles of curriculum construction," Tyler once contended. "It is one way by which you can develop rationally, and infer principles to follow. There are other ways, although they do not seem rational to me."[6]

CHAPTER 5

Appraising the Nation's Schools

When President John F. Kennedy's second commissioner of education, Francis Keppel, began work in his Washington office in 1962, he noticed on one wall a framed copy of the charge to the commissioner dated 1867, when the U.S. Congress established the Office of Education.[1] The duty of the office, he read with interest, was to "collect statistics and facts showing the condition and progress of education in the several states and territories and to diffuse such information respecting the organization and management of schools and school systems and otherwise promote the cause of education throughout the country."[2]

Yet no commissioner of education had really fulfilled that responsibility, Keppel soon realized. The data that the office had been receiving were of limited value. Each state submitted a hodgepodge of facts and figures, from various sources, providing no grounds for showing "the progress of education." As a result, the Office of Education could do no more than report to Congress on such superficialities as the numbers of administrators and teachers, investments in buildings, and so forth.

Such has been the state of affairs since the first schools in America were founded, or at least since the federal government first took an interest in the country's schools. Without a systematic, comprehensive, and reliable way to evaluate schools, colleges, and universities, citizens and professionals have had little to go on besides the reputations of their teachers and programs, their buildings, facilities, and financial support, or high school students' college-entrance test scores.

Keppel was convinced that Congress and the public needed to know what the nation's students were learning. He was particularly eager to provide Congress with such data as a means to help improve the achievement of poor and disadvantaged students. Keppel was preoccupied with the issue for a long while before he asked an old friend of his, Ralph Tyler, in July 1963, to devise a plan to find out what progress in education, if any, the nation was making. Tyler agreed to try.

Two decades had passed since the completion of the Eight-Year Study, and during that time Tyler had been indefatigable in his efforts to reform American education; the energy he devoted to publishing and lecturing seemed scarcely diminished even by his administrative responsibilities at the University of Chicago, as chairman of the Department of Education and then as dean of social sciences. In 1953, after serving five years as dean of social sciences, the faculty voted unanimously to offer him another five-year term. No other dean there had ever received such total faculty approval.

Another term, however, was not to be. Chicago's president, Robert M. Hutchins, had left Chicago in 1951 for a vice presidency of the Ford Foundation. His successor, Lawrence Kimpton, was in Tyler's opinion more concerned with establishing serenity than with facing up to the controversy that inevitably accompanies forward motion with a free and contentious faculty. So Tyler decided to leave Chicago in 1953 to accept the founding directorship of the Center for Advanced Study in the Behavioral Sciences, a think tank he helped establish atop a hill across the road from Stanford University.[3] He conceived it as a center for social scientists considered to be of great promise as well as for those who were already distinguished.

At the time Keppel approached Tyler, in 1963, he was still director of the center. As Tyler drafted a plan, two eminent statisticians also happened to be there—John W. Tukey of Princeton and Fred Mosteller of Harvard—as well as the psychologist Clyde H. Coombs of the University of Michigan, whose book *A Theory of Data* was to be published the following year. Tyler asked the three to look over his draft. What he was proposing had to be not only educationally sound but statistically rigorous as well.

Keppel and his staff liked Tyler's proposal and thought it worth a try. Like most of his predecessors in the commissioner's office, Keppel had neither training nor day-to-day experience in practical school matters. But he knew enough to accept Tyler's suggestion that the appraisal instrument he was proposing should be called an "assessment." This term would differentiate it from standardized tests, which are not designed to show what students have actually learned. Ultimately, the Keppel/Tyler project came to be known as the National Assessment of Educational Progress (NAEP).

Keppel and Tyler knew that by far the biggest challenge they would face would be not logistical but political. Any sort of venture in national assessment would spur outcries among school officials and the public that the assessment was actually a Trojan horse concealing the federal government's intention to control the schools. No matter how much Keppel argued that he was simply carrying out a duty of his office, long disregarded, to monitor the progress of American education, he would be met with suspicion and outright hostility on the part of the local schools.

Indeed, whether the federal government ought to impose itself on the nation's schools had been a controversy of long standing. The Constitution says nothing about education, and according to the Tenth Amendment, powers unspecified in the Constitution devolve to the states. The states, in turn, delegate schooling to the localities. Until the beginning of the 1960s, the federal government's involvement in education was minimal.

All that changed, as did so much, when the Soviet Union launched Sputnik in October 1957, shaking Americans out of their complacency. They became concerned, even fearful, that they were falling behind their nuclear rival, particularly in science and technology. In response, the U.S. government initiated and funded educational programs in foreign languages, mathematics, and the sciences. Schools renewed their efforts to identify and separate those deemed to be intellectually gifted.

So the federal government had recently established beachheads in local schooling, but the matter remained a touchy one. In order to avoid suspicion that the NAEP was an attempt to control the schools, Keppel asked the Carnegie Corporation to finance development of the program. Keppel had clout at Carnegie; his father, Frederick Paul Keppel, had been a highly regarded president of the corporation from 1923 to 1942. Carnegie was interested in launching a national assessment, and the program was taken over by Carnegie's president, John W. Gardner, a trained psychologist who later served as Secretary of Health, Education, and Welfare from 1965 to 1968—formative years for the NAEP.[4] He was also later to be chairman of President Lyndon Johnson's Task Force on Education and chairman of the 1965 White House Conference on Education.

On December 18 and 19, 1963, Gardner assembled an informal group of testing specialists to seek their opinions about the assessment plan. This was to be the first of a series of small, unpublicized conferences on the various methods of assessing educational attainment in the United States. No doubt a second, if unstated, purpose was to build consensus among professionals and opinion leaders. The first group, led by Everett F. Lindquist of the University of Iowa, who had a good deal of experience in large-scale testing, concluded that, unusual though the proposal was, it could be made to work.

The second unpublicized conference gathered leaders of the most influential educational organizations, over dinner at the Century Club in New York City on January 27, 1964.[5] The participants, who continued their discussions the next day at Carnegie headquarters at 589 Fifth Avenue, included the president of the American Council on Education, Logan Wilson; the president of the National Education Association, Robert Wyatt; the chancellor of New York University, George Stoddard; the president of Teachers College at Columbia University, John H. Fischer; Oregon's superintendent of public instruction, Leon T. Minear; and the commissioner of education of New York State, James E. Allen. This group concluded that whereas the proposed assessment could be done, it was potentially dangerous—it was a double-edged sword. The results of the study could be used either to help or to harm the schools.

Although no unanimity resulted from those two meetings, John Gardner thought that there was enough consensus to justify moving ahead, at least on a preliminary basis. He authorized funds for an exploratory committee, which he asked Tyler to chair. Lloyd Morrisett, a staff associate at Carnegie, would represent the corporation on the committee. Other members would be Paul Johnston, the state superintendent of public instruction in Iowa; Mabel Smythe, principal of the New Lincoln School in New York; Katherine E. McBride, president of Bryn Mawr; Melvin Barnes, superintendent of the Portland, Oregon, schools; John J. Corson, a professor at Princeton's Woodrow Wilson School of Public and International Affairs; Devereux C. Josephs of New York Life; the journalist Roy E. Larsen of *Time;* Paul C. Reinert, president of St. Louis University; and Jack C. Merwin, the staff director of this exploratory committee.

After explaining the details of the assessment proposal, Tyler laid out the groundwork that remained to be done before the program could be launched. Misconceptions had to be corrected and support had to be built among educational institutions, testing specialists, government agencies, and the general public.

Then there was the major issue of what specifically should and should not be assessed. The exploratory committee had to determine first—consistent with the Tyler Rationale—what the "thoughtful public" expected the schools to teach before it could find out what competencies the project should assess.[6] The committee convened a meeting of scholars in an array of school subjects to ascertain what these specialists believed their subjects could contribute to the education of people who were not necessarily planning to become, say, professional historians, mathematicians, or literary critics. Then, with a list of these scholars' suggested aims, the committee brought together a national cross-section of school superintendents, principals, and teachers, presented them with the list, and asked whether their schools were teaching those things. After all, there was no point in including in a national assessment subjects that were not being taught in the schools. The responses of the teachers and principals trimmed the list only slightly.

Next, the committee met with representatives from the U.S. Chamber of Commerce and the AFL-CIO, from agricultural associations, and the League of Women Voters. Then there followed conferences with a wide cross-section of concerned lay people in each of four regions of the country: Northeast, Southeast, Central, and West. In each region, twenty-five or so people assembled in a motel over a weekend. In all of these meetings, members of the exploratory committee displayed the list of what schools around the country said they were teaching, then asked three questions: "What do these objectives mean to you? For each objective, do you think it is important for all students to learn? Would you want your child to learn it?"[7]

The idea underlying these many gatherings was to ensure that the assessment covered subjects that scholars thought the schools *should* teach, that school professionals thought schools *were* teaching, and that the concerned public, including parents, deemed important. By canvassing opinions so widely, and among so many different interest groups, Tyler hoped to avoid a problem common to most tests—evaluating what one particular person or group believes schools should teach without regard to whether this is what a community wants and expects.

But the great, perhaps even insurmountable, problem with any such national assessment is that no one can actually know what goes on in every classroom in the nation. This would require competent observation in every single one, which is, of course, impossible. Surveying textbooks and curriculum guides is useless, given the likelihood of misuse, misreading, misinterpretation, and plain disregard. Tests and assessments may reveal what Johnny knows and can do—but whether he actually learned those things in school or somewhere else requires further investigation.

So a relatively small but representative number of students would be preliminarily assessed. The committee decided to sample students at ages nine, thirteen, and seventeen. Age rather than grade was the basis for selection because Tyler had found that numerous schools in several southern states failed to promote many black students; as a result, by the end of high school, only the high achievers remained. Age, therefore, was the most reliable indicator of the progress that all students were making. The committee arrived at these particular ages by considering some rough and general relationships between grade level and learning. By the end of third grade, most learners are nine and able to read simple materials. By the end of seventh grade, typical students are thirteen, can interpret what they have read, and can use reading to learn about matters that interest them. At age seventeen, most students are still in high school. Then, to judge the permanence of learning, there was to be a sampling of young adults.

The exploratory committee's next job was to develop tasks to which learners were to respond. Tyler preferred to call these "exercises." Terms like "questions," or "items," Tyler believed, tend to imply responding with paper and pencil, yet some learning cannot be readily assessed by paper-and-pencil responses. Assessing social attitudes and interests in reading, for example, requires direct observation; assessing someone's ability to conduct a lab experiment calls for demonstrations.

Tyler and others on the various planning committees that grew out of the exploratory committee were at pains to set up the assessment so that competition among schools, school districts, and states would not come into play. It is no secret that education in America is not conducted on a level field, that there is no contest between a state of high scorers like North Dakota and of low scorers like Mississippi. Besides, Tyler's years of experience had convinced him that competition only harms schooling—competition puts the emphasis on winning, not on learning, thus polluting the educational process.[8] He believed that advocates of competition in schooling, who were plentiful, were presuming a false analogy, that the utility of competition in athletics or business might profitably apply also to education. Tyler had found, however, that in the classroom a stress on winning only promotes feelings of superiority and inferiority, envy, and strife, all of which affect morale and thus interfere with the process of educating. Nor was Tyler alone in this. The late industrial consultant W. Edwards Deming left a legacy of writings on the harmfulness of competition, in both industry and education. A more popular treatment of the topic, specifically with respect to education, appears in the writings of Alfie Kohn, in particular his book *No Contest: The Case against Competition*. Nevertheless, the supposed worth of competition in schooling is so deeply ingrained in the American culture that many leaders of education regard it as a universally accepted truth.

Among the advocates of competition with whom Tyler contended were both John Gardner and Francis Keppel himself. Keppel recalled later that in urging this national assessment he was "eager to encourage competition between states and districts with the goal of improving the quality of student learning. Without comparative data, the possibility of emulation and real competition was lacking."[9]

Keppel repeatedly expressed this opinion in committee meetings during the planning of the assessment, but in the end Tyler prevailed in his argument against turning learners into contestants. Not only did rivalry do nothing to increase achievement, Tyler asserted, producing empirical evidence to support his claim, but it ran counter to the fundamental aims of the assessment.

Therefore the planners avoided the use of school districts, cities, states, and other political demarcations. Instead, they divided the nation into the four broad regional areas already noted. To reflect the wide differences among the nation's communities and learners, a number of demographic aspects were chosen: boys and girls, type of community, socioeconomic status, and others. There would be no individual scores; some exercises required the responses of more than one student. "No meaningful [in-dividual] scores can be obtained," Tyler insisted.[10] A number itself does not tell who learned what.

Instead, "meaningful" reports were to be expressed in this manner. For the sample of seventeen-year old boys of higher socioeconomic status from rural and small town areas of the Midwest region, it was found that:

- 93 percent can read a typical newspaper paragraph
- 76 percent can write an acceptable letter ordering several items from a store
- 52 percent take responsible parts in working with other youth in playground and community activities
- 21 percent have occupational skills required for initial employment.[11]

Specific examples were provided of each kind of task.

The idea of a national assessment of educational progress continued to excite controversy, however. In 1965, at the White House Conference on Education, John I. Goodlad, then director of the University Elementary School at UCLA, presented a paper on the proposed NAEP, at the request of the conference's chairman, John Gardner, and Commissioner Keppel.[12] Goodlad's paper aroused a good deal of argument at the conference, particularly from Harold Hand of the University of Illinois, who attacked the idea of a national assessment as a dangerous federal attempt to impose educational uniformity on the nation's schools. After the White House Conference ended, Harold Hand embarked upon a speaking tour of sorts assailing the NAEP. Tyler, who tended to ignore his critics, found himself forced to defend the proposal at numerous public appearances, arguing that the NAEP did not in fact involve national testing and would not lead to federal control of the nation's public schools; that was not the point at all.[13]

After several testing organizations had prepared a set of exercises, it was time for a tryout. Tyler wrote to a small number of superintendents in different parts of the nation, in a variety of kinds and sizes of school districts, asking for their cooperation.

Harold Spears, the superintendent of the San Francisco schools, received one of the requests. He had recently gone through a troubling experience with another assessment, which had soured him on the idea altogether. Some time earlier there had been a statewide test in California, the results of which were to be kept confidential. But a member of California's Department of Education had leaked the results to the media. The scores from the San Francisco schools were predictably among the lowest, because of the vast numbers of students in the area who were unfamiliar with English and whose parents were poor and badly educated, if at all. At that time Spears happened to be president of the American Association of School Administrators (AASA), deepening his embarrassment. Tyler thought that this unpleasant experience led the AASA Executive Committee to send a letter on January 9, 1967, to all members "requesting them not to cooperate with the assessment project, not even to permit the pilot testing of assessment exercises in their schools."[14]

Spears's lobbying incensed many of the superintendents and other educators involved in planning the assessment. One early participant, James Allen, wrote to the executive secretary of the AASA suggesting that any decision be postponed until the next annual meeting, to find what the wishes of the full membership really were. AASA's officials acceded. At that annual meeting, held as usual in Atlantic City, Tyler, a life member, addressed the opening general session, speaking on February 12, 1966. He succeeded in allaying some of the membership's fears. Swayed by his explanation and his reputation, the AASA passed a resolution endorsing the assessment and asking that a member of their organization be placed on the NAEP's exploratory committee. The request was granted, the hurdle overcome, and the project was able to move ahead.[15]

Still, there remained widespread concern that the NAEP would be used as a tool for the federal government to run the schools. Gardner, in response, suggested that the assessment be conducted by the Education Commission of the States, an interstate organization created in 1965 by Harvard's James B. Conant and Governor Terry Sanford of North Carolina (later president of Duke) to foster cooperation among the states, and thereby discourage attempts by the federal government to control the nation's schools. The ECS, which was underwritten by the Carnegie, Danforth, and Ford foundations, agreed to conduct the assessment.

In 1969, fully six years after Tyler conceived the idea, Carnegie financed the first administration of the exercises.[16] When the NAEP's leaders reported to the Education Commission of the States, at its annual meeting in the summer of 1970, it was impressed enough with the value of the study's findings to vote to continue cooperating with the NAEP. NAEP's leaders sought support from the U.S. commissioner of education, Harold Howe III, who authorized Office of Education funding through the National Center for Educational Statistics to underwrite the second round. Since that time the federal government has funded the NAEP; it has evolved into a legal federal obligation that has received continuing bipartisan support.

But the course of U.S. government support for the NAEP has not been without its controversies. Over the years, several government agencies have jockeyed for ownership of the study. "When something turns out to be popular," Tyler recalled, "everyone wants to take it over, you know."[17] Later, the National Center for Educational Statistics announced that since it was the vehicle for the funding, it would be taking over the assessment from the Education Commission of the States.

The "Nation's Report Card," as it is often called, is a congressionally mandated project of the U.S. Department of Education's National Center for Education Statistics. The commissioner of education statistics is responsible by law for carrying out the NAEP project. The National Assessment Governing Board, appointed by the secretary of education but independent of the Department of Education, governs and sets policy. Since 1985, the Educational Testing Service (ETS) has been responsible for developing the assessment instruments, overseeing the scoring, analyzing data, and reporting the results.

Tyler was dismayed that the ETS had taken over the assessment. He recalled, "The NAEP was given to ETS by a man briefly in the U.S. Office of Education. A man who resigned shortly afterward for using federal funds to pay for his private trips. He knew nothing about educational evaluation and did not understand that psychometricians do not learn much about educational objectives. I spent weeks with committees of scholars and groups of laymen to define the original objectives of the NAEP. ETS just took items off their shelf."[18] Tyler regarded that powerful organization as a redoubt of psychometricians preoccupied with the bell curve. "The strong position in national testing of ETS, made up primarily of psychometricians with few educators, headed by an honest man who knows little about testing, makes it problematical," he wrote in 1989. "I hope that my speaking and writing helped to clarify the difference between tests seeking to identify what students had learned from tests seeking to find out where students were to be placed in a hypothetical distribution of students from those who are 'best' to those who are 'worst.' I have continued to remind educators and parents that American schools are trying to help every student learn what the schools are expected to teach and that the preoccupation with where the students stand on this hypothetical distribution distracts attention from an effort to understand what students have learned and where they are having difficulty in learning."[19]

Since it was taken over by the ETS, in 1985, the NAEP has been a methodological hybrid. While still adhering to the original purpose of the study in that it specifies what students are learning, it also classifies scores on a bell curve, without reference to the areas of learning that the NAEP originally sought to address. It has become for the most part just another standardized test.

Tyler regretted, too, another distortion of the NAEP's mission, which resulted from a congressional law of 1988—the introduction of competition. The law permitted statewide administration of NAEP exercises, and because statewide results are accessible, they encourage invidious comparisons between the states.

These and other problems have continued to bedevil the NAEP, and it is likely that they always will. In this regard, the NAEP is no different from any other complicated human enterprise. Still, imperfect and beleaguered though it may be, the assessment continues to provide Congress and the public with the most reliable data it has on the progress of the nation's vastly different local schools. Under the No Child Left Behind Act of 2001 (PL 107-110, Title VI, Part C, Section 411 (5)(A)), the commissioner is charged with ensuring that authorized NAEP tests "do not evaluate or access personal or family beliefs and attitudes or publicly disclose personally identifiable information."

While NAEP is indeed voluntary, the No Child Left Behind Act clearly provides strong incentives for school districts and states to participate in NAEP. Beginning with the 2002–2003 school year, states that wish to receive Title I grants from the federal government must participate biennially in the fourth-grade and eighth-grade NAEP reading and mathematics assessments. The federal government assumes the full cost of administering these assessments.[20]

CHAPTER 6

Contrarian Views

During the more than six decades of Ralph Tyler's career, he was repeatedly invited to sit on or chair committees, act as a consultant to schools or educational groups, conduct surveys, and render his opinion. He was constantly in demand, his advice widely sought, for after years of experience, research, and teaching, he had developed a set of strongly held views on any number of controversial subjects. His views on standardized testing, on tracking and class size, and on minimum competency testing put him at odds with the prevailing orthodoxies, but in every case his views flowed not from prejudice but from careful analysis.

Schools are often faced with pressure to teach driver education, sex education, vocational education, and other educational demands of the moment. Having analyzed the school as an institution, Tyler concluded that schools are set up to perform some but not all educational tasks.

For example, he noted that most teachers are educated in the arts or sciences and have considerable, yet limited, time at their disposal. Most schools have libraries, some have laboratories. Therefore, he concluded, schools are obligated to impart the kind of learning they are uniquely able to perform. Other social institutions, such as home, church, and youth-serving organizations, are responsible for imparting other kinds of learning. Failure to encourage these agencies to bear their responsibilities weakens our total social structure.[1]

Standardized tests have become a multimillion-dollar industry in this country; they have grown steadily in popular acceptance since the Army Alpha Test of World War I. Today they enjoy almost a sacred-cow status in much of the teaching profession and the general public.

Tyler condemned the use of standardized tests as instruments of assessment in teaching. Often they have been labeled "achievement tests" (the Stanford Achievement Test, for example), whereas Tyler argued that achievement was the one thing they did *not* measure. They are designed not to assess the results of teaching, he insisted, but to rank and classify.[2]

A standardized test must be written, Tyler pointed out, so that there are few high scores and few low scores, and most scores fall in the middle—the classic bell curve. For statisticians, this "normal distribution" of scores reflects random departures from a norm. This was precisely why Tyler deemed the curve unsuited to assessing teaching. As he often observed, if you select one hundred men off the street purely at random, their shirt and shoe sizes will fall into the same distribution pattern—few large sizes, few small, and most medium. Yet if the results of teaching should follow this pattern, the teaching must be deemed unsuccessful; schooling, after all, is not a random but rather a *purposeful* endeavor. A standardized test, then, has nothing to do with evaluation.

The public and even many in the profession fail to understand this distinction, Tyler found, a situation that has led to serious misinterpretations. Between 1965 and 1975, for example, there was a marked decline in Scholastic Aptitude Test scores across the country. When an employee of the Educational Testing Service, which produces and administers the SAT, leaked a report of this decline to the media, it predictably excited widespread concern.[3]

Sidney Marland, the president of the College Entrance Examination Board (CEEB), which sponsors the SAT, was delighted with the resulting publicity. Marland was a Marine Corps general in World War II and later superintendent of Pittsburgh schools; he had served as U.S. commissioner of education before assuming his position as CEEB's president. Seeking to capitalize on this publicity, he asked his friend Willard Wirtz, former secretary of labor, to chair a "blue ribbon committee" to "investigate" the decline in SAT scores.[4]

Tyler was chosen for this committee but was surprised to find that only three of the committee members actually understood the technicalities of testing.[5] These testing specialists inquired into whether there was any qualitative or demographic change in the kind of students who had been taking the SAT during the ten years in question; they learned that there had been a substantial increase in the number of students from the bottom half of their classes. This had resulted from BEOG (Basic Educational Opportunity Grants) legislation, the intention of which was to encourage lower-performing students to apply to colleges, which meant taking the SAT.

When the testing experts analyzed the SAT examination itself, they discovered that the decline had been greatest in the vocabulary section, which tested students on words not commonly used in high school. They concluded that the SAT had little or no connection to high school curricula. What was more, they realized that among those types of students who normally took the SAT, there was no evidence of any decline in actual educational achievement during the ten-year period studied.

But when the test specialists, including Tyler, presented their findings to the entire committee, buttressed with some statistical technicalities, Marland seemed less than interested. He asked the committee to issue a nontechnical report, avoiding statistics as much as possible, and he proceeded to take his message about the putative national decline in test scores to the public in speeches, public appearances, and articles. He restated the popular wisdom about how high school students watched too much television. Recognizing the futility of contending with a chairman who, in Tyler's words, "knew nothing about tests," he and the other test specialists decided not to write a dissenting report.[6]

Tyler similarly found himself at odds with the popular wisdom when it came to the notion of "tracking" or "ability grouping" in the schools. Tracking derives from the belief on the part of teachers or administrators that they are able to recognize "native abilities" and develop suitable instructional programs for groups of differing abilities.[7] Tracking in one form or another, whatever name it went by, had been studied since the 1920s, Tyler insisted, and he believed it had been roundly discredited.[8] Based on his research and his own experience, he did not believe that children learn more when placed in groups with others like them. In fact, he had found that variety within a group can stimulate discussion and thought, whereas uniformity stunts intellectual development.[9] Ability grouping was more suited to athletics, he thought, than to education.

The always contentious issue of class size was another matter on which he had done much thinking. Tyler had concluded that the number of students in a class in itself has no direct connection with the quality of learning. All that counts is what is done in class. If a teacher merely lectures, then obviously class size is irrelevant; a creative and enterprising teacher with a large class can always teach well through the use of such devices as peer-group teaching.[10]

On the question of teacher preparation, Tyler's view was bracingly simple—the best way for teachers to learn to teach is to observe and participate in classroom teaching, report on problems they see or encounter, and discuss these with whoever is guiding them. He was wary of teacher supervisors, who tended to think of their job as telling teachers "the way I would do it."[11] Skilled supervision requires a thorough knowledge of the principles, not mere unanalyzed experience.

Tyler believed that virtually all children can learn. He had a striking opportunity to demonstrate the potential even of the children whom many teachers were inclined to write off when the superintendent of the Detroit public schools, Norman Drachler, invited Tyler in to see what he could do about four particularly troubled, mostly black, elementary schools in Detroit's worst slums, near the Chrysler plant. In August 1968, Tyler established a workshop for the schools' teachers that enabled them to observe and talk with students playing in the streets and talk with their parents in their homes. Having observed the students' lives outside of school, the teachers began to realize how the subjects they taught might be adapted to the concerns of both students and parents. By the end of the three-year trial period, in 1971, the students in the four schools were doing as well as, or better than, those in Detroit's mostly white middle-class schools.[12] (The supervisor of the four inner-city schools, Hugh Scott, later became dean of the School of Education at Hunter College in New York City.)

Tyler was an opponent of "minimum competency testing," state policies requiring students to pass achievement tests at a minimal level. Presumably, this approach is supposed to boost achievement overall—or so taxpayers often believe. When the Florida Education Association asked Tyler to study the effects of the state's minimum competency legislation, he discovered that such testing had perverse consequences. The state's schools responded to the testing by deeming the new minimum standard an acceptable aim—and thus achievement declined. The policy was, he found, a disaster.[13]

CHAPTER 7

The Mentor

"I like to help people find ways of using their talents most effectively," Tyler once said, "and that's usually by giving them an opportunity for a time to do what they think is important."[1] This view proved a hallmark of his career. As the late Lee Cronbach, professor of education at Stanford University, once pointed out, "While Ralph has made notable intellectual contributions, perhaps his main contribution has been in his development of people."[2]

In the mid-1930s, while working as a director of the Eight-Year Study's evaluation staff, Tyler happened to meet "a wonderful teacher of history and social studies" in one of the thirty participating schools.[3] The teacher later recalled that Tyler "brought a cool scientific attention to problems relating to experimental education."[4] This teacher was James A. Michener, who was at the time teaching history and geography at the George School, a private Quaker boarding school in Newtown, Pennsylvania, near Philadelphia. Tyler, taking note of Michener's talents, persuaded him to accept a research assistantship at OSU and get a master's degree.[5] Michener went on to teach in Greeley, Colorado, at what was then Colorado State Teachers College. Later, Tyler recommended Michener as an editor of social studies textbooks at Macmillan. After the outbreak of World War II, Michener joined the navy and wrote *South Pacific,* the novel that Rodgers and Hammerstein adapted into the successful musical. Later, of course, he went on to write such best-selling novels as *The Source, Hawaii,* and *Texas.*

Michener was perhaps the first prominent person for whom Tyler was a mentor; he was hardly the last. Another scholar involved with the Eight-Year Study was the controversial writer and Holocaust survivor Bruno Bettelheim. Tyler's contribution to Bettelheim's career was significant; his pivotal behind-the-scenes role in bringing Bettelheim to this country has never been disclosed.

In an essay in the *New York Review of Books* on February 27, 2003, Robert Gottlieb, the former editor in chief of Alfred A. Knopf and *The New Yorker,* wrote of Bettelheim: "In 1938, he was deported by the Germans first to Dachau, then to Buchenwald. Surviving through his determination and strong sense of self, he was rescued through the efforts of his family and friends."[6] Two of the Bettelheim biographies Gottlieb reviewed in his essay, Nina Sutton's *Bettelheim: A Life and Legacy* (1996) and Richard Pollak's *The Creation of Dr. B: A Biography of Dr. Bruno Bettelheim* (1996), also discuss the question of how exactly Bettelheim was released from the camps, contending that the answer may never come to light.

Bettelheim himself claimed that he never knew. Unproven rumors and suppositions had circulated for decades that certain prominent Americans, including Eleanor Roosevelt and New York governor Herbert Lehman, had intervened with the State Department, which had in some mysterious way managed to secure the young scholar's release from the Nazi regime.[7]

But Ralph Tyler, who was closely associated with the circumstances of Bettelheim's release, dismissed these speculations. The story he recounted, many years later, was rather different.

Beginning in the 1920s, the Rockefeller Foundation initiated a program in the social sciences to bring eminent Europeans to America for periods of time to teach American social scientists the various concepts and methods then emerging in Europe, particularly those rooted in Freudian concepts. The foundation's European representative kept a list of Viennese psychologists to be invited to the United States. But with Hitler's 1938 *Anschluss,* the annexation of Austria by Nazi Germany, most of these psychologists were sent to concentration camps.

The Rockefeller Foundation's representative then learned that the Nazis would release these men if a suitable ransom was paid—Berlin needed foreign currency to build up its war machine. Tyler recalled being told that Hitler demanded a ransom of half a million dollars for the eight men.[8] The Rockefeller Foundation's officers proposed to the foundation's board of trustees that they pay this ransom, Tyler later recounted, and thereby bring eight Viennese psychologists to America.[9] The president of the Rockefeller Foundation, Raymond Fosdick, told Tyler that he had been the one who brought this morally fraught issue before the board, recalling that "it took a lot of soul-searching to get the Trustees to approve paying ransom . . . to Hitler."[10] By law, the foundation was permitted to contribute only to nonprofit organizations, not directly to individuals—

and certainly not to help Adolf Hitler, who, though not yet at war with the United States, would surely use the money to build up his military.[11] The debate was, naturally, heated: Should they save eight men—and thereby contribute to Hitler's war preparations?

At last they decided to pay the ransom. The psychologists would be released, but the U.S. Immigration Service would not admit them to the United States unless they were guaranteed employment. When the foundation asked the directors of the various projects it was funding whether they would promise to employ these men, Tyler pledged to hire Bettelheim.[12]

Tyler, then the director of the evaluation section of the Eight-Year Study—the evaluative work of the study, recall, had been underwritten by the Rockefeller Foundation when the Carnegie Foundation had pulled out—was at the time seeking a specialist to assess art appreciation. Told that one of the imprisoned psychoanalysts, Bettelheim, had a doctorate in aesthetics from the University of Vienna, Tyler was interested.

Bettelheim had also professed credentials as a professional psychoanalyst, falsely claiming to have practiced psychoanalysis in Vienna. (Tyler assumed, mistakenly, that Bettelheim had received formal certification in psychoanalysis, a matter on which Bettelheim never set Tyler straight.) In his *New York Review* essay, Robert Gottlieb writes that "Bettelheim began to exaggerate his professional qualifications when he first arrived in America, immediately after his release from Buchenwald. He was without a job—without, really, a profession—and desperate to gain a foothold in a new world."[13] In fact, Bettelheim had claimed these false psychoanalytic credentials before his arrival in the United States, a crucial distinction; he may have known of the Rockefeller Foundation's willingness to intervene to rescue psychoanalysts. By styling himself as a psychoanalyst, Bettelheim would have made himself eligible for the Rockefeller Foundation's help.[14]

In 1939, Bruno Bettelheim began his long career in the United States, as a member of the evaluation staff of the Eight-Year Study. He was to devise evaluation methods for assessing students' appreciation of art, particularly paintings. The procedures he conceived, Tyler recalled, were innovative and, appropriately, nonverbal.[15]

Later, as chairman of the education department at the University of Chicago, Tyler in 1944 appointed Bettelheim principal of the Sonia Shankman Orthogenic School for autistic and other troubled children, a responsibility of Chicago's education department. Bettelheim remained head of the school until his retirement in 1973. He became renowned internationally as a specialist in the treatment of autistic children and as a prolific writer of articles for the profession as well as for the general reader. As sole author, he wrote thirteen books, including *The Uses of Enchantment, Love Is Not Enough, The Informed Heart, The Empty Fortress,* and *The Children of the Dream.*

On March 12, 1990, after suffering a stroke and other physical and emotional problems, Bettelheim committed suicide. Following his death, some former patients at the Orthogenic School publicized reports about Bettelheim's mistreatment of and cruelty toward them and other patients. Tyler, however, remained a defender of Bettelheim and gave little credence to these reports.[16] He wondered why such accusations arose only after Bettelheim's death, when the man was no longer able to respond.[17]

Daniel J. Boorstin, a 1934 graduate of Harvard with highest honors, a Rhodes scholar who later received his J.S.D. degree from the Yale Law School in 1940, was appointed assistant dean of the University of Chicago Law School in 1944. Also a teacher of legal history at the law school, Boorstin, whose scholarly interests extended beyond the legal to the broader social, political, and economic aspects of history, nevertheless lacked the paper credentials expected of an academic historian.

Shortly after his arrival at the law school, Boorstin wrote a book-length manuscript on Thomas Jefferson, on the basis of which he sought an appointment to the university's history department. Boorstin asked the chairman of the history department to read his manuscript and judge his competence as a historian, but the chairman refused, insisting that every member of his department had to have a Ph.D. in history.

With manuscript in hand, Boorstin then went to see the dean of the social sciences division, Ralph Tyler. Tyler, though no historian, read the manuscript and judged it promising. He sent it on to his friend Paul Buck, the Harvard historian, for his opinion. Buck was impressed by the manuscript, an intellectual history of Thomas Jefferson's political philosophy; thus assured, Tyler appointed Boorstin to Chicago's prestigious Committee on Social Thought, one of several interdepartmental committees that Tyler had fostered.[18] Boorstin's manuscript was published in 1948 as *The Lost World of Thomas Jefferson.* Boorstin went on to become a member of Chicago's history department. His *The Americans: The Democratic Experience* won the Pulitzer Prize in 1973. He retired as Librarian of Congress in 1987 and continued to write critically acclaimed, best-selling works of history.

The economist Theodore W. Schultz came to know Ralph Tyler during the Second World War, when Schultz was at Iowa State College (now Iowa State University), in Ames, and the college had brought Tyler in as a consultant. Schultz, who was chairman of the college's combined department of economics and sociology, asked Tyler to help improve the quality of undergraduate education in his department.[19]

Some time later, Schultz's department, with a grant from the Rockefeller Foundation, began preparing a series of pamphlets on issues of farm and food policy during wartime. One of the graduate students in the department, Oswald H. Brownlee, wrote a pamphlet urging that the public use margarine instead of butter, on the grounds that margarine was as nutritious as butter, cost half the price, and required less labor to produce. When the pamphlet was first published, in 1943, it received little attention. Within a few weeks, however, the National Dairymen's Association ran a full-page ad in the *Des Moines Register* attacking the booklet as mistaken in its assertion that margarine was as nutritious as butter. The dairy farmers were so incensed that they exerted pressure on the president of the college, Charles E. Friley, to rescind the pamphlet and put out a revised one that conformed to their interests. Friley caved in to the farmers. Theodore Schultz fired off a letter to Friley vigorously defending the author's freedom to express his views, deploring the president's failure to protect intellectual freedom at the college, and submitted his resignation.[20] Within a year, fifteen other social scientists had also left the college over the controversy.[21]

Tyler, learning of Schultz's resignation and admiring his distinction as an agricultural economist, helped arrange for Schultz's appointment to Chicago's economics department. Later, when Schultz was a fellow at the Center for Advanced Study in the Behavioral Sciences at Stanford, during the 1956–57 academic year, and Tyler was still the center's director, he told Tyler that he was interested in investigating the economics of some field other than agriculture. Tyler suggested education. Schultz, intrigued, began studying the economics of education and determined that investments in education yielded higher rates of return than investments for purely economic purposes. Furthermore, investments in elementary education yielded higher rates of return than investments in secondary education, which in turn yielded higher returns than investments in tertiary education.[22] In 1979 Schultz received the Nobel Prize in Economic Science for this work.

The first black person ever appointed to a regular-status faculty position at a predominantly white university was the illustrious educational sociologist and anthropologist Allison Davis, who owed this landmark appointment to Ralph Tyler.[23] Davis was born in 1902 in Washington, D.C., to an educated, middle-class family with wide intellectual and cultural interests. His father was an official in the Government Printing Office until President Woodrow Wilson, under pressure from southern politicians, widened the segregation of federal workers; Davis's father was demoted, along with other black employees. Allison Davis attended a segregated high school in Washington, which he later recalled was "quite well known and had a very good faculty. This is important because it shows that not all segregated schools are poor schools."[24] He received a B.A. from Williams College, class of 1924, graduating summa cum laude, Phi Beta Kappa, and class valedictorian. After his graduation he applied for a teaching assistantship at Williams but was rejected by the president of Williams, on the pretext that the presence of four or five southern students at the school made the appointment of a black teaching assistant untenable.

Davis then went to Harvard and, in 1925, received a master's degree in English. In his first teaching position he taught English at the Hampton Institute in Virginia. There he concluded that it was the prevailing social order, not ability, that accounted for many of the obstacles that he and other blacks faced in education. He decided that English literature was the wrong area of study for him if he wished to understand the American social system and its undemocratic aspects. He returned to Harvard to do graduate work in anthropology and received a second M.A., then undertook further anthropological study at the London School of Economics.

His mentor at Harvard was W. Lloyd Warner, who arrived at the University of Chicago in 1935. Warner analyzed American society in terms of associations among people. In his description of social relationships, Warner classified people as members of higher and lower social classes. Because social classes are likely to state or imply superiority of some over others, Warner and his social class analysis became controversial. Academics and others assailed him as undemocratic and un-American. In response, Warner explained that he was not advocating social classes; rather, he was describing what he observed. Warner had arrived at his conclusions empirically from firsthand studies of American communities. He treated class distinctions in America not in terms of wealth and power but of sociability and consumption.[25]

Allison Davis followed him to Chicago and received his Ph.D. there in 1942. Tyler, then head of the education department, was looking for a faculty member qualified to teach and conduct research into the problems of teaching the rural and urban poor. John Dollard of Yale had brought Allison Davis to his attention; Dollard had directed a study of youth problems during the Depression and had employed Davis and his wife to interview black families. Davis's report, published as the book *Children of Bondage,* impressed Tyler.[26]

He considered Davis the leading candidate for such an appointment, and Robert M. Hutchins, the university's president, agreed. But even at the ostensibly liberal, tolerant University of Chicago, the appointment of a black professor to the faculty was controversial. Recognizing the trouble ahead and predicting that the university's board of trustees would reject Davis's appointment using the excuse of a lack of funds, Tyler and Hutchins turned to the Julius Rosenwald Fund, located on Ellis Avenue near the Chicago campus. The Rosenwald Fund had as one of its objectives eliminating barriers that institutions, including universities, impose on blacks and other minorities. Tyler and Hutchins asked the fund to underwrite Davis's salary and expenses for the first three years. The university board would then not be able to reject Davis on economic grounds. The case for Davis's appointment could be made solely on merit.

Even at the Rosenwald Fund, however, the plan ran into trouble. A member of the fund's board of trustees, Edgar B. Stern, objected to Davis's appointment. He insisted that Davis could do more for his race by teaching at a Negro university. He also maintained that it was improper for the fund to underwrite a university position, that it should be financed by the university itself. The president of the fund, Edwin R. Embree, responded that the very function of foundations is "to bring about higher standards and wiser practices than would occur in the normal course of events."[27] Stern was outvoted, Tyler's and Hutchins's plan worked, and Davis was appointed an assistant professor of education and anthropology in 1942.

Though Allison Davis went on to conduct significant research in education and race, he continued to face discrimination in his personal life. He was unable to buy a house in Hyde Park, the university's neighborhood, and instead had to live in the racially mixed Kenwood area, farther from the campus. He was unable to gain admittance to the university's faculty club, the Quadrangle Club, until 1948, when women were first admitted. When conducting field research in the South and Southwest, Davis faced problems finding living quarters; although he was often the lead investigator, he and his white staff members had to resort to surreptitious meetings, such as in wooded areas.

Davis's race and middle-class background gave him a distinctive and important vantage point in examining education in both lower and middle-class American society. He pointed out, in much of his teaching and writing, that schools are fundamentally middle-class institutions— most teachers are middle class, and most textbooks and school curricula make reference to middle-class experiences. This conflict between the schools and their pupils, many of whom come "from people who work with their hands," was, he believed, "a major problem in public education."[28]

Davis also concluded from his research that the lower-class child was penalized by intelligence tests, many items of which require middle-class experience to be comprehensible. His analysis of the individual items in IQ tests was groundbreaking and led to the abolishment of IQ testing in New York, Chicago, Detroit, and San Francisco, among other major cities. "This was one time," Davis later told an interviewer, that "I got what I wanted: a direct effect on society from social science research."[29]

To replace IQ tests, he began to develop what he called a "culture common test"—a test that referred to experiences common to all cultures or social classes. Ultimately Davis decided to abandon this project. One reason, according to Tyler, was that Davis came to agree with the emerging view among educators and psychologists that human intelligence cannot be expressed in a single score, that people have different kinds of intelligence, including verbal, mathematical, social, spatial, musical, and artistic.[30] Also, Tyler had told Davis of his observation that the schools often use IQ scores as a reason for neither expecting much from, nor seriously teaching, low-scoring students.

Davis's ten books, all dealing with how minorities are affected by the dominant society, included *Deep South* (an analysis of the lives of blacks in Natchez, Mississippi) and *Children of Bondage*, a study of how the personalities of black urban youth are formed in the urban South. He did research as well into the notion of ability grouping in the classrooms. In his 1948 Inglis Lecture at Harvard, he was critical of homogeneous grouping, which he argued actually

> sets up different social and cultural groups within the school and thus establishes different learning environments. . . . Because selection is based upon reading scores and/or intelligence scores, many abilities and problem-solving activities are not considered. Segregated from each other, unable therefore either to stimulate or to imitate each other, each group fails to learn well those problem-solving activities and insights in which the other group excels. Both groups lose more than they gain.[31]

One of the most renowned sociologists of the twentieth century—David Riesman, the author of *The Lonely Crowd*—credited Tyler with altering the direction of his own work entirely, inspiring Riesman to do the kind of work he actually wanted to do. In the mid-1940s, the late Edward Shils, a social scientist at the University of Chicago, read an article on civil liberties by Riesman, then a law professor at the University of Buffalo. At the time, Shils was developing a social science III course. The article convinced Shils that Riesman could make a substantial contribution to the school, and he arranged for Riesman to move to the University of Chicago.

Born in Philadelphia in 1909, Riesman was a child of well-to-do, educated German-Jewish parents. His mother, a Philadelphian by birth, was

a Bryn Mawr graduate and had a lifelong enthusiasm for music and literature. His father, also named David Riesman, was a native of Germany,
a professor of medicine at the University of Pennsylvania, and a noted
internist who acquired considerable wealth through his medical practice.
The younger David Riesman therefore never lacked for money.[32]

As a Harvard undergraduate, Riesman majored in a field that failed to
arouse his enthusiasm—biochemistry. His father had told him that he
could learn other subjects from books. During his senior year, Riesman
became a friend and student of Carl Joachim Friedrich, then a young
political philosopher early in his career at Harvard. Friedrich broadened
Riesman's interest in the social sciences, particularly in public opinion and
the Gallup Polls, which were just beginning. Riesman graduated in 1931
with a degree in biochemistry, attended Harvard Law School, and after
graduation served as law clerk to Supreme Court Justice Louis Brandeis.
There followed a succession of jobs in law and government and a professorship of law at the University of Buffalo, before he came to Chicago in
1941 as a visiting associate professor of social science at the university.

While still on the Chicago faculty, Riesman spent a year, 1947, at Yale,
where he began an investigation into the effects of society on the character of its members. Along with Nathan Glazer and Reuel Denney, his
coauthors, Riesman reported his findings in his now-classic study on the
American post–World War II urban middle class, *The Lonely Crowd*. An
all-time best-seller for the Yale University Press since its publication in
1950, *The Lonely Crowd* popularized such incisive descriptions of social
character as "inner directed" and "other directed."[33]

Yet Riesman had no degree in any of the social sciences. Several members of Chicago's social sciences division, most prominently Philip
Hauser, a sociologist with a specialty in demography, decided that
Riesman was unacceptable because he lacked a Ph.D. and disregarded
the accepted methodology. There was mounting opposition to keeping
Riesman on. Tyler, however, who was by then dean of the social sciences division, thought that Riesman, despite his unconventional background, offered a distinctive and valid perspective. Realizing the strength
of the opposition to Riesman in the social science department, Tyler
instead appointed Riesman to the Committee on Social Thought in
1949.[34] There Riesman remained until 1958, when he was appointed
the Henry Ford II Professor of Sociology at his alma mater, Harvard.
It was Tyler's intervention, Riesman later recalled, that was largely instrumental in urging him along the path of sociology, where he would
attain such remarkable success.

Another of Tyler's students, and later a colleague, was the scholar of
education Benjamin S. Bloom. Bloom is perhaps best known for his

"taxonomy" of educational objectives, which described the cognitive aims of learning in hierarchical terms. In his account, the pupil begins with the recall of learned material, which leads to comprehension of acquired knowledge, generalized application of concepts, synthesis (the assembling of knowledge into a new pattern), and finally evaluation, in which the pupil is able to judge the value of material based on specified criteria.[35] Although Tyler was unpersuaded of the taxonomy's usefulness, many have found it a useful model for curriculum development and the teaching of critical thinking skills. Bloom's other work, which Tyler did admire, dealt with the development of talent, mastery learning, and the various domains of learning (cognitive, affective, and psychomotor).

A native of Pennsylvania, Bloom was born in 1913 and graduated from Pennsylvania State University, where he earned B.A. and M.A. degrees in psychology. He then worked in social research during the Depression, first for the Pennsylvania Relief Organization, then for the American Youth Commission in Washington, D.C. While working for the AYC, he attended a talk given by Tyler that inspired him to begin doctoral study at the University of Chicago under Tyler's guidance, in the summer of 1939. In order to pay his expenses, Bloom worked as Tyler's assistant in the university's Office of Examinations while completing his Ph.D., which was awarded in 1942. It was at the examiner's office that Bloom found himself working on the problem of how to organize educational objectives according to cognitive complexity, in order to devise a reliable method to assess students as well as educational practices—work that led to the development of his cognitive taxonomy. Bloom succeeded Tyler as college examiner in 1953, when Tyler left Chicago to become the founding director of the Center for Advanced Study in the Behavioral Sciences in Palo Alto.[36]

Bloom remained at the University of Chicago's education department for more than fifty years, rising through the ranks from instructor (in 1944) to the Charles H. Swift Distinguished Service Professor of Education (in 1970). His research into the importance of the first four years of a child's life in promoting cognitive development—a subject about which he testified before Congress—proved influential in the establishment of the Head Start program. Tyler particularly admired Bloom's work with Torsten Husen of the University of Stockholm in founding the International Study of Educational Achievement, work that led a number of nations to launch centers for curriculum research.[37]

Had it not been for Ralph Tyler's influence, Ernest Boyer, the U.S. commissioner of education from 1977 to 1979, would have been not an educator but an audiologist. In 1957, Boyer was an academic dean at the now-defunct Upland College in California. Discouraged with the field of education, he had decided to quit and resume the practice of medical audiology, for which he had previously trained. At a series of conferences for small-college deans, sponsored by the Fund for the Advancement of Education with financing from the Ford Foundation, Boyer attended a workshop given by Tyler.[38]

"For the first time," Boyer later wrote, "I saw education as an intellectually compelling field. Because of Ralph, I began to see education not as a bureaucratic process, but as an intellectual quest."[39] He abandoned his plans to return to audiology. With Tyler's help, he devised a program in which each student undertook his own project rather than attending classes, a program that met with great success.[40]

In 1963, when the chancellor of the University of California at Santa Barbara, Samuel B. Gould, was looking for someone to direct a project that would institute some degree of coherence in the nation's schools, he asked Tyler for a recommendation. Tyler suggested Boyer, who accepted on the condition that Tyler become a member of the project's board.[41] The following year, Gould became chancellor of the State University of New York and asked Boyer to join him in Albany to develop innovative programs, including the Empire State College. Ultimately, Boyer became chancellor of the state university himself in 1970. President Jimmy Carter named Boyer as his first commissioner of education, in 1977, after which term Boyer became president of the Carnegie Foundation for the Advancement of Teaching.[42] At the Carnegie Foundation, where he served until his death in 1995, he, along with his research team, published a number of influential studies, including *High School: A Report on Secondary Education in America* and *College: The Undergraduate Experience in America.*

Lyle M. Spencer, the founder and president of the educational publishing firm Science Research Associates (SRA), arrived in Chicago in 1933, a Phi Beta Kappa graduate of the University of Washington, to pursue graduate work at the University of Chicago's sociology department. It was the depths of the Depression; half a million Chicagoans were unemployed, banks were closing, and a strike at Republic Steel had just been broken by the Illinois National Guard.

In 1938, at the age of twenty-seven, Spencer started SRA as a nonprofit company. In 1939, after almost going broke and receiving subsidies from friends and family, he reorganized the firm as a commercial venture. During the years before World War II, SRA published guidance materials and obtained contracts for distribution in the schools.

When the United States entered the war, Samuel Stouffer, then a professor of sociology at the University of Chicago, was asked by Brigadier General Frederick H. Osborn, chief of the Morale Division of the War

Department, to head a research branch of the army's Information and Education Division. Stouffer asked Spencer to be his deputy. Commissioned a lieutenant colonel in the army, Spencer became interested in testing; he also formulated the point system for demobilizing World War II soldiers. When he returned from the war, he decided to start a test-publishing business.

In need of capital to launch his enterprise, he approached the Harris Trust Bank, which urged him to get an education specialist to advise him. Spencer, who had never studied education, went to see Tyler, with whom he had never studied, to ask his help. He and Tyler spent hours discussing the problem of testing, and soon Tyler became a supporter of Spencer's efforts.[43] He envisioned SRA as (in the terms of a later decade) the Bloomingdale's, rather than the Kmart, of educational publishers. Among the tests published by SRA were the Primary Mental Abilities Tests, written by L. L. Thurstone and Thelma Gwynn Thurstone.[44] Another was the Iowa Test of Educational Development, developed by Everett Lindquist of the University of Iowa.[45]

Spencer came to rely heavily on Tyler's advice and direction, particularly as to where to allocate funds. Some years later, in 1961, Spencer invited Tyler to join the SRA board to replace Irving Harris, a wealthy Chicago businessman whose Harris Trust Bank had lent Spencer the money to start SRA. Spencer had found Harris's suggestions on how to run SRA intrusive. For instance, Harris insisted that SRA pursue the adoption of its tests by the states, which was where he felt the money was; Spencer, on the other hand, thought that state adoptions would impose mediocrity on SRA's products. The two men clashed over the issue until Spencer finally decided to force Harris's ouster.[46]

SRA's directors were required to be shareholders in the corporation; Tyler borrowed six thousand dollars to buy his shares, at a nominal price.[47] When Spencer sold SRA to IBM in 1964 (he remained as president), IBM made the purchase with a block of 250,000 shares of its stock, a value at the time of fifty-five million dollars. Tyler's shares were suddenly worth two million dollars, though by the time of his death the value of his IBM stock had dwindled to a fraction of that.

Lyle Spencer died in 1968, leaving an estate worth eighty-eight million dollars, much of it in IBM stock. In a handwritten note found after his death, Spencer had written, "All the Spencer dough was earned, improbably, from education. It makes sense, therefore, that much of this money should be returned eventually to investigate the ways in which education can be improved around the world." Most of the Spencer estate went toward funding a new incarnation of the Spencer Foundation, which had been founded in 1962 and focused on the improvement of educational research and practice. The first president of the reorganized Spencer Foundation was H. Thomas James, the dean of the Stanford University School of Education; the chairman of the board was Charles Dollard, a former president of the Carnegie Foundation and a friend of both Spencer and Ralph Tyler.[48] Dollard had been, like Spencer, a deputy to Samuel Stouffer in the Army's Information and Education Division. He was also chiefly responsible, as an officer of the Carnegie Foundation, for creating the Educational Testing Service, by merging several educational entities.[49]

Tyler, who served on the board of the Spencer Foundation for some twenty years, was influential in setting the foundation's policy of funding researchers, not subjects—encouraging researchers to determine the areas they wish to pursue, rather than putting out "requests for proposals."

The most widely influential of Tyler's students, certainly in the realm of education, is John I. Goodlad, the author or editor of over thirty books, including *A Place Called School* (1984), *Teachers for Our Nation's Schools* (1990), and *Educational Renewal: Better Teachers, Better Schools* (1994). A leading educational thinker and proponent of public education as a cornerstone of democracy, now president of the nonprofit Institute for Educational Inquiry in Seattle, Goodlad has also been a professor of education at Agnes Scott College; at Emory University; at the University of Chicago; at the University of California at Los Angeles, where he spent twenty-five years, sixteen as dean; and at the University of Washington's Center for Educational Renewal.

Born and raised in western Canada, Goodlad received a teaching certificate from the Vancouver Normal School (1939) and a B.A. (1945) and M.A. (1946) from the University of British Columbia. After working as a teacher and administrator at the Provincial Industrial School for Boys in British Columbia, where he dealt directly with juvenile delinquency, he became interested in learning more about problem juveniles and decided to pursue his interest at graduate school. He enrolled at the University of Chicago and signed up for a class on secondary education, though the instructor was not listed. The professor turned out to be Tyler, who was at the time the department chairman and was substituting for someone else. Though Goodlad was astonished by his professor's "incredible mind," he found Tyler's classes "rather boring" and Tyler's rationale, at the time, incomprehensible.[50]

Nevertheless, Tyler became Goodlad's dissertation advisor. An appointment with Tyler was both hard to get and limited to about ten minutes. "But he was absolutely superb," Goodlad later recollected. "One had his attention for the entire ten minutes and always walked out of his office with a clearer head."[51] Goodlad's dissertation was an investigation into which first and second graders were promoted, and which were not. He concluded that there was no educational advantage to holding pupils back.

Only six years later, Goodlad says, did he come to understand explicitly what Tyler's rationale implied. His thinking was strongly influenced by Tyler's approach, though he and Tyler had their philosophical differences. In the matter of educational reform, for instance, Tyler generally worked within the status quo, believing that schools, as they stand, offer vast opportunities for increasing achievement. Goodlad, on the other hand, assumes that schools have to change fundamentally in order to improve. Goodlad and Robert H. Anderson's *The Nongraded Elementary School* argues that since children do not grow in grade-level spurts, the conventional grade-level organization of schools is at odds with the nature of child development. They advocate eliminating grade levels altogether.

As educational administrators, both Tyler and Goodlad initiated teacher preparation programs that involved cooperation between schools and universities, approaches in which the prospective teacher watches and takes part in classroom teaching, then attends a seminar guided by a university specialist. Goodlad's particular concern lies in preparing teachers to succeed in schools where the students are children of immigrants. Still, on the subject of teacher preparation, as on so many other matters, Tyler's influence upon his views is apparent.

Asked about his role in "nurturing" so many colleagues, students, and other such acolytes, Tyler would reply with typical self-deprecation. "Well," he said, "when a sow is suckling a pig, the sow enjoys it as much as the pig." But then Tyler was the last person to draw attention to his accomplishments. Characteristically, he resisted being labeled the "father" of educational evaluation. "If naming the child, as the godfather names babies, makes you father, then I am," he said. "I invented the term 'evaluation' when applied to educational procedures. And when it began to be a cliché, and evaluation meant so many different things to different people, I invented the term 'assessment,' and that's what we used next . . . . You can't take responsibility for what other people do, so the only thing you can do when anything becomes a cliché is to get a new word."[52]

Over the course of his career Tyler served as an advisor on educational matters to seven presidents, beginning with Franklin Delano Roosevelt, in whose administration Tyler served on a commission charged with finding a home for national educational affairs more suitable than the Department of the Interior. Harry Truman, rattled by General Douglas MacArthur's insubordination during the Korean War, asked Tyler to study how the education of military officers could be improved. (Tyler never had the opportunity to undertake the study; when Truman found out such a study could not be completed quickly, he told Tyler not to bother, since he would not be in office long enough. Tyler then realized, long before it was announced publicly, that Truman had decided not to run for reelection.) Dwight Eisenhower asked Tyler to serve on a committee to study the serious problems of children and to help establish an agenda for the White House Conference on Children and Youth. John F. Kennedy appointed Tyler to the National Science Board. Lyndon Johnson appointed Tyler to his 1964 Task Force on Education and named him vice chairman of the National Advisory Council on the Education of Disadvantaged Children. Tyler was reappointed to the council by Richard Nixon. Jimmy Carter appointed Tyler to a committee to formulate policies for the Peace Corps, Teacher Corps, and Vista.[53]

Ralph Tyler would minimize his own historical importance in the history of American education. It is difficult to know, he said, whether "people with ideas" produce change or whether the needs of a particular time produce the people who lead the change. When it was suggested to him that he was "one of our most important educational statesmen," he demurred. He was simply a product of the times: "Look back at the times that we've had people that we call statesmen. For example, in the case of Horace Mann, it was when there was a great expansion in the elementary school system of Massachusetts. They did not have enough teachers, and he had to solve the problem of how to educate teachers. He invented the normal schools, and he did a number of other things. But during the periods before that, when there wasn't a great expansion and when there were not problems in educating teachers, they didn't have any demands in that sense for persons to lead them in new ways." In his view, "some situations produce more statesmen than others."[54]

Man is essentially a problem solver, Tyler went on to say, citing the words of one of his intellectual forebears, John Dewey. "He's not a cow that chews its cud after a nice meal in the pasture and just enjoys that. Men and women are essentially made to deal with problems, and that's why civilization advances." His strength, he believed, was simply in approaching problems with common sense. "The only problem with common sense," he maintained, "is that it's so uncommon."

PART II

Conversations with Ralph Tyler

A Talk with Ralph Tyler

Phi Delta Kappan, October 1967, pp. 75–77.

The current interest in national assessment has brought the amiable and sensible Ralph Tyler, winner of the second PDK-AERA Outstanding Researcher Award, once again into the limelight. Interviewed for the *Kappan,* Tyler discussed some of the many ways he has been involved in education since he started as a high school teacher in Pierre, S.D., 46 years ago.

Ralph Tyler's retirement last July from his position as director of the Center for Advanced Study in the Behavioral Sciences at Stanford did not reduce in the least his involvement on the frontiers of educational thinking. It merely shifted the focus. This month he is serving as an American representative to an International Conference on Curriculum at Oxford. In November he will lecture at the Hebrew University in Jerusalem. In January and February he will be one of the visiting scholars at the State University of New York, working with the faculties of the state colleges that are moving toward stronger liberal arts programs. In April he will go to Seattle to serve as visiting professor at the University of Washington.

Since he left the University of Chicago in 1953, where he was dean of the division of social sciences, his major interest has been directing the Stanford center. When he was asked which of his many interests would become his major activity now that he has another opportunity to choose, he replied that he must wait a few months to see how it all works out.

"I know I will stay in teaching," he said. "Ever since I began my teaching in the high school at Pierre, South Dakota, nothing has been as exciting as teaching. That was an exciting school, too, with a truly heterogeneous student body. About one-fourth were Indians, one-fourth children of cow-punchers, another fourth from the families of government officials, and still another fourth belonged to the local service people."

As Ralph Tyler leaves the Stanford center about which his professional life has revolved for 15 years, his thoughts naturally center about this unusual institution over which he has presided with a devotion and a kindliness that has endeared him to the staff and to the hundreds of scholars who have been selected for a year of self-directed study there.

Tyler served as chairman of the committee that planned this unique study center and secured Ford Foundation support for it. When he described the center, it was apparent that he had a large emotional investment in this venture. As he talked, his enthusiasm mounted.

"The original purpose—and the continuing purpose—was to secure better teaching in the behavioral sciences. Even after a man has secured his Ph.D. and has had substantial experience, growth must continue, based upon reflection. The center is a place for reflection for 50 outstanding students of human behavior, both the younger men and some who are well-established. One scholar celebrated his 26th birthday at the center; another his 80th. Scholars are selected with an eye to age distribution, roughly one-third being under 40, one-third between 40 and 50, and one-third over 50. They are also selected to obtain a balanced distribution among the disciplines and to secure a four-to-one balance of Americans and foreign scholars.

"The center tries to provide these scholars with the ideal environment for study and reflection; to make it easy for them to accomplish what would be difficult or impossible in the home setting. Here they have extended opportunity to work alone and uninterruptedly or to converse with top scholars in their own fields. When the center invites a scholar it is able to assure him with confidence that he will find at least half a dozen others there with congenial interests. The urge to communicate with one's fellow scholars creates a lively conversational tone in the dining room which carries over to informal group discussions in the lounges and frequently to the establishment of scheduled seminar sessions. Whatever scheduling is done is arranged by the scholars themselves, not by the administration. The visiting scholar at the center has complete freedom to be alone or to associate informally."

Ralph Tyler's talents are divided among many organizations. Among the advisory bodies on which he serves are the National Science Board, the Research and Development Panel of the U.S. Office of Education, the National Advisory Council on Disadvantaged Children, and the National Academy of Education, of which he is president. He is also an active member of the Social Science Research Foundation, the Armed Forces Institute, the National Society for the Study of Education, the American Association for the Advancement of Science, and the American Educational Research Association.

Tyler gives unqualified praise and support to the purposes of the Academy of Education, which has been in existence only two years. "It exists," he says," to focus attention on scholarly work, in much the same way that the National Education Association exists to focus attention on practical school problems. It emphasizes the notion of the deferred value of research, so that people will learn to understand that research has a much wider role than the direct, immediate solution of specific problems."

The academy includes members of four categories: 1) The History and Philosophy of Education; 2) The Politics, Economics, Sociology, and Anthropology of Education; 3) The Psychology of Education; and 4) The Study of Educational Practice. Group four will soon publish a monograph prepared by Roald Campbell dealing with the relation of education to political and social forces.

The original roll of 27 members appointed by James Conant, John Gardner, and Francis Keppel will ultimately be expanded to 50. Vacancies will occur only by death, resignation, or retirement.

When asked about the influence of the Eight-Year Study, the first of the national programs with which he has been associated, Tyler cautioned against attributing change to any specific influence unless the relationship can be clearly demonstrated. "There is little doubt," he suggested, "that we are more understanding of the needs of young people today, and this understanding is reflected in our more flexible educational programs, but there is no way of knowing how much of the advance can be properly attributed to the Eight-Year Study. And of course our problems have multiplied as fast as our knowledge, so we appear to be no wiser now than we were a generation ago. One of the most conspicuous advances lies in our learning to look ahead. And the *Kappan* and other educational journals are most useful in focusing attention on what lies ahead."

As we talked about the successes and failures in education and the prospects for the future, Tyler was reluctant to identify any single area as exemplifying outstanding advancement. Instead he elaborated on the theme of ceaseless change.

"It is impossible to compare the quality of the job we are doing today with what we did in an earlier time, because our job has changed. Until World War I our job was essentially to provide educational opportunity for students who were already motivated. Since then, and especially since the Great Depression, we have assumed an entirely different task. We have learned to teach those who could not and would not have learned under the old scheme. Some persons still fail to grasp the fact that our great task is still to reach those who are not themselves actively seeking education. By far the easiest part of the teaching task is to teach the student who comes to school eager to learn."

When the conversation turned to the possibilities of extending the opportunities of college to all youth, Tyler's agile mind ranged over a wide spectrum of relevant knowledge.

"Our colonial colleges started with an effort to reach a wider clientele than was served by the English university," he said. "Then somehow our colleges became stuck in a pattern of selectivity that was broken only by the Morrill Act of 1862, which extended collegiate offerings to the vast middle class of youth whose intellectual concerns were tied to the arts, agriculture, and mechanics. Later the junior college movement extended the opportunities still further. Last year 60 percent of the graduates of the University of California were students who had started at junior colleges.

"The extension of college education, like the extension of high school education, is primarily a problem of learning to provide rigorous offerings appropriate to the backgrounds and the motivations of the students you wish to serve. Years ago W. W. Charters and I developed a new program for the Rochester Institute for engineering students who were reluctant to tackle the usual abstractions in that curriculum. We developed a work-study program that brought the abstractions closer to the practical applications. We also had the student move from the concrete to the abstract, from the laboratory and the workshop to the calculus class, for example. Engineering still frightens many students because of its abstractions.

"We can reach far more students at the college level than we have reached in the past. Geneticists continue to report data that suggests that we can raise the ability level of most students to accepted college levels. We have not begun to approach the potentials of student abilities. We must learn the basic wisdom of letting the individual learn, but at the same time we must learn how to demand successfully that he learn more. It is commonly recognized that most persons use only a very small portion of their intellectual capacity. So far we have only been tinkering with administrative arrangements in our efforts to achieve more effective learning. For example, it may be that reducing class size is only a kind of feather-bedding. There is no evidence that smaller classes necessarily result in more or better learning.

"We need faith in the ability of the individual student to learn. We have been badly misled by our misinterpretation of I.Q. scores. An I.Q. score measures what a person has presently learned about how to learn, but it says nothing about the limits of his ability to learn. Possibly we have frequently tried too hard to teach instead of providing freedom, encouragement, and materials for learning.

"We try too hard to reassure ourselves that we the teachers are working hard enough and doing the right thing. We focus too hard on ourselves, on teachers as the actors, as if they were the central figures in the play."

Tyler leaned back and reminisced briefly about the University of Chicago under Hutchins, when students were granted more freedom to progress at their own speed than is usual on college campuses. He regretted the retreat from the Hutchins plan, but was unwilling to suggest an explanation for the discarding of so useful an arrangement.

Pressed to identify areas where it is reasonable to expect early progress in our educational efforts, Tyler replied with a comparison to the business world. "A manufacturer," he said, "cannot expect to be able to control both the volume of production of his product and the volume of his sales. That would be a forced and unnatural situation. Nor is it natural for a teacher to control both the teaching-learning situation and the grading of the learning product. Outside accounting or grading is essential in every kind of operation. Schoolmen are in an untenable position when they resist having a competent professional team assess their product. This just isn't realistic."

As the time allotted for our conversation drew to a close, Tyler alternately reminisced and philosophized about the big issues in education. "Our job is to be aware of reality, to understand reality and learn to manipulate reality in order to work effectively. I remember well my conversations with John Dewey during the course of the Eight-Year Study. He said to me, 'An educational experience is one that provides a balance between things the learner cannot control and those he can at least partly control. If the learning situation was so controlled that the learner could only rebel or be conditioned, or if, on the other hand, it was so free that there were no restraints and he could respond with pure whim, little learning would take place in either event. A learning situation must offer a nice balance between discipline and freedom. Neither one is first or most.'

"A friend of mine was complaining recently that it has become almost impossible for a college dean or president to operate with all of the student dissent to cope with. Actually, if the college administrator accepts the reality of dealing with activist students he can be quite happy in his job, just as some business executives have learned the reality of dealing with organized labor. Again it is just a matter of facing reality."

Whatever educational challenges Ralph Tyler accepts, he is sure to take with him to the job an enthusiasm, an optimism, an agile and trained intellect, and a well-developed acceptance of reality.—DWR

The Father of Behavioral Objectives Criticizes Them: An Interview with Ralph Tyler

Justin M. Fishbein

Phi Delta Kappan, September 1973, pp. 55–57.

Ralph Tyler is known as one of the truly great elder statesmen of education. He first came into national prominence as director of the famed Eight-Year Study of Secondary Schools, 1934–42. After a distinguished career as professor and author, he became director of the Center for Advanced Study in the Behavioral Sciences of Stanford, California, in 1953. He was awarded the second PDK-AERA Award for Distinguished Research in Education in 1965. After retirement from the Stanford center, Tyler became chairman of the Educational Advisory Board for Science Research Associates in Chicago, a position he still holds.

The interview reported below came about last spring when Justin M. Fishbein, senior project editor for SRA, discovered that Tyler is known as "the father of behavioral objectives." Since Fishbein was a member of the Citizens Advisory Committee to Establish Objectives for the Lake County (Illinois) High School District 125 and was aware of the continuing controversy over behavioral objectives, he determined to interview Mr. Tyler.

Q: Dr. Tyler, I read an article of yours in a 1931 issue of the *Educational Research Bulletin* in which you emphasized the value of defining educational objectives in behavioral terms. How did you arrive at that idea?

A: When I went to the Ohio State University in 1929 to head the Division of Accomplishment Tests in the Bureau of Educational Research, I was asked to work with those faculty members who wanted to construct better examinations and improve the effectiveness of their instruction. First, I worked with teachers of undergraduate biology courses.

At that time, the usual procedure followed in constructing educational achievement tests was to identify the textbooks being used in a given subject and to write a set of questions that sampled the content of these books. It was assumed that the extent to which the student remembered specific items of content was a measure of his attainment of the objectives of the course. I found, however, that these biology teachers were seeking to help students learn to use the subject in their own contact with biological phenomena and did not consider memorization of details of content a major purpose of the course. From their experience with students, they had found that some who could answer questions on content details could not use biological concepts and principles in explaining the phenomena that they encountered in the laboratory or in the world outside.

This led me to realize that it was important in constructing an achievement test to identify the one or more kinds of things that students were expected to learn so that test exercises would be designed to furnish an opportunity for students to show the extent to which they had learned these things.

Q: What do you mean, "kinds of things students were expected to learn"?

A: Keeping in mind the psychological definition of learning as "the acquisition of new patterns of behavior through experience," I asked the biology teachers what kinds of *behavior* they *hoped* their students would acquire through their study of the college biology courses. I also pointed out that the term "behavior" includes all kinds of reactions people carry on—thinking, feeling, and acting. I was not using the term as it was used by the school of behaviorism, which restricted it only to overtly observable acts and ruled out much of human behavior that is subjectively experienced but not directly observable by others.

Q: Could the teachers describe the kinds of behavior the students were expected to learn?

A: As they worked to clarify and formulate their intentions as teachers, they agreed upon five kinds of behavior: 1) recalling information, 2) understanding concepts and principles, 3) applying principles to concrete

situations, 4) interpreting experimental data, and 5) employing laboratory skills. These were defined more fully to be useful in guiding the teach-
ing/learning process as well as in building valid tests and exercises for their
courses. "Recalling information" was defined as "stating the facts" and
also "recognizing factual statements." Furthermore, they listed the facts
that they believed to be important to remember.

"Understanding concepts and principles" was defined as "stating them
in one's own words, giving illustrations of them, and recognizing examples
of them." They also listed some 34 concepts and 91 principles that they
considered important in understanding biological phenomena.

"Applying principles to concrete situations" was defined as using one
or more of the important principles in explaining concrete biological
phenomena or in predicting the course of biological processes.

"Interpreting experimental data" was defined as drawing reasonable
inferences from experimental data and criticizing the inferences drawn by
others. They also outlined the range of experiments relevant to these
biology concepts.

"Employing laboratory skills" was defined as skillfully carrying on laboratory exercises. They also defined the laboratory activities they considered important for the biology courses.

Q: Did the teachers see any value in formulating objectives this way?

A: They found that the exercise of identifying and defining their educational objectives in terms of behavior helped them to recognize more
clearly what they expected their students to learn. It also helped them to
plan their teaching and the learning assignments. For example, if students
were to learn to apply principles, their learning experiences should have
included practice in explaining concrete biological phenomena in terms
of relevant phenomena. If the students were to learn to interpret experimental data, they would have needed experiences in examining data and
drawing inferences from the results and in reviewing and criticizing inferences drawn by others. Moreover, these definitions furnished the basis
for diagnostic and summative tests, since they pointed out the nature of
the test exercises which would give students a chance to show the extent
to which they were acquiring these patterns of behavior.

The assistance which these teachers of undergraduate biology reported
that they had gained by this work led me to write the article in 1931 on
defining objectives in this way.

Q: Did you follow up this kind of activity with other groups?

A: Yes, I worked with other departments of the university. Then when
I served as director of evaluation in the Eight-Year Study, from 1934 to
1942, this procedure guided the development of new curricula in the 30
high schools as well as the program of evaluation. Working in all the ar-

eas of secondary school instruction, we encountered a great range of behavior patterns that students were expected to acquire. For example, in English, teachers sought to help students to interpret literature, develop interests in a wide range of mature reading materials, and appreciate various kinds of literature. In social studies, teachers planned courses that they thought would help students understand certain concepts developed by social scientists, analyze in terms of these concepts concrete social problems they encountered, interpret social data, and be concerned about the public good. A description of these objectives emphasized in the Eight-Year Study is found in its five-volume report. The volume that deals with defining objectives and the evaluation instruments that were developed is called *Appraising and Recording Student Progress.** This procedure was also followed in the construction of the comprehensive examinations at the University of Chicago when I was university examiner there from 1938 to 1953; in the development of the tests and examinations for the U.S. Armed Forces Institute, while I was director of the examinations staff from 1943 to 1953; and in the curriculum and evaluation programs of the Cooperative Study in General Education, the so-called "Twenty-Two college study," which I directed from 1939 to 1945.

Q: What has happened to the "behavioral objectives movement" today?

A: It seems to have bogged down between the conception of learning as limited to the acquisition of specific patterns of behavior and the notion of learning which includes the development of generalizations. Or it may be hung up on the confusion between "clarity of definition" and "specificity" when applied to educational objectives. Let me illustrate each of these.

When Thorndike and his associates demonstrated experimentally that transfer of training did not automatically take place and that the doctrine of formal discipline (the idea that when a student took a subject like mathematics or Latin his mind was disciplined to deal with any kind of intellectual task) was not substantiated empirically, association theories of learning became popular. Typically, these theories viewed learning as the building of connections between specific stimuli and specific responses. This led to the listing of literally thousands of objectives for a school subject. For example, Thorndike's *Psychology of Arithmetic* listed more than 2,000 objectives for primary school arithmetic. Each of the 100 addition combinations taking one-digit numbers two at a time was a specific objective. As another illustration, Pendleton listed nearly 3,000 objectives for high school English. However, this effort to state specific objectives was short-lived both because teachers could not keep in mind such a long list of aims and because further studies of human learning demonstrated

*Eugene Smith and Ralph Tyler, *Appraising and Recording Student Progress* (New York: Harper's, 1942).

that students could generalize their learning from concrete experiences. Judd and Freeman conducted several crucial experiments on generalization, and Thorndike's later work led him to formulate laws of transfer of training based on the theory of identical elements that the learner could recognize in varied learning situations. By 1927, the notion of guiding teaching by using specific objectives was no longer widely accepted.

Q: Your explanation gives me some idea of the earlier history of specific objectives emphasized by educational psychologists in the early part of this century, but what is the "confusion" you mentioned between "clarity of definition" and "specificity"?

A: If a teacher is to use his statement of objectives to guide his planning and teaching, he needs to know what they mean, and if tests are to be constructed to assess the extent to which students are achieving the objectives, these aims must have a clear meaning. But clarity is not the same as specificity. One can be clear about a more general objective such as applying biological principles to concrete phenomena, yet it is not a specific objective. It is clear when "applying principles" is defined as "using the principles to explain the biological phenomena that the student encounters," when the principles dealt with in the course are listed, and when "concrete phenomena" are defined as "the biological phenomena in which the principles are relevant." Such an objective assumes that the student can generalize the ways in which principles serve to furnish a scientific explanation. The validity of these assumptions is in harmony with many studies of student learning in science subjects. An educational objective does not need to be specific in order to be clear, attainable, and capable of assessment.

Q: If "specific association" is no longer accepted as the only kind of human learning possible and if studies of human learning in various fields have demonstrated the potential of generalized objectives, how do you account for a substantial number of efforts today to state educational objectives of schools in specific terms?

A: I see two factors that account at least partly for this. One is the success in the business and industrial world of management by objectives. The other is the achievements in military and industrial training of programs focused on specific objectives.

Many industries have been able to respond positively and profitably to the rapid changes in modern society by identifying attainable goals, developing a strategy to reach them, and building an annual operating plan to implement the strategy. Thus, a producer of automobiles might identify a market for compact cars among lower income families and establish objectives to obtain 20% of that market within a five-year period. This would require a strategy involving the development of new designs, the construction or modification of factories, and the training of a certain number of production workers and salesmen who would be required to produce and sell the number of automobiles projected as the goal. From this strategy, a plan for each year can be devised that becomes the operating plan for that year. Managers can be assigned their various roles in the plan, and—of special note—their responsibilities in terms of production or marketing can be allocated in concrete terms with definite numbers of persons to be trained and cars to be produced and sold. The assignment of responsibility in terms of these concrete objectives has proved to be a strong incentive and guide to improved management and performance of the firm.

It is not surprising that laymen who have been impressed by the success of this system of management by objectives should press school administrators and boards of education to adopt it. However, in the response to these pressures, too little attention has been given to the nature of human learning and the purposes of education. Specific learning objectives have often been confused with clear and *appropriate* educational objectives that could be used as guides to the school's management and performance.

Q: Can you clarify further just why educators have gone wrong in adapting successful programs?

A: During the second world war and since, new products, new tools and machines, and new technologies have called for sharp and rapid shifts in the ways in which industrial work is performed. Also, the great increase in population and the extension of employment opportunities to minority groups have greatly increased the numbers of persons who need training to undertake the changing jobs in industry.

In a large number of cases, the initial training required acquisition of very specific skills like those involved in assembling electronic equipment, or in winding small coils, or in testing miniature circuits. By defining specifically what the worker was to do, the training program was precisely designed and the tests of the worker's learning were established. These programs, in most cases, greatly shortened the period of training required. Moreover, the trainers found that most training programs previously had defined only vaguely the skills to be developed and had not devised specific tests to determine when the trainee had acquired and could use the skills. Hence, several trainers published manuals on defining objectives in terms of specific observable behavior. A number of educational leaders were impressed by the success of these training programs and sought to follow the recommendations of the training manuals. Apparently, they failed to distinguish between 1) the learning of highly specific skills for limited job performance and 2) the more generalized understanding, problem-solving skills and other kinds of behavior patterns that thoughtful teachers and educators seek to help students develop. As a result, these training manuals and some of the trainers themselves have served as guides for many of the current efforts to write behavioral objective.

Q: You mentioned earlier the reliance you placed on the ideas of teachers regarding desirable and attainable educational objectives. Can't experts write better objectives than teachers can?

A: My attempt to answer this question will require some preliminary comments. There are far more "good things" that students could learn than their time in school permits. Certainly, the choice of aims—that is, the decision about the kinds of learning that the school should emphasize and devote its resources to—is such a major matter that it is of concern to parents, children, and the general public as well as to teachers and school leaders. The judgments coming from all these sectors of our society can be improved by data regarding the changing demands and opportunities of contemporary life, about the interests and needs and talents of particular children, and about the continually developing resources, knowledge, and skills on which the school can draw. Systematic study of these matters is an important part of curriculum development.

But I believe we must also recognize that teachers working closely with children often have a notion of the ways in which their students have gained new ways of looking at things, ways of attacking problems, new skills, new interests, and new ideas. I find that such teachers, as they participate in a sympathetic discussion, can state these kinds of behavior so that the real meaning will not be lost. Specialists in writing objectives often seem one or two steps removed from actual experiences with children. A sympathetic discussion of what things teachers had observed children learning was the chief source for developing the objectives of the Eight-Year Study. The discussion also helped to clarify the meaning of the statements, and it reinforced the idea that the objectives are attainable. Unless the teacher understands the objectives he is supposed to be helping students attain, and unless he believes that students *can* attain them, it is unlikely that he will give real attention to them.

Q: Do you believe that teachers, educators, parents, children, and the public as well will benefit if educational objectives are clearly stated in terms of behavior to be learned?

A: I do. The discussion and clarification of important objectives can be a source of help to teachers and a way of building better understanding of the school's mission in the community.

Ralph Tyler Discusses Behavioral Objectives

June Grant Shane and Harold G. Shane

Today's Education, September–October 1973, pp. 41–46.

Today some educators focus on a humanistic-ethic model for schools while others favor a model which states all goals in explicit behavioral terms. To bring the issues into focus for the readers of *Today's Education,* we interviewed Ralph W. Tyler, a pioneer in the study of behavioral objectives. Dr. Tyler is a distinguished senior educational statesman and director emeritus of the Center for Advanced Study in the Behavioral Sciences at Palo Alto.

Q: Is our impression correct that while you were involved in the Eight-Year Study* you practically "invented" performance objectives by stressing the need for schools to define their educational targets operationally?

A: I was involved even before that study began in 1933. When I first went to The Ohio State University in 1929, I was asked to work with various departments in improving instruction. Even then, some faculty recognized that a college education was more than simply absorbing facts. They wanted measures of effectiveness that went beyond mere memorization.

I soon realized that "learning" is a process by which people acquire new patterns of behavior—*behavior* meaning all kinds of human reactions like thinking and feeling as well as overt reactions. Thus, in talking with

*Ed. Note: The Eight-Year Study (1933–41) was designed to find out first whether it was necessary for high school students to meet traditional college entrance requirements in order to ensure their success in college; and second, what secondary schools would do with their curriculums once their students no longer had to meet the customary requirements.

the various science departments, we included ways of thinking as human behavior, and behavior patterns. We then were able to talk about students' understanding of principles and about their being able to apply them. This illustrates what I mean by behavior.

Although we decided that we must define our objectives in terms of behavior if we were to evaluate students, we did not use the term *performance objectives*. *Performance* at that time was a term used in testing to refer to a test where one did manipulative things like work with blocks to show one's ability to visualize concrete objects.

Q: In general, Dr. Tyler, you have reviewed the experiences and the circumstances that led you to conclude that the concept of expressing sought educational outcomes in terms of behavior was desirable. But if you had tried to give a definition of behavioral objectives at the time you first created them, how would you have stated it?

A: I would have said something like this: As teachers try to state what they are attempting to do, they should formulate this in terms of what the student is supposed to learn, and state this in terms of the kinds of behavior which they hope the student will acquire as a result of instruction. These become behavioral objectives.

Q: Would you change that definition in any way today?

A: No, I think not. But please keep in mind two things that many people now overlook when they talk about behavioral objectives:

One: I am using the term *behavior* in the broadest psychological sense. It includes any reaction a human being is capable of making. It includes attitudes toward subjects or things. It encompasses being able to solve problems and to acquire intellectual skills like reading or physical skills like running.

Two: We must recognize that human beings are capable of generalizing behavior, whereas it is generally necessary to be highly specific when training an animal. A dog, for example, has got to jump so high; he's got to do so and so. But the human being can learn how to go about problem-solving—not just how to deal with a specific task that you have trained him to do as you might train a dog.

I think many current uses of the term, *behavioral objectives*, imply procedures that are too specific. I believe that the individual human being is able to solve many of his own problems and so I think that more of our educational objectives should be general in nature—like learning how to go about attacking problems, finding out where the difficulties are, getting information, analyzing the data, and drawing inferences from data.

Hence, in my view, many behavioral objectives should be set at a considerably higher or more general level than the extremely specific things I find in many current efforts to write them.

Q: Would you please make some distinctions between behavioral objectives and performance objectives? Also, how do you interpret criterion-referenced performance?

A: One has to remember that, unlike the sciences, education does not have a highly standardized terminology for technical terms. So the dictionary is no help when we try to explain what is meant by behavioral objectives. Also, usage changes quite rapidly.

But let me try to make a distinction. What I mean by behavioral objectives is a statement of what teachers are trying to help students learn from their instruction—the ways of thinking, feeling, or acting that they want students to develop.

Performance objectives tend to pertain only to matters of overt behavior, to what students do that one can see. If this is all the school attempts, it seriously limits school learning. Humans can also learn ways of thinking; they can learn ways of responding emotionally to literature. They can learn a lot of things that transcend overt performance objectives.

Q: What about criterion-referenced performance? Is it related to performance objectives?

A: I think the term *criterion-referenced* has assumed importance today because, in the past, testing in the United States has been norm-referenced. Two kinds of events influenced the so-called "Modern Testing Movement" in Western Society.

One was the effort to identify people who were subnormal or superior in human functioning—the work of Binet which, in this country, resulted some 50 years ago in the development of the Stanford-Binet test.

The other was the development of the Army Alpha group intelligence test, which was created by psychologists during World War I to select out of several million men those who were most likely to benefit from quick instruction and who would be able to go into the many kinds of jobs the military required.

This test was so successful in identifying people who subsequently succeeded in various military roles that group intelligence tests and achievement tests as well began to be used in the schools.

The basic purpose of this testing is to take a total group and arrange them in some kind of order so that you can say here is the top 10 percent and here is the bottom 10 percent. The population is arranged on a linear scale from the best to the worst. This is called norm-referenced testing.

When this type of test is being made, various test items are tried out. If the items differentiate among the persons tested, they are retained. So a typical achievement test has about 80 percent of its items in the narrow range of difficulty, where between 40 and 60 percent of people tested get the answer right.

If the purpose is to identify those who do best on the total test and those who do poorest, this is an efficient way to go about it. But if you are trying to answer the question, "What have students learned?" you run into difficulties. This is because (a) almost all items that most persons can answer correctly are dropped from the typical achievement test because they do not discriminate and (b) those items that almost no one can answer correctly are also dropped because they don't discriminate either.

Actually, instead of testing what our students have learned, we have been using test items to differentiate some students from other students.

Now, in this era of accountability when we are being asked such questions as "Are pupils learning to read?" or "Can they compute?" we need a different approach. We must set up questions or exercises that are related to a particular question—that is, they are criterion-referenced: the criterion being whether or not pupils can read, compute, understand, etc.

In other words, the new tests that are coming out are criterion-referenced because they are judged for their validity in terms of whether they really test what the schools are trying to teach and not whether they differentiate the better students from the poorer students.

Q: How would you account for the fact that your views regarding behavioral objectives, which go back over 30 years, were not more generally accepted sooner? Indeed, many people seem to feel that behavioral objectives are new educational tools which were discovered in the early and middle '60s.

A: This phenomenon is not associated just with my work. Each generation tends to forget to look at the past (and this is especially true of those preoccupied with recent rapid changes). I think it is a natural phenomenon. In fact, the Bible talks about young people having forsaken their elders. They were not listening in those times, either.

Q: In general, what is your reaction to educational practices done in the name of behavioral objectives since the early 1960s? In other words, what is your reaction to such developments as competency-based teacher education, performance contracting, lists of performance objectives for the teaching of reading, and so on?

A: As a young man, I had the good fortune to be a research assistant to W. W. Charters when he was in charge of the influential Commonwealth Teacher-Training Study. It was designed to identify the activities of teachers upon which their preparation should be based. In other words, the Commonwealth Study was performance-based.

In the Study report, which was published in 1929. Charters identified the 1,001 activities which teachers must learn how to perform if they were going to be effective in the classroom. We have the same thing coming up now in 1973, and I fear we are back where we were almost 50 years ago. Apparently, we keep on *rediscovering* ideas rather than *building* on them. That applies to behavioral objectives and performance-based objectives.

Q: Were you really speaking of 1,001 activities or were you using that number metaphorically?

A: As I recall, the number turned out to be 1,017. However Mr. Charters thought that 1,001 sounded better, so that was the number commonly used. As a statistician for the whole enterprise, it was my role to find statistical ways of classifying these activities so there would be a finite number to deal with. We developed a series of categories that came out. I believe, that with perhaps 27 major objectives that would now be called performance-based objectives for teacher education.

Q: Would you agree or disagree with the statement that widespread use of behavioral objectives tends to substitute "specific answers" for general education, such as defined in the Harvard Report, *General Education in a Free Society*, that was published after World War II?

A: The faculty discussions that culminated in the Harvard Report were actively under way during the latter part of the Eight-Year Study, which ended in 1941, and were greatly influenced by it. If you look carefully at that report, you will see that they, too, were trying to formulate general education in terms of major aspects of human behavior.

I think many people who are trying to use behavioral objectives today perceive them as very specific kinds of behavior. If they consider that's what schools are all about, they are confusing knowing *answers* with being *educated*.

Let me cite an example. Between 1939 and 1945, I worked as Director of the Cooperative Study of General Education. This involved some 22 colleges that were being aided in developing general education programs under the auspices of the American Council on Education.

One of the things these colleges were continually concerned about was establishing objectives that would help students attack larger problems. Although various students may come out with different solutions to problems, the important thing for each of them is knowing how to approach the problem, what kinds of issues are involved, what sorts of data should be collected, and how the data could be interpreted. These are the kinds of things that can be taught so that students become inquirers rather than possessors of pat answers.

I think we should be less concerned with specific behavior and more concerned with human capabilities. We should be less interested in whether students have acquired a bunch of little answers to little questions and more concerned with whether they conceive of human learning as a means by which they are able to work out answers to their own

problems because they have acquired intellectual tools. Equally important is whether they have the attitude toward life that enables them to
approach the tasks of living with initiative and creativity.

Q: What is your opinion of depositories of behavioral objectives—
depositories from which one can obtain lists of such objectives?

A: Records of what people have chosen as objectives or of how they
have formulated them can be useful as a guide. However, if the objectives are taken mechanically, I think this is as bad as becoming a convert
to a religion without knowing what the religion stands for.

Q: Recently someone described a school system in which two teachers were released full time to spend the entire school year preparing behavioral objectives to match the content of textbooks the school was
using. Is this a desirable way of developing behavioral objectives?

A: As you describe it, it sounds mechanistic. However, if the objectives were compiled to stimulate the thinking and understanding of those
involved, then it could be quite helpful. Knowing what you think and
trying to be clear about it is a good thing, whereas simply substituting
someone else's wording is bad.

Q: In some of the small brochures that are available to help people write
behavioral objectives, there sometimes are lists of words that are considered more "desirable" than others. For example, "to understand" or "to
appreciate" are not as favored for use in preparing behavioral objectives
as are "to list" or "to write." Is this differentiation in terminology important?

A: I think it unfortunate to talk about "good" words or "bad" words.
If you want to develop some kind of meaning for a term or concept that
involves more than just memorizing a definition, and if you mean by the
word *understand*—then I prefer that word.

If, however, the word *understand* is used in order to be vague or because the person hasn't thought through what a student would do, and
if you start testing him simply by checking memorization, then it is a
"bad" word.

Q: Educators like James MacDonald and Arthur Combs have expressed
concern lest behavioral objectives and criterion-based performance de-
humanize education. Is this a real or fancied cause for alarm?

A: I would say that if the current interest in behavioral objectives im-
plies only specific training, then I agree with all the criticisms of this type
of activity. It ignores the notion that learning involves acquiring new
behavior.

Q: What is your appraisal of efforts that personnel at the U.S. Office
of Education have made in the last year or two to see that funded projects
have their outcomes expressed in behavioral terms? Does this seem de-

sirable or does this practice limit or even stifle some of the work we ought to be doing?

A: I do not have concrete cases on which to base an answer. However, if any USOE personnel think of behavioral objectives as very specific types of objectives that are not adequately representative of what the schools ought to be doing, then I think it is a bad thing.

On the other hand, USOE employees have to be concerned about people who get money for a project without a clear idea of what it is they hope to accomplish. To insist that they state their objectives in clearer terms is certainly desirable.

Q: Recent legislation in California and Ohio has led some local districts to conclude that specific instructional goals must be stated precisely in terms of the behavior sought from young learners. Since the law, at least in California, requires that the competence of educators with permanent status be assessed at least every two years and that of personnel with probationary status every year, do you think use of behavioral objectives will become an indirect way of rating teachers?

A: I can imagine some laymen who have not really examined what goes on in schools and education thinking that there is some simple device by which they can determine whether to promote teachers, transfer them, or have them do something else. But I am certain that if they attempt to carry out such a policy, it will prove futile.

Q: Michael Scriven's name is sometimes associated with the term *evaluation*. He has emphasized what he calls "goal-free" evaluation, where the outcomes of instructional experience are evaluated without any consideration for what the planner intended. What are your views on goal-free evaluation?

A: Let me say why I think Michael emphasized goal-free evaluation. When the Office of Education asked him to look at projects and their potential for the improvement of education in various parts of the nation, he discovered that in some cases the persons who had designed projects had rather limited vision—that their objectives were much less ambitious than they might have been.

As a result, he suggested that evaluators look at an ongoing educational activity from the point of view of their own knowledge of how learning takes place to examine what its potential might be for good or bad. In this connection I consider goal-free evaluation as being worthwhile.

My usual role, on the other hand, has not been to appraise things in general, but to work with schools in specifically improving what they are doing. Here, it is very important to begin with what the schools see themselves attempting to do *now*: to examine what goes on, to discuss it, to see if there are greater possibilities than they thought, to see if they have been vague in places or have lost impetus because they haven't brought their work into focus.

Q: Do you feel that having a nationwide agreement on certain behavioral objectives would reduce children's problems as they moved from one place to another within the United States?

A: We should think about this question at two levels: the secondary and the elementary school level. I think it is desirable that almost all of the states in the United States permit a person to demonstrate that he qualifies as a high school graduate by taking standardized tests such as those we devised under the guidance of E. F. Lindquist for returning veterans—the Tests of General Educational Development.

These examinations were based on behavioral objectives—upon students' being able to handle various kinds of concepts, being able to read carefully and critically a variety of materials, and being able to analyze and solve certain quantitative problems.

At the elementary school level, we face greater difficulty. In our National Assessment program, we find great agreement among educators and laymen about certain ends of education—for example, being able to comprehend newspapers and other kinds of reading materials, being able to handle certain quantitative problems in arithmetic, being able to understand the operations of our system of government, and so on. However, in the early years of school, there are no standard sequences for developing them.

Some schools start children reading with a look-say approach; others start with a phonic approach; still others start with a linguistic approach. As a result, if you were to test children in the second and third grade, prior to their having attained competence, some would have a broad vocabulary while others would have a limited one.

Therefore, if a child's family moves while he is at this age level, he may find he has quite a different background and may have difficulties for a while. However, as you move up in the grades, you often find more differences between two schools in the same city than there may be between schools in two different states.

Another point enters in here. America increasingly is acquiring a common culture. Its television and other mass media help to provide a national and world view of what is going on. Our citizens are beginning to become concerned with the same values; they consider the same skills important. As time goes on, mobile children will probably have fewer and fewer problems in finding very different purposes in the schools they attend.

Q: At the turn of the century, we thought of America as a kind of melting pot where the friendless and homeless would, at least in some respects, be homogenized and Americanized. In the 1960s there was a growing emphasis on pluralism. How can you reconcile the emphasis on a pluralistic culture with the comments you have made about a growing common culture in America?

A: Let me make two comments. First, a crucial problem in any society resides in the continued tension between individualism and socialization. The individual needs to be different from others; his uniqueness must be preserved. Yet, paradoxically, in order to live today with our great interdependence, he must be able to participate in a mass society.

Today, the various places where individualism and socialization come into conflict are seen all about us. I do not see this conflict ever disappearing. We may always have to struggle with the problem of how we can have a society which is both effective as an organization and yet provides a great deal of opportunity for individual uniqueness.

Second there is this to say about membership in groups: An ethnic group may be concerned—and rightly so—about its unique characteristics, but this still gives the individual an ethnic problem. He doesn't want to be considered too much like every other person who comes from his ethnic group.

The melting pot concept represented an effort to emphasize socialization. Now the pendulum has swung the other way, but we must continually keep both objectives in mind: the need to develop the individual, yet to be sure that his socialization is not sacrificed in the regular educational process.

Q: In the perspective of our discussion, how would you summarize your present attitude toward evaluating the curriculum in the light of predetermined and definitely stated behavioral objectives?

A: Let me go beyond our conversation. The great impetus to look at the curriculum in a different fashion developed after the First World War and came to fruition with the publication of the two-part 26th *Yearbook* of the National Society for the Study of Education. These significant volumes were presented to members of the association who gathered at Dallas in February 1927. Here, many of the things that we are talking about today were expressed for the first time.

Much of my thinking was strongly influenced by this publication because I had worked with a number of people who had been responsible for its preparation.* They pointed out that we were talking about subjects as though they were ends in themselves. That is, you studied Latin because it presumably would improve your language; you took geometry supposedly because you would become a better thinker. Rather, these pioneers said, we should look at the questions—What is it that students

*On the *Yearbook* Curriculum Committee were William C. Bagley, Franklin Bobbitt, Frederick G. Bonser, W.W. Charters, George S. Counts, Stuart A. Courtis, Ernest Horn, Charles H. Judd, Frederick J. Kelly, William H. Kilpatrick, Harold Rugg, and George A. Works.

can learn? How can they develop into persons who can take responsible positions in a rapidly changing society?

This made me and many other persons in the field of curriculum begin to realize that we had to look at the *outcomes* of learning rather than to look at the *labels*.

The Eight-Year Study was a final demonstration at the high school level that what had been holding the high schools back was the reluctance of the colleges of that era to accept a nontraditional pattern of subjects.

The Study showed that it wasn't the subjects that determined whether young adolescents were ready to go on to college; it was whether they had acquired certain kinds of behavior. Could they read critically and effectively? Could they understand important concepts, and could they handle quantitative ways of thinking?

In the end, the teachers' responsibility comes back to this: "What is it that students can learn?" And *learning* means not just talking about topics but determining what students can *do* with them. This kind of guided human development transcends behavioral objectives per se.

Each generation has to learn to get beyond the labels and to understand the deeper significance of content. Let me say in closing that it is important, I think, for parents and educators alike to keep their minds continually concerned with what it is that education can be doing.

What can young people learn that is transferable to the world beyond the school so that they are truly educated for living and doing things of value in this world? Behavioral objectives are of value only insofar as carefully phrased ones serve as tools in helping instruction attain its real goals.

June Grant Shane is professor of education and Harold G. Shane is university professor of education, Indiana University, Bloomington.

An Interview with Ralph Tyler

Kevin Ryan, John Johnston, and Katherine Newman

Phi Delta Kappan, March 1977, pp. 544–547.

Kappan: Let's begin with a horribly general question: What is your assessment of the general state of education today? Many people are discouraged with the schools. They look at the dip in achievement scores. They feel that public support for education is eroding. They think teacher organizations are becoming a part of the problem rather than part of the solution.

They suspect that there is no intellectual vitality in the schools. Do these concerns fit with your assessment of the way things are?

Tyler: I think this is *not* the way things are. I think that education, like other important social functions—such as the maintenance of health or the provision of a nice combination between law and freedom—is something that has to be worked on continually. The tendency to be disillusioned grows out of inadequate understanding or unreal expectations.

Let me look for a moment at history and then come back to talk about current questions. Historically, we have moved in 200 years from a country made up very largely of farmers and pioneers. When the Declaration of Independence was signed, probably less than 15% of the people were literate. Now, according to our national assessment program, 80% of our 17-year-olds can read and comprehend simple materials. Bit by bit we have been achieving literacy. As long as a considerable fraction of our people didn't need literacy, we didn't think about it. When I was born, 61% of the labor force was unskilled and didn't require education in order to work. When I was young, half the children in Nebraska dropped out of school by the time they were 12 and got jobs because education was compulsory only to that age.

When we begin to get discouraged, it's either because we don't know the facts or because we are expecting to achieve 100% literacy in one great leap.

This leads me to a second point: We look at the school as if it were the only educational institution in our society. The real educational system of any society is a combination of all the institutions that provide constructive learning experiences. Most of us have learned more at home and at work and in relations with others than we have learned in school. That doesn't mean that the school doesn't serve a very important function—one that probably could not be served by any other institution. But we should remember that the process of becoming a constructive, disciplined, mature adult involves a tremendous range of influences, including the home and the work place.

If you ask yourself realistically, "What has changed in recent years?" you will find, in the first place, that the influence of the home has been greatly reduced. Second, opportunities to learn through work are more limited. In 1950 something like 80% of our young people had opportunities for work experience before they finished high school; now the figure is about 25%. Opportunities to learn from adults in the larger society are more restricted as we tend toward segregation by age. Although the average elementary child continues to spend about the same amount of time in school—1,100 hours a year—he doesn't have as many other educational experiences as he once had.

Schools were established at a time when the stimulation and the need for schooling came from sources outside the schools. The situation has now changed. For example, schools still teach kids to handle arithmetic, but outside of school they aren't forced to use it as much as they once did. Take another illustration: The National Assessment of Educational Progress shows that children up through the third grade are reading better than ever before; but at the sixth grade they are reading less well. I take this to mean that we have taught them to read in school, but the opportunities for reading that used to be provided in the home are replaced by television. So instead of looking at the NAEP findings simplistically and saying, "Oh, my God, how bad education is!" let's look at the question "Where is education less adequate? What can we do to strengthen it?" And of course our answer must cover the need for a better relationship between the schools and other educative institutions. Our failure to look at the total educational system results in a lot of useless expenditures and a lot of misdirected energy.

Kappan: Many of today's critics of the schools have the idea that students are not doing as well in the basic or tool subjects as they used to. What are the facts?

Tyler: First, let's look at national assessment program findings. In the second round of reading assessments, 9-year-olds—kids at about the end of the third grade—did slightly better than 9-year-olds did in the first round. By and large, primary-grade tests of other sorts show that scores have improved. At age 13 there is not so much increase.

Achievement test scores are not as easy to interpret as the NAEP data, because they have been designed to measure individual differences and to drop out items that everybody can answer. Thus one can't really tell what things everybody is learning from an achievement test as normally constructed. However, I would say in general that achievement in the primary grades is improving more than in the middle grades.

In mathematics the picture looks somewhat different. Practically 90% of 17-year-olds can add, subtract, multiply, and divide with whole numbers. However, only about 40% of them can apply this knowledge to a variety of problems—how much tax you have to pay, for example, and other problems that you and I encounter in using math.

Still looking at 17-year-olds, the second round of reading assessment shows that they are slightly better in reading than they were in the first round, about five years ago. So in this area there isn't any deterioration.

Kappan: Why, then, are critics disillusioned with schools' ability to teach basic skills?

Tyler: I think the disillusionment comes from two sources. One is that many older people tend to have a rosy view of the past. Second, people expect much greater achievement than is reasonable. Few of them remember that at the time of World War I an equivalent of our 9-year-old test of reading comprehension was administered to the draftees; only about 45% of the 17- and 18-year-olds could read at that level. Now about 80% of them can. Even in World War II only about 65% of this group could read. So we've been moving ahead, reaching a larger and larger proportion of the population. But the public often expects 100%, and this is an unreasonable expectation. We are not likely to realize it for another 15 or 20 years, if ever.

Kappan: There has been considerable concern in the last year over reports that high school students' scores on the Scholastic Aptitude Tests are going down. What is your view of this matter?

Tyler: The College Entrance Examination Board has established a panel to study the test score decline. I'm a member of this panel, and we are looking at both the populations and the tests. It is not yet clear what accounts for the decline. The data are somewhat inconsistent. PSAT

[Preliminary Scholastic Aptitude Test] scores have been rising, and it appears that a good many of the kids who consider themselves best prepared for college are taking only the PSATs, so that in the final SAT we don't have the same strata of the population that we had 10 or 15 years ago. The panel is considering how much difference this factor could make.

We are also looking into how well the tests were equated from year to year. We have proposed actually administering this year anchor items that were used in 1964, to see whether adding together the slight drops observed each year yields an accurate measure of the 12-year decline.

A third factor, revealed when we look at particular test items, is that the decline in the verbal SATs is not primarily in reading but in vocabulary. And here the decline is in understanding antonyms rather than synonyms. This fact suggests that the vocabulary of our young people may have changed in 12 years. If so, it does not necessarily mean that they are less bright.

One disturbing thing about the SAT is that it is validated in terms of college grades, not in terms of an effort to say what intelligence really means. For example, an item is kept in if the kids who get it right tend to get higher grades in college (primarily in their freshman year) and dropped if they don't. The interesting logic of the problem is that the kids who have taken the most recent tests are getting higher grades than those who took the test 12 years ago did. If the tests measure something important because the kids get higher grades, and they keep getting higher grades, how can we say that there has been a drop? It's very confusing. Of course one might then say—immediately shifting the logic—that college grades are inflated. But this would discredit grades as a criterion.

Kappan: What do you think the contribution of the National Assessment of Educational Progress is or can be?

Tyler: Since it is a census-like collection and presentation of data related to educational accomplishments, its value, like that of any other census, lies in providing dependable information. Until we had the NAEP, we had no basis for criticizing Rudolph Flesch's book, *Why Johnny Can't Read,* which caused many people to believe that most Johnnys can't read. The parents who were most impressed and who demanded new reading programs were in the middle-class communities where the kids *could* read.

The need to have dependable information about phenomena of social importance is always with us. That's the purpose of the national assessment program. A lot of the tests are not adequate yet; it is difficult to find a contractor capable of making tests for some of these objectives. But it's imperative that we keep demanding them and that we don't settle for less than meeting the real needs for these kinds of information.

Kappan: To what extent is the information provided by the NAEP used by educators to help the child in the classroom?

Tyler: It isn't intended to give immediate help in the classroom. The difficulty is in the people who think that planning is only done by the person operating the classroom. They ignore the fact that it is really the larger community that sets the expectations. It's the general public for which national assessment was first planned. Anything that can be useful to the teacher is a good thing, but national assessment doesn't take the place of the teacher's effort to know about his children any more than public health data on the incidence of tuberculosis relieve the doctor from finding out whether his patients have tuberculosis.

Kappan: A frequently voiced criticism of national assessment is aimed at federal involvement resulting from federal funding. Could you comment?

Tyler: Well, all the schools are getting federal funding now. Are they all corrupted by it? I am reminded of the time in 1933 shortly after Franklin Roosevelt became president. There was no social security apparatus. Roosevelt immediately established a Federal Emergency Relief Administration and offered each state money in accordance with need as revealed by the unemployment rate. This offer came to the legislature of Louisiana. One of the leaders said, "Huey [Huey Long was governor of Louisiana], this is federal money. Tainted, ain't it? Should we accept it?"

Huey said, "You know, when I was a small boy up in northern Louisiana, I went to a poor Baptist church. None of us had much money, but one Sunday somebody put a $100 bill in the collection. Now we knew that nobody in that town had a $100 bill. But one of the deacons had a wayward son who was a big-time gambler in New Orleans. He had come back to visit his folks that weekend, and we knew that the $100 bill came from the gambler. So the Board of Deacons came to the parson and said, 'Parson, that's tainted money, ain't it. Can we accept it?' The parson said, 'I'll pray on it.' He went into his study and prayed and came back and said, 'The Lord said that $100 bill had been doing the devil's work for so long that now it was time to do the Lord's work.'"

To answer your question more specifically, the federal government's support of the national assessment program has not brought about federal interference with the school curriculum.

Kappan: If you were to offer a group of school superintendents advice on how they might best use national assessment data, what suggestions would you have?

Tyler: I would of course want them to conduct similar assessments in their own schools. If a superintendent can relate a local problem to a national problem, he doesn't have to be ashamed that it's there; others have it, too. If the facts can be faced frankly, it really helps. Facts are not things to be ignored or brushed under the table. A good administrator has to face them and say. "What does it mean? Could we do something about it? Should we apologize for the lack? Shouldn't we say frankly that it's consistent with the national picture, that it's something American schools haven't learned to do, but that we're going to start working on it?"

Kappan: In recent years many innovations have been presented to the education community. In general, how do you view innovations in education?

Tyler: First, let me comment on bandwagon psychology in a mass society like ours. People hear about something that looks new and exciting and becomes popular; without necessarily understanding it, they want to climb on the bandwagon. This reaction is unfortunately common in education, just as it is in many other areas. But most education innovations have a particular purpose. It is my understanding, for example, that the open classroom was a reaction to the education of working-class children in England, where the homes were pretty rigid and structured; the school was, too. For an open classroom to be effective, not only did it need to provide freedom for children who didn't have much freedom outside of school, it also had to achieve the basic purposes of education.

I saw an illustration in my own hometown of Lincoln, Nebraska, not long ago. I visited two schools with what they called open classrooms. One of them was a parochial school in an area of working-class people, mostly second-generation Irish and German. Their homes were pretty rigid, but the open classroom, conducted by nuns, was highly creative. The kids thrived on it; it gave them a sense of freedom that contrasted with the more restricted environment outside. Then I visited an open classroom in the poorest part of town. The children were mostly blacks and Mexican-Americans from disorganized homes. A great many of the children came from homes where only the mother was present, and she was so distracted that there was very little structure. In the open classroom these kids were just completely lost. They had no sense of direction and nothing to live up to. The open classroom for these children seemed to me to be a great mistake.

This example illustrates the fact that most innovations begin as responses to a particular problem. There is no use in an educator's saying, "We should have an innovation" until he has identified the problem.

Kappan: It is often said that educational change occurs slowly because the adult public is captured by its own school experience. People have spent a good part of their formative years in school, and they don't have any sense of what the alternatives are for their children.

Tyler: Your comment suggests that the public is less anxious to change than the teachers. With most social institutions, the recipients of the services are more anxious to get improvements than the people who operate the bureaucracy. It is easier to understand this in terms of the rigidity of bureaucracies. Any association tends to try to protect itself; to avoid making demands of its members, it continually says that what it's doing is the right thing. I'm not attacking teachers—bureaucracies operate in the same fashion among all groups. But part of the role of a good administrator is somehow to get outside influences to come in. Some say that administrators must get parents to come into contact with the teachers. Teachers are not so belligerent when they meet individual parents. In some fashion, education leaders need to keep opening up that bureaucracy. The more a bureaucracy is sheltered, the more difficult it is for teachers to talk together about *common problems*, and the more they develop a shell which prevents communication outside.

Kappan: Mr. Tyler, we know that you have been involved in and concerned about graduate study in education. What is your view on the essential contribution of the university to the study of education?

Tyler: The greatest contribution the university can make is to figure out how systematic, tested knowledge can improve education—and how some people can be educated to apply it. First, a university is devoted presumably to getting accurate and dependable knowledge in contrast to dependence upon tradition without examination. Second, the university is different from a teacher-training institution of the old style; it can draw upon a variety of disciplines, all of which can add something. Just think of how much we have learned since we've begun to add to pedagogy the kind of insights we might get from psychiatry, from sociology, from anthropology, and more recently from the economics of education. We are getting more help as we go along from other disciplines. The university should equip educators with a number of different lenses through which to look at education—from the standpoint of the learner, from the standpoint of a psychologist, from the standpoint of a sociologist, and so on—enabling them to look at problem areas from different perspectives, to see different ways to explain things, and to focus on where to get a hold on and do something about problems.

Kappan: What is your view of the controversy surrounding the question whether the federal government, as opposed to the university, should set the research agenda for education?

Tyler: One question is the extent to which we expect to get federal support for the basic research that we carry on. The persons who are really going to get new knowledge through significant basic research are relatively few. In the first place, the demand for new knowledge is not nearly as great as the demand for educating people, and the proportion of our resources to be devoted to getting new knowledge is always going to be less than that for public instruction. I think that is wise. One or two creative, highly influential ideas don't cost much to get, by comparison with the cost of educating millions of people every year. But the notion that every professor should be a researcher, no matter how pedestrian he may be and how limited he may be in his own outlook, has had a bad effect.

I think that there is enough money to support the persons who really are dying to do significant research and can do it, and there is perhaps less money for development of programs in which you utilize research. I'm not worried about the federal government's targeting a lot of money in areas it is concerned with (disadvantaged children, the handicapped, and so on), because I think the public wants resources so targeted. The nature of our society is such that political leaders (the persons who are able to capture the interests and attention of people) are going to spend governmental resources where they think the people want them spent. I accept that we live in that kind of society, and my great interest has been in how to help that society move ahead in desirable directions. This is better than saying, "I just don't like it. I would like to create a wholly different society." I have a feeling that if I *did* create it, the new society would be unable to survive in the kind of environment that the natural selection process may have worked out quite well for human beings as they are. Now that kind of optimism is, perhaps, unbecoming at my age, but I have it.

Kappan: In your long and distinguished career, you have acted as teacher, writer, administrator, and consultant. How do you interpret your role in these activities?

Tyler: I like Lord Acton's observation: "Administration is the art of the possible." He was trying to consider goals in terms of what is possible. How are we going to move just a little closer to the ideal? If I've any success in curriculum, it's been because we start working on it. I can't answer other people's questions. But I do say, "Can we do it this way?" or "Let's try this."

The first question people have when I come in as a curriculum consultant is "What is it he's trying to sell us?" But I do not have an ulterior view. I'm not trying to sell anybody anything. My role is to help people work out their own philosophies.

Many people don't understand what I call the skills of administration, which are to help people get the things done that they want to get done and to help them understand more thoroughly where they're going. I know there is a place for prophets; I used to read Amos and Hosea and Isaiah with great wonder. But it isn't my role to see the time when we will beat our swords into plowshares. My role is to see how we can get less conflict next year, to see whether there is something I can do. Where does the trouble lie? Where do the strengths lie? Instead of letting people say, "Well, we just can't get there from here; it's just too long a road," and not doing anything about it, I try to ask them, "What steps can we take to make progress?" That's the art of the possible.

An Interview with Ralph Tyler

Jeri Ridings Nowakowski, Ed.D.

Occasional Paper Series, No. 13, Evaluation Center, College of Education, Western Michigan University, Kalamazoo, 1981.

This interview will be of interest to those entering the field of education as well as for those who have made their home within the field for some time now. In the interview, Ralph Tyler discusses work in education and educational evaluation that spans over a half a century. He describes issues that were important at the beginning of his career (those related to his work with the Bureau of Accomplishment Testing at The Ohio State University under W. W. Charters, and issues emerging in the Eight-Year Study), and issues he thinks are important to education and educational evaluation today.

I asked Dr. Tyler questions about his early career, middle career, and his present activities. He discussed the progress he felt was being made, the problems that still exist, and the resources he thinks are available to the field of education. Throughout, he captures a sense of the history and perhaps even the inevitability of public education. He is essentially optimistic—he sees the gains in public education outweighing the problems, and the promises still attainable.

Whether the reader is an old or new friend of Ralph Tyler's, the conversation that follows will help you get to know this man a little better. As he discusses a lifetime of effort and multiple professional responsibilities, a sense of continuity and direction becomes apparent. Here is someone who deliberately chose public education some sixty years ago, and has spent, and continues to spend, most days in pursuit of its improvement. He is not at all smug, but he seems sincerely to enjoy the idea that his work has made some important differences.

The interview took place in November 1981 when Dr. Tyler made a three-day trip to Western Michigan University at the request of Kappa Delta Pi, an honorary fraternity for students in education. Ralph spent three days in classrooms and auditoriums, and at luncheons and wine and cheese bashes. Throughout he was approachable—always giving the same attention and the same quality of response to whomever he was talking to. And whenever anyone began taking Ralph Tyler or the topic at hand too seriously, you could begin to see his eyes light up as he dropped a saucy joke or line on an otherwise unsuspecting fan. The interview, I think, gives you a feel for the combination of levity and seriousness that makes Ralph Tyler good company as well as an educational legend.

I am indebted to Dr. Tyler for his willingness to share his thoughts with me. I am, in turn, pleased to share this interview with other educators.

THE INTERVIEW

Ridings: I'd like to begin with some questions about your history and your education. Were you born in Nebraska?

Tyler: No, I was born in Chicago while my father was in the theological seminary. And when I was two years old he graduated and we moved to Nebraska, where I was raised.

Ridings: You attended Doane College in Nebraska.

Tyler: Yes, I received my bachelor's degree there in 1921 and went to Pierre, South Dakota, the capital of the state, to teach science in the high school.

Ridings: Did you go from there to the University of Chicago?

Tyler: I first went to the University of Nebraska to get further training in science teaching, and they employed me as a supervisor of practice teachers in science. I was an instructor there for four years until 1926. Then I went back to the University of Chicago and got a doctorate in educational psychology.

Ridings: You would have finished your doctorate then, when you were 25 years old. I heard you say the other day that dissertations shouldn't be a student's magnum opus; what was your dissertation study?

Tyler: I was studying educational psychology, but because of my background in mathematics (I had an undergraduate major in mathematics as well as in philosophy), I was employed on the Commonwealth Teacher Training Study as a research assistant, and the title of my dissertation was "Statistical Methods for Utilizing Personal Judgments to Evaluate Teacher Training Curricula." Sounds quite complicated, but that was the time when Professor Charters was heading the Commonwealth Teacher Training Study; I had collected some two million cards from each cooperating teacher, who wrote down on a card an activity that he was engaged in. We had two million cards. In those days there was no automatic sorting equipment or computers. My role was to classify those two million cards and finally to get statistical methods for identifying what were the important and crucial, or what is often called now the "critical incidents" for teachers. That was my dissertation. The classification reduced the two million cards into "The Thousand and One Activities of Teachers in America."

Ridings: How do we use that information today?

Tyler: Well, the Commonwealth Teacher Training Study is a report upon which competency-based teacher education in those days was developed. You know, about every 20 years or so the uneasy tension between theory and practice in professional education (whether it be doctors or teachers or others) alternates between emphasizing the activities within the profession or emphasizing the theory that may help to guide the profession. This was one of those times when, as now, the emphasis was on finding the competencies of teachers and trying to focus on them.

Ridings: Did you move from the University of Chicago to Ohio State?

Tyler: No, my first position, after I got my degree, was at the University of North Carolina, where I worked with teachers in the state on the development of more effective curricula. Because Rex Trabue, who had founded the North Carolina State Testing Program, was on leave, I was also in charge of the testing program of North Carolina at that time. Then in 1929, Mr. Charters, who had left Chicago and gone to The Ohio State University to head the Bureau of Educational Research, asked me to join him there to head the Division of Accomplishment Testing, as it was called, in the Bureau of Educational Research.

Ridings: The group of young people who went with Charters to Ohio State turned out to be a pretty exciting group of people. What was it like working at the Bureau at that time?

Tyler: Charters was a very stimulating person to work with. Every other Monday evening beginning at 7:30 the heads of the different parts of the Bureau met at his home. I was in, as it was called, accomplishment testing; there was Edgar Dale in curriculum, W. H. Cowley in personnel, Earl Anderson in teacher education, and Tom Holy in buildings and school surveys. We met, with each one of us previously submitting a written report on what we had accomplished during the two weeks, what we saw ahead, and what were the new problems, so that we had a chance continually to see ourselves at the cutting edge in developing new ideas and new research.

Ridings: You worked on something called "Service Studies" with professors across campus, didn't you?

Tyler: Yes, my role in the Bureau of Accomplishment Testing was to spend half time or more than that working with the colleges of The Ohio State University to try to increase student retention and improve the teaching. The legislature had become concerned because half of the students that were enrolling in the freshman year never came back for the sophomore year. The legislature appropriated funds to devote to improving teaching and learning in the university. Half my time was devoted to working with faculties there (actually, more than half), and the other half of the time with schools in the state.

Ridings: What were some of the studies conducted with the schools in the state?

Tyler: Let me begin by describing the public mood at that time. The Great Depression began in the fall of '29, shortly after I arrived in Columbus. People began to worry about their material losses and blamed much of it on the banks, the government, and the schools. A big conference was held in 1933 on "The Crisis in Education: Will the Schools Survive?" The papers were reporting how bad the schools were. Since these accusations included no evidence of school decline, I wrote to the superintendents in Ohio asking them whether they had any of the tests and the papers left that were given 25 or more years before. I offered to get them reproduced if they would give the tests again to see whether the students are really better or worse than those 25 or more years earlier. We found a number of communities where old tests were available, and we gave them again. We found, as was discovered in Indiana a few years ago when they repeated the Stanford Achievement Tests after 25 or 30 years, that the students of today either did the same or better than those of the past. The public acceptance of the notion that in some way things are deteriorating seems to be due not to a presentation of facts but the feeling of people that things are bad because they are not as well off as they expected to be. They are not able to get a second car or to make other purchases that they had planned. So they blame their social institutions, such as the schools, and think they aren't doing their job, for the kids are not as submissive as they used to be.

Ridings: That's basically an optimistic note, and you feel that's true in 1981 as well?

Tyler: Yes, I do. You've seen it around . . . people saying it. When you look at the National Assessment, for example, you find that there are more children able to read in 1981 than there were ten years earlier. But the public doesn't pay as much attention to the National Assessment results as it does to the College Board report that the SAT scores were declining slightly, 30 points, which is only 2.4 points in raw score. The standard scores of the SAT are based on a scale in which the mean is 500 and the standard deviation is 100. And the standard deviation of the vocabulary test that fell so much was 8, and so 30 standard score units is 3/10ths of 8, or 2.4 points. This is the extent of the decline in ten years. Now that's not a serious decline, but it looks severe to those who don't know what the SAT standard score means. A more important College Board result was that the subject examination scores were going up. Nor was it generally brought to public attention that the SAT is taken by more and more students in the lower half of the class because they want to get Basic Education Opportunity Grants. And, so, in 1975 no publicity was given to the fact that many more young people from the lower half of the high school classes were taking the test than in 1965. Nothing was reported to the effect that we're testing a larger proportion of students who didn't do very well in high school. The public jumped to the conclusion that the youth of today are not doing as well as those in earlier years. The eagerness with which this conclusion was accepted, I think, is because many people are now not as well off as they hoped to be and they blame their disappointment on the failure of schools and other public institutions.

Ridings: You've brought up National Assessment, a project you began working on in the early sixties. Was the National Assessment Project your brainchild?

Tyler: Well, I was asked to design the plans and was chairman of the exploratory committee to develop an effective operation so that it could be taken over by the Education Commission of the States that now operate it.

Ridings: Has it turned out to be all that you'd hoped that it could be?

Tyler: Oh, nothing is ever all that one hopes for. But certainly it has turned out to provide helpful data about the problems and progress of education in the United States.

Ridings: Do you think the change in funding base from a federal to a state nexus is going to have an impact on National Assessment? Will it make national data more important for us?

Tyler: I think it is very important before we spend much money on educational programs to have a picture of where we really are. This is particularly true now when pressure groups are trying hard to get funds for these purposes. So I think the National Assessment is always important—especially in difficult times when funds are rationed and should be focused where they are going to be most needed. However, the National Assessment is being supported by federal funds, and this year they were sharply cut. The Secretary of Education at the annual meeting of the Education Commission of the States in Boston this last August promised that he would do what he could to try to get some of that restored, [but] it hasn't yet been restored. This raises the question of whether the National Assessment can be adequately continued, but I hope it will be.

Ridings: Let's move back to the end of your work in accomplishment testing at Ohio State. Was it then that you began to work on the Eight-Year Study?

Tyler: I began my work on the Eight-Year Study in 1934. I went to Ohio State in 1929, so it was five years later. Perhaps I should give you the background. When I came to Columbus I worked with faculty members in the university in departments that had a required course for students—e.g., botany, zoology, and agriculture. They were having large numbers of failures and they wanted help, and so it seemed important to find out how much students were learning. The instructors would usually say: "We'll give them a test." Then I would point out the problem: "*What* do you want tested? The typical so-called achievement test is simply a test of what students remember about things that appear in their textbooks, and surely that isn't what you're after . . . you are not just teaching them to memorize." This conclusion led us to talk about what the instructors' objectives were, that is, what they really hoped their students would be learning. And then they said that a test should provide evidence of whether students were learning those things or not. Because the term "test" usually was interpreted as a collection of memory items, I suggested the use of the term "evaluation" to refer to investigating what students were really learning. As we developed evaluation instruments with those departments and began to use them, we obtained information about what students were learning and were not learning; how permanent some learnings were; how quickly they forgot information; and how long they remembered basic principles. Things of that sort were part of our experimentation. Then we moved on into other subject areas—chemistry, accounting and business, history, and various other departments. This was going on during my first five years at Ohio State. Without going deeply into the background of the Eight-Year Study, one could say that it was a project which developed from a realization on the part of many secondary schools that the Depression had brought into the schools many young people that did not plan to go to college; in fact, they didn't really want to go to high school, but they went because there was no place else to go. Youth unemployment was nearly 100 percent. By 1929 we had reached a point where about 25 percent of an age group went to high school. In my day it was only 10 percent of an age group, and suddenly, as the Depression went on, 50 percent of an age group were in high school. It doubled the enrollments. Many of these young people didn't find the curriculum for college entrance meaningful to them. And the other common program, the Smith Hughes Vocational Education Program, was highly selective. It enrolled persons who were definitely planning a particular occupation like garage mechanics, or homemaking, or agriculture.

High school principals realized that the schools should have a different program for these new students who were now in the high schools because they couldn't find work. But the course requirements of high schools then were pretty largely determined by, on the one hand, college entrance requirements and, on the other hand, the requirements of State Education Departments. These determined what subjects were taught and how many units were to be taken. Leaders among the principals brought attention to their problems, and the Progressive Education Association, which was interested in innovations, took the responsibility of getting together a conference of school and college people, including the state departments, to determine what could be done.

Out of that conference emerged the idea that a small number of schools (ultimately 30 schools and school systems) should be encouraged to develop programs that they would design to serve the high school students of that period. These 30 schools were to be given eight years in which to develop and try out new educational programs. During that time they would be freed from meeting the specific requirements of the state and of college entrance subjects in order to provide freedom for experimentation.

But there was a stipulation in the arrangement agreed to by the colleges and the state department; namely, that there would be an evaluation, and the evaluation was to include the following: One, there would be records available about the performance of students that would furnish information to help colleges make wise selections. Second, there would be an appraisal of what students were learning year after year in the high school so that the school would get continuing information as to whether they were learning something important. Third, there would be a follow-up after graduation to see how well they did in college or in other post–high school areas employment, marriage, or whatever it might be. This was the threefold task of evaluation.

The first year of the Eight-Year Study (1933–34) the directing committee expected to use the General Culture Test developed by the Cooperative Test Service for the Pennsylvania Study of School and College relations. But this was just a test of information students recalled about the things presented in widely used textbooks in the various so-called basic subjects. The schools rebelled; that wasn't what they were trying to teach, therefore it would not be a fair measure of their efforts. They threatened to drop out of the study. This produced a crisis in the summer of 1934 at the time of the annual meeting of the participants.

At this point, a member of the directing committee, Boyd Bode, a well-known philosopher of education who had his office across the hall from me in The Ohio State University said, "We've got a young man in evaluation at Ohio State who bases evaluation on what the schools are trying to do. He works closely with them and doesn't simply take a test off the shelf. Why don't you see if he will take responsibility for directing the evaluation?" I was reached by telephone at Chapel Hill, where I was teaching in the summer at the University of North Carolina. I came up to the Princeton Inn, where they were meeting. They interrogated me all morning and then I had lunch with them. They went into executive session in the afternoon while I twiddled my thumbs and watched people playing golf outside the Inn. At 4:00 P.M. they came and said, "We would like to have you be the director of evaluation for this project." I agreed to do so after making arrangements with The Ohio State University to spend half time at the University, half time on the Eight-Year Study.

Ridings: Would you say that Tylerian Evaluation, as we understand it, was born during the Eight-Year Study?

Tyler: Well, I don't know, it depends on what people want to call Tylerian Evaluation.

Ridings: That brings up an interesting point. Yesterday I heard you describe the evaluation process in the context of training evaluators, and it sounded a good deal richer than the six or seven steps often used to describe objectives-based evaluation.

Tyler: Oh, surely you can't use just the objectives as the basis for comprehensive evaluation. But certainly it was very important for people starting a program to reach new students and find out whether they were accomplishing their purposes. But it is also important to find out many other things in order to understand what's going on in a program and to guide it. I think when people say "Tylerian" as a single process it's like saying Dewey only mentioned child interests; there is no way of summarizing very simply any human being's notions about something complex. But for convenience we are likely to give a procedure a name, rather than describing it more fully.

Ridings: As you worked with teachers to produce objectives that reflected their classroom goals, you must have realized that you had an impact on curriculum.

Tyler: I think so. Especially in the areas where there had not been much clarity in the curriculum descriptions and explanations. For example, in the case of literature, the teachers of literature would usually repeat some trite phrase like "the students should learn to appreciate literature." I said, well, that sounds sensible. What do you mean by that? What have you observed that you are trying to help young people learn that you call "appreciation"? Is it that they can tell you about who wrote a book? Is it that they can make critical judgments of a literary work in terms of some criteria, such as unity or illusion of reality, or what not? We discussed such things until we began to agree that ultimately with literature we were concerned with comprehension, interpretation, and appreciation. They meant by appreciation that the reader responds emotionally to some literary works and thus his life is richer by reason of these emotional reactions. Reading is not just a dull sensing of meaning. All that came out of discussions, and from continuous reminders, "Don't look at some taxonomy to define your objectives. A taxonomy is what someone else states as the meaning of educational objectives. You're a teacher working with students. What have you found students learning that you think is important?" We formed a committee of teachers on appreciation of literature from the 30 schools and their discussions became a very rich way of trying to clarify what one could help students learn with literature. We were aided, of course, too, during the Eight-Year Study, by committees of people outside of the schools who had ideas. Louise Rosenblatt wrote *Literature as Exploration,* and that gave a new vision of what literature could be; or the book written by Alberty and Havighurst, who was then teacher of Science at the University School in Ohio State, on *Science in General Education,* gave new insights into that. So we were trying to help get a vision of what educational objectives could be. These discussions guided both the teaching and the evaluation.

Ridings: When we hear criticism of objectives-based evaluation, it's typically that the objectives are not evaluated. Yet in listening to you over the last two days, it's apparent that you have had a good deal of communication with teachers, and respect for their skills. . . .

Tyler: They're the ones who have to do it. Nobody else can tell you what you're trying to do as well as you yourself. Especially when you try to probe the unconscious intuition of things that teachers are doing that have been sensible, yet they haven't really worded them before.

Ridings: So it's a matter of articulating some things that you think teachers do know how to do, have been doing, but probably need to refine. You approach educational problems with a great deal of common sense.

Tyler: The only problem with common sense is that it's so uncommon.

Ridings: One could say that while there might not have been a formal step for assessing the worthwhileness of objectives, that was in fact always going on in the "Tylerian" evaluation process.

Tyler: Yes, of course. The schools were helped not only by the evaluation staff but by a curriculum staff working under Professor Alberty. In 1938, the curriculum staff complained that the schools were saying they were getting more help for the evaluation staff than from the curriculum staff. Alberty explained this by saying: "Tyler has a rationale for evaluation and there isn't any rationale for curriculum." So when we were having lunch, I said to Hilda Taba, my right-hand associate, "Why, that's silly, of course there's a rationale for curriculum." I sketched out on the napkin what is now often called "The Curriculum Rationale." It indicates that in deciding what the school should help students learn, one must look at the society in which they are going to use what they learn and find out the demands and opportunities of that society. To learn something that you can't use means that in the end it will be forgotten. One must also consider the learner—what he has already learned, what his needs are, and what his interests are, and build on them; one must also consider the potential value to students of each subject. After lunch I said to the curriculum people, "Here's a rationale you might want to follow," and that kind of outline of a rationale began to be developed.

Ridings: Dr. Tyler, when I was reviewing for this interview, I looked back at your work, and I looked at Cronbach's piece in 1963 on course evaluation. It was apparent that you really couldn't talk about evaluation in the early days of educational evaluation without talking about curriculum; that they were in fact completely intertwined.

Tyler: Well, if you are talking about evaluation of education, of course.

Ridings: It seems, as educational evaluation has grown, in some ways we have seen the parting of education and educational evaluation; that is, educational evaluation has taken on a life of its own, is going in its own direction, and is really not attending to curriculum.

Tyler: That happens in all professional fields; medical research has often forgotten the patient, who has become clinical material, and forgotten the role of the physician as a health counselor. It was as if in some way, once the physician knew what was going on in the human body, automatically the patient would get well; but we know that only the patient can get himself well—just as only the child can learn. You can't learn for him. So there is all this evaluation business up here, without considering what it is the learner is doing. The same problem exists with social work; they sometimes think of clients as having no minds of their own. But, when for instance, people discover that money can be had in the aid to dependent children, some are tempted to say, "That's the way to make my living. I'll just have more children and get more money." You've got to consider the social situation and what it means to the so-called clients. They're not inert objects out there to be worked on. You can do that if you're working on plants, but you can't do that with human beings.

Ridings: Ironically the federal dollars that moved evaluation forward brought us . . .

Tyler: Has it moved us forward?

Ridings: Well, it brought us large funded programs and with them program evaluation which has grown and become more methodologically diverse. I guess the question is whether program evaluation has co-opted curriculum evaluation in the public school system.

Tyler: Well, I think there will be much less money from the federal government for that kind of evaluation, and that may help people to stop chasing dollars and try to consider what is really involved in effective evaluation and who are the clients for evaluation. One of the problems is that they see the clients as being federal government, the Office of Education, NIE, or the Congress, instead of the clients that you're going to improve—the teachers and the people who operate schools, and the parents and children. When you have those clients, you have to have different considerations.

Ridings: The evaluation components for many large-scale funded programs are still focused on outcome measures. . . .

Tyler: And often inappropriate ones.

Ridings: They don't reflect the literature that we have available in evaluation. Who's in control of educational evaluation in our country? Why don't we see what professionals and academics are doing reflected in evaluation as it's legislated?

Tyler: You're not asking that as a question, are you?

Ridings: You mean, it's so apparently government influence.

Tyler: Well, the evaluations that make any difference are those that reach the people that really care about education—the teachers, the parents, the children, and citizens who are concerned with the welfare of the country. Much program evaluation has been directed at Congress which, because it's controlled or greatly influenced by high pressure groups, doesn't really care as long as it has satisfied its pressure groups. And if it's an act of law, they will not change the law just because something is found not to work—not unless the pressure groups no longer press for it.

Ridings: An abstract of a recent dissertation study on the University of Chicago evaluation group proposed, after looking carefully at you and Bloom and the students that you had touched, that perhaps the most significant aspect of that group is the communication network that was set up and continues between you and your students.

Tyler: How do they determine what is the most significant, what's their criteria [*sic*] for significance?

Ridings: I didn't read the whole study. I would speculate that it might mean the characteristic that has been most instrumental in keeping evaluation alive and growing within that group, and perhaps influencing the general development of evaluation.

Tyler: Well, that's a theory of history, and there are other theories, such as the need for some things will cause the persons who produce it. The question, for example, of whether it was the automobile industry, as an industry, that made the great use of cars, or the discovery that cars were so helpful to people. It's hard to determine whether it's people with ideas that produce—rather than the need of a time—and obviously it's some kind of interaction. You can have people pressing for some things and nobody feels the need for it, and it disappears in due time. In some way it's a combination, but it's too simple a theory to talk about. These "networks" haven't changed the world generally when they've been in existence, unless at that time there was a need for one.

Ridings: Do you keep in active communication with most of your students?

Tyler: I certainly see them quite often and I live not far from Lee Cronbach. My two right-hand research assistants getting their doctorates in Chicago, in those early days, were Ben Bloom and Lee Cronbach. And then there was Chester Harris, and, of course, Hilda Taba had already finished her doctorate, and I was able to help her stay in this country when she was about to be deported back to Estonia because she came on a student visa.

Ridings: In 1938 you made the move from Ohio State back to the University of Chicago, where you became the chairman of the Department and later Dean of the Division of Social Science.

Tyler: I came first to do two things. One was to take Mr. Judd's place, who was then retiring, and so to be Head of Education. And the other was to head the Board of Examinations responsible under the Chicago plan for determining the student's completion of his educational program. Under that plan, all the degrees are based on passing various comprehensive examinations. So that I was University Examiner half time and half of my salary was paid by the Examiner's Office, and half was paid by the school of education.

Ridings: Egon Guba said to me that while people know you as a researcher, a theoretician and a statesman, you were also a wonderful administrator and a very good dean. Did you enjoy administration?

Tyler: Yes, if you define administration as Lord Acton does, "the art of the possible." I like to help people find ways of using their talents most effectively, and that's usually by giving them an opportunity for a time to do what they think is important. Then, from that experience, thus try to clarify what they really feel they can do best in that context.

I think that Guba is especially influenced by his own major Professor Jacob Getzels. I found Jacob Getzels teaching social psychology in the Department of Human Relations at Harvard and brought him to Chicago. He said he was a social psychologist. He said, "What do you want me to do?" I said, "I want you not to teach anything until you feel you've got something to teach. I'd like to have you go around to schools, see what you see going on in education that could be understood by utilizing social psychology." Well, he told me later that he didn't really believe me, so when the quarter started he said, "What am I to teach?" I said, "Whatever you feel is important to people in education." "Well, I don't know." "Until you find that, just go on observing schools and talking to school staff." And so this went on until he felt he had something to teach teachers. And he also worked with people in administration on the theory of organization. I conceive a task of the administrator to find what appears to be a bright and able young man, then not to put him into a niche but to help him find himself and where he could use his talents, and then support and encourage that.

Ridings: So you were the true facilitator?

Tyler: That's what an administrator should be, a person to help people accomplish; it is the art of the possible—helping make possible what others dream and hope they can do.

Ridings: It's a nice definition.

Tyler: I might name a good many others I tried to help. For example, Herb Thelan—I found him teaching chemistry in the university high school in Oakland, and again I had him, before he taught anything, observe what was going on in teaching. He became interested in the interaction of students and teachers. He said he wanted to work on that, so I set up a laboratory in which interactions in the classroom could be observed and recorded; a place in the laboratory school where he could study different groups of students. We didn't have videotape in those days, but we had audiotape and we had ways of looking through one-way mirrors, and so on. So he began to have a chance to do what he had discovered to be interesting after looking at education for a while . . . and study what he wanted to learn about. Some of his students never went beyond that. Ned Flanders, for example, always wanted to have just interaction-counting. But Herb, if you've seen his recent book just published, has gone a great distance in his understanding of the human influence involved in teaching.

Ridings: I'm moving you through your life way too rapidly. I was about to move you into 1953 when you became the director of the Center for Advanced Studies.

Tyler: But you may want to understand that during the war I was also the director of the Examinations Staff for the Armed Forces to develop educational testing. The GED Test was originally developed there, guided by Everett F. Lindquist of the University of Iowa.

Ridings: Didn't Dan [Stufflebeam] also work on the GED?

Tyler: After I left Chicago, the responsibility was contracted out to Ohio State when Guba was director of the Bureau of Educational Research, and I believe Dan was working on the GED Tests then. We originally developed the examination so that young people who were returning from military service after the Second World War would have a chance to demonstrate what they'd learned and get some credit for it. So we also developed a series of subject examinations and course examinations for that purpose. When the war was over I was asked to serve as director of the Veterans' Testing Service for the American Council of Education to develop centers where veterans could take the tests, and demonstrate what they had learned in the armed services. Those were some administrative responsibilities to try to make possible something that seemed important.

Ridings: You were also instrumental, you and Frank Chase, in beginning Regional Labs in our country.

Tyler: Well, in 1964 Mr. Johnson set up a task force to see what needed to be done in education, if he were elected, as he was in 1964 to the presidency. The task force was headed by John Gardner and included a number of very able persons like Edwin Land, the inventor and head of Polaroid. He suggested the idea of Supplementary Education Centers in order for children to learn from museums, libraries, and other educative agencies in the community. Unfortunately, this section of ESEA was construed by the educational bureaucracy as another task for the schools, and most projects supported under this title involved school activities, instead of sending kids out where they could learn from other experiences. I was responsible for writing the section on laboratories, the substance of which was included in the Elementary and Secondary Education Act of 1965. We viewed laboratories as the "middleman" between research and schools. We already had the R and D Centers in which educational research and development was supported. What we did need was a way by which the consumers, the schools, could identify problems they had and seek help from research of the past as well as the present. The laboratory was to be based with the consumer, but the laboratories that were actually funded were, with some exceptions, either R and D Centers or oriented toward the producers of research rather than the consumers. The result is that we still lack the "middleman" in most regions.

Ridings. Like the National Assessment, it would seem that the regional labs could be jeopardized by lack of funding.

Tyler. Yes, but it is possible that this could be a constructive result. They might then seek to serve the consumer more fully and get support there. For example, the post office looks to Congress, it doesn't worry too much about its consumers; but if the post office were responsible to their consumers then there could be more concern for good service. It is possible that if the federal government doesn't support the labs, they will seek support for their consumers. That may make the labs more responsive to the needs of schools rather than to becoming a sort of second level of R and D Centers.

Ridings. From 1953 to 1963 you were the director of the Center for Advanced Studies. What do you think were the Center's major contributions during that decade before you began work on National Assessment?

Tyler. Providing an opportunity for very able behavioral scientists to spend time to think and to study when they were not responsible for teaching and other services based on their previous work. At the Center they could think about what they needed next and they could get ideas for future development.

The idea of the Center was suggested first by Haus Speier in a communication to the Ford Foundation. The Foundation, in the autumn of 1951, appointed a committee to explore the idea. It consisted of ten leading behavioral scientists. I served as chairman of the committee. We met in New York for Saturday all day and Sunday until noon each weekend from January until June, 1952, working out possible ways to help able people to keep growing.

One of our members, Robert Merton, had been studying the careers of Nobel Prize winners and noted that they rarely produced anything new after they were awarded the Prize. We recognized a need for scholars and scientists to get new stimulation and new ideas in mid-career. To this end the Center was founded. Outstanding students of human behavior were invited to come there with no assignments other than their own restless energy. The Center administration's responsibility is to help each scholar to do what he believes will give him new lines of work. That the Center has been a constructive influence is shown in the visible career lines of those scholars and scientists who have spent a year there. Each year the Center invites about forty people from the United States and ten from abroad to be in residence there.

Ridings: So once again you played the role of facilitator and nurtured people so they could do good things in education and research.

Tyler: Well, "nurture" is a term that depends on how suppliant you think they are. And, of course, don't forget the basic political principle that has guided many pressure groups in seeking government funds—when a sow is suckling a pig, the sow enjoys it as much as the pig.

Ridings: [Laughing] I like that one. Tell me, when you look back on a career that has already had so many pinnacles . . .

Tyler: I don't think there are pinnacles.

Ridings: Would you buy tiny hills?

Tyler: I don't think of them that way at all. I think about moving along doing the things that seem important.

Ridings: Just plodding through with Ralph Tyler. Is there something you feel a greater sense of personal accomplishment over?

Tyler: I never thought of it in those terms.

Ridings: If you don't think about accomplishments in a personal sense, what about as contributions to education?

Tyler: I thought they were useful; but I never tried to examine them.

Ridings: You don't rank order?

Tyler: No, I certainly don't.

Ridings: Okay. I'm going to turn to some specific questions about the field of educational evaluation and start with what I think is the obvious one. You've often been referred to in the literature as the father.

Tyler: I invented the term "evaluation" when applied to educational procedures; so if naming the child, as the godfather names babies, makes you father, then I am. And when it began to be a cliché and evaluation meant so many different things to different people, I invented the term "assessment," and that's what we used next.

Ridings: Well, that's what I wanted to ask—the amount of paternal responsibility you take for this offspring that is credited to you.

Tyler: You can't take responsibility for what other people do, so the only thing you can do when anything becomes a cliché is to get a new word.

Ridings: And that's "assessment?"

Tyler: Right now it's "assessment," but that will become a cliché, because many people quickly catch on to forms and to labels without understanding the substance of what something is. I was at a meeting yesterday in Chicago for the Board of the Institute of Philosophical Research, and one of the group had been making a study of the influence of the Committee of Ten's report on secondary education. That report was headed by Charles Eliot, the president of Harvard, and it was sponsored by the NEA. It outlined a program of education which in form set the structure of American education for 1893 until at least the Eight-Year Study, or about 1933—at least 40 years. But what this researcher had discovered, Mrs. Van Doren, was that most of the things that were carried over were forms. The schools offered those subjects named in the committee report, but they did not usually believe in such courses, the aims and the content suggested by the committee. Many of the committee's suggestions are fresh ideas today. I was not surprised. Why was it that PSSC and the other science courses, supported in their preparation by many millions of federal dollars, never really reformed much of the curriculum? Because the people who quickly took it on took on the form; they were taking PSSC and using the books not as aids to inquiry but as stuff for kids to remember. You may have seen the report of the use of these materials prepared by the University of Illinois committee led by Robert Stake. The problem is that something is labeled, like the Tylerian rationale, and pretty soon it is the form that is in people's minds, not the substance. Forms, like cosmetics, are so much easier to adopt than changing your personality. And that kind of business makes it necessary periodically to change labels because the labels become clichés representing something like Dewey's "Do-I-have-to-do-what-I-want-to-do" sort of cliché—which was not what Dewey said at all, but a way of quickly labeling it. And then it's lost.

Ridings: It's also much easier to dismiss an idea after you simplify that greatly.

Tyler: There was a woman, very set in her ways, who taught in the schools of Tulsa during the Eight-Year Study. Every time we had a workshop, she'd say, "We've been doing that for 13 years in Tulsa." Of course she didn't understand what was being talked about except for the label she could quickly attach and, of course, then dismiss because "We've been doing it for 13 years in Tulsa."

Ridings: Speaking of labels, there are a growing number in evaluation. I think Michael Scriven said that, at one count, there were over 50 evaluation models; we have at least two bona fide professional evaluation organizations, and probably more; we have a number of evaluation journals, and a number of sets of standards now. Do you think this is progress?

Tyler: Probably not. It depends on whether evaluation has become so popular that it's a fad and is likely to fade. However, there will be people who really are concerned with finding out what is going on in our educational program and want to understand it. These people will be seeking ways of evaluation. That's what science is about—trying to distinguish between the ideas you have about phenomena and what's really going on.

Ridings: If you were to run a major project tomorrow, would you hire someone called an evaluator to work with you on the project?

Tyler: It depends on whether they could do what needed to be done.

Ridings: What kind of a job description would that be?

Tyler: "Evaluation" is a very broad term—what is it that needs to be done?

Ridings: Well, right now you're helping to educate evaluators, working on training programs for professional evaluators, is that right?

Tyler: Well, what I do now, of course, since I have no permanent job, is what's expected of me, growing out of my background and where I'm employed. For example, this semester at North Carolina State University I'm employed by the Division of Adult Continuing Education and Community College Education. Now, for example, the evaluation of general adult education requires the kind of person who understands what learning and teaching involves and can design a learning system and evaluate parts of the learning system that are working or not working. But they need to do this with a good deal of understanding of what that means in the context of the community college in North Carolina, or adult education that ranges from the basic education of illiterate adults, of whom there are a lot in North Carolina, to the adults who have graduated from college. They need to have gotten well along in a job and understand what life is really about, or, as Marvin Feldmen says, "Is there life after work?" Then there are the trainers, people in continuing education who I meet on Fridays from IBM and a good many other industries in that area involved in textiles, electronics, and printing. There the problem is identifying what is to be learned and how to evaluate it. Now there are some general people who can do that, but my own experience in evaluation is that except for the generalists like you and Dan, most of the people are going to be in a particular situation where their understanding of the particular situation is terribly important. Hence, I would choose someone very familiar with the context and teach them how to evaluate, or choose an excellent general evaluator and immerse them in the context. Christine McGuire, one of my students at the University of Illinois Medical School, is a good illustration. She is a general evaluator but very familiar with teaching and learning in the various areas of medicine, pediatrics, psychiatry, and the like.

Ridings: You said yesterday that it was hard for you to believe that people involved in educational evaluation of schooling would have much insight or be very productive if they hadn't been in a public school classroom.

Tyler: Yes, if that's where they're evaluating—or medical schools if they are there, or training stations if they are there.

Ridings: That brought to mind, however, the many new people who are being graduated and have degrees in evaluation; some are a new breed of professional with technical skills and quantitative backgrounds, but they are not necessarily educators.

Tyler: They're like the economists of today who can tell you what's wrong with the economy but can't figure out what you're going to have to do about it.

Ridings: In other words, such evaluators are playing a role in finding problems but not in solving them.

Tyler: Well, it depends on what the purpose is; there's a place for finding problems. There's a place for the diagnostician or the person who runs the blood tests in the clinic, but he is not the one who is going to tell you what to do with the information.

Ridings: Let me ask you about the *Standards*. As you know, the Project to Develop Standards for Educational Evaluation is housed here at Western Michigan at the Evaluation Center and has been chaired by Dan Stufflebeam. That group dedicated their *Standards* to you.

Tyler: That was nice of them.

Ridings: Certainly it was a sign of respect. What do you think about the quality of the *Standards*? Do they hit the mark now? Do we need them?

Tyler: I think it's very helpful for the kinds of program evaluation that have been done under federal support to have this set of standards. Standards for anything have to be in light of the context and where the problems lie. There are different problems if you're talking about the evaluation of medical school curriculum in order to produce general practitioners, rather than people who are primarily research people in medicine.

Ridings: Do you think the *Standards*, or a profession searching for standards, will bring up some issues that will have to be resolved?

Tyler: Oh, I think that anything that causes you to look critically at what's going on will help you to identify places that have to be examined very carefully. Put another way, a professional occupation is one where there is continuous effort in the research of the profession to identify both the proper ends and the effective means of that profession. Research on the proper ends is concerned with the ethics of the profession relating the professional's work to the common good rather than the notion that what's good for General Motors is good for the country.

For example, there needs to be a continuing study of the nature of medical ethics as new ways are developed for keeping people alive a long time at a great cost. The ethical issue is: How much can society spend, if it has limited resources, on keeping some person of age 65 alive for ten years at a cost that would cover the health services to children for perhaps

20 or 30 times that many children? This is an ethical question not easily answered, and should be a matter of continuing study. Correspondingly, for the profession of evaluation, the questions of who are the clients and what proper service can be given clients are raised. Is it proper for some people to get information that might be wrongly used? These are kinds of questions in evaluation that are continually going to come up, and they change with time.

One role of the research profession, the important one, is the continuing study of ethics in the light of changing situations. The second is trying to understand the processes and trying to characterize them in ways that others can understand so they can do more than simply follow what the "master" does. They need to understand what goes on and be able to solve new problems as they arise. Evaluation needs to continually try to examine the appraisal process and to find principles rather than setting up models to be followed. If you look at science, it has not benefited by structural models alone except as an illustration of principles in which the models keep changing as new situations and applications of the principles require.

Ridings: Whether you look at medicine, or fields like accounting and auditing that deal with information, if those fields don't revisit their principles and the impact of those principles on their audiences, instead of a guiding set of principles they end up with a very restrictive set of expectations.

Tyler: And with limited time and resources, an important question for applied research in evaluation is to discover how far a further refinement of evaluation data is justified in terms of the cost, and how much difference it would make in the actions to be taken. A number of researchers seek more refinement but, because they think only of general group data, are happy to talk about a correlation, say, of .6. Many testers were jubilant when they found a correlation of .6 between the SAT and first-year grades. But they did not examine the question as to whether this correlation was a sign that college teachers should change their ways of teaching so that they could reach students who had not learned to study before, or whether they select only students who have already learned to study. That's an ethical problem in connection with testing for admission. Testers did not consider another question: What does the admissions committee do about the SAT score when the correlation is only .6? How many individuals are misplaced, and does the college care about the misjudged individuals? If one only cares about the institution getting its share of good students, one can disregard the errors which individual students suffer. What is the ethical responsibility of testers? Don't they need to learn more about the person than is provided by an instrument giving a correlation of .6? This ethical question is the one on which the Communists and Fascists differ most from avowed democracies. Communists and Fascists say, "We don't care as long as we get what we need to keep the state going. It's too bad that an individual suffers; but people serve the state." However, we believe in the individual; we believe in equality, and what right have we to say that we're satisfied to be guided by a .6 when we could go and try to learn more about the individual and get to a point where we could make fairer decisions? These are ethical questions that arise from a statistical method which applies only to groups. Don't we have a responsibility to learn more about the individuals within the group? [Interruption for a photo session]

Ridings: During the photo session, we were talking about statesmen. I made the statement that you were, if not the premier educational statesman, one of our most important educational statesmen.

Tyler: Well, flattery doesn't get you everywhere. Let's go on with the questions.

Ridings: Let's talk about the necessity of statespersons and how to groom them in education.

Tyler: Well, of course, there are different history theories, too. One is the necessity of statesmen, and the other is the English theory, during the time of the First World War, that you can muddle through without statesmen some way and the civilization survives. But, in any event, it's nice to have them. Whether they're necessary is another question.

Ridings: We mentioned a few; Frank Chase was one of the people we were talking about, and Horace Mann. You also included Hilda Taba. These are all people who are or have been national and sometimes international leaders in education. We were talking about the problems of why sometimes we seem to lack statespersons in education and suggesting that it might be, in fact, the educational process or training process. Could you talk a little bit about what makes a statesperson and what kind of activities they're involved in?

Tyler: You might want to talk first about why some situations produce more statesmen than others, and that, of course, has been a concern of religious writing for many many years. Amos advanced a theory in his book of the Bible that in periods of affluence (he described vividly how women flaunted their jewelry), people were no longer interested in God because they could satisfy their wants easily. The great ethical period for the Jews was in their Babylonian captivity. The general theory, which is hard to refute because it seems to fit so many historical periods, is that the human being is both an animal that, like other animals, depends upon various physical things—food, for example—and is greatly attracted to material possessions but also is capable of immense efforts to attain goals that are nonmaterial (concern for others, unselfishness, altruism, and so on). In times when it's easy to satisfy the material wants, people generally become greatly attached to material things so that in affluent times people spend more than they need, they're satisfied and get happy about all the things they can get, and they pay little attention to the nonmaterial because they spend little time in reflection when enjoying physical gratifications. In difficult times, when the physical gratifications are not easily obtained, more time is spent in thinking about seeking nonmaterial goals.

John Dewey pointed out that man as a human being is essentially a problem solver. He's not a cow that chews its cud after a nice meal in the pasture and just enjoys that. Men and women are essentially made to deal with problems, and that's why civilization advances. People have been able to meet new environmental problems when other organisms have often perished because they couldn't adapt. Which suggests that the environment in which people can continue to develop is one where goals require effort and problems must be solved, and not one of relative ease. Now that's a theory of history that I think may be useful in this connection. Look back at the times that we've had people that we call statesmen. For example, in the case of Horace Mann, it was when there was a great expansion in the elementary school system of Massachusetts. They didn't have enough teachers, and he had to solve the problem of how to educate teachers. He invented the normal schools, and he did a number of other things. But during the periods before that, when there wasn't a great expansion and when there weren't problems in educating teachers, they didn't have any demands in that sense for persons to lead them in new ways.

Ridings: If times are getting bad, are we about to see the emergence of some new statesmen?

Tyler: If they're viewed as bad by those for whom the measure is money and physical satisfactions, then the times ahead are likely to be austere times. But that has nothing to do at all with the question of whether there will be good times for education or for people who care about others, who are concerned with some sense of satisfaction in serving others as well as being served, and those who care about a closely knit family. Those are things that can become better during periods of austerity.

Ridings: So the funding hiatus in education might in fact help us?

Tyler: It's probably going to produce better education. You might ask yourself if you got 25 percent more salary would you do a better job than you do now?

Ridings: No.

Tyler: So really money has nothing to do with how well you do, does it? Money helps because it provides for your physical satisfactions and it may be nice for you to have other clothes or other physical things. But if it causes you to be so interested in such things that it distracts you from thinking about your work, then it can be distracting. The point is, when is physical well-being such that you don't worry about it? People who are starving certainly can't think about things because in some way they have to get food. So there's some line between which a situation is so devastating that people can't rise to it, or so satisfying that they don't worry about anything else. There is some line which promotes the problem-solving characteristic that we should try to attain.

Ridings: You have seen a number of crises or what people characterized as crisis periods in public education. You've also seen enormous amounts of gain made in education, and probably experienced some disappointing losses. . . .

Tyler: That's life.

Ridings: Something must have motivated you all those years to stay active in public education, to still look forward to another decade or more of active work in education. What keeps you going?

Tyler: Well, I think, like all people, if you feel your experience and your training gives you a chance to make contributions to important things, you want to be right in there fighting.

Ridings: And you're optimistic and believe in the public education system?

Tyler: There isn't any alternative. Public education didn't come first, you know. When we first really had formal education it was supported by the family. You remember that in the English law from which our English ancestors came in the 1600s, the family was responsible. Every person had to be with a family; if someone had no relatives, he had to be attached to a family under law, or bound over, if he was a child, to somebody or to an orphanage. And the family was responsible for seeing that the person respected the law and obeyed it, for deciding which occupation to carry on to make his living, for his religious duties, and all those things that followed the requirements of the state for citizenship—that was all left to the family. People who came from upper classes were destined to be the rulers, so they were sent to secondary schools in England, Eton and Harrow, and so on, and then those of them who were going to be scholars and intellectuals were sent on to Oxford and Cambridge Universities.

But what happened with this group who first came to the New England colonies? They were Congregationalists. They did not believe that a priest could lead them to salvation; they thought you had to read the Bible and understand what Christianity meant and make a voluntary decision to be Christian. Now that was a new conception; a view that a person had to make himself good meant they had to teach the children to read the Bible. It became a community responsibility because they were a religious community. So the first schools founded in New England were not just families tutoring children. The first schools were based on the need to have everybody learning to read.

Now we've got the same corresponding business. Less than 5 percent of the population can work at unskilled labor; that's the present proportion of the labor force that is unskilled. All the other jobs require some education. The people who don't have some education are typically on welfare and they can't get jobs. So that makes another requirement and reason for why public schools are important. The largest percentage of private schools we ever had in my time was just before the Depression hit—we had around 20 to 22 percent of our students in private schools. Now we've got about 11 percent, about half that number. In those days, the parochial schools were the largest; nuns belonged to orders in which they had taken a vow of poverty and so it didn't take very much tuition to go to a parochial school. Now, of course, fewer young people are going into the orders, so that most of the parochial schools have to pay higher salaries and they are more expensive for the family than the public schools. And then also the people who were moving up in social class felt their kids should have a better education than the public could provide, so they had private schools for them.

When it came to secondary education, the last state to have public secondary schools adopted them in 1912, so public high schools were relatively rare. They started out as the Latin grammar school, so most learning was in Latin. Then when Benjamin Franklin recommended that the time for a person to be educated was while carrying on business activities of that sort, they established academies. Still, they were usually private academies. And finally public schools began to be adopted after the Civil War, and the first public high schools were adopted around 1870.

This evolution is not likely to go backwards because the requirements of managing a system privately, making it capable of accomplishing or getting along, is too great for people to handle. When I was director of the laboratory schools at the University of Chicago and later when I was helping to put the Dalton School back on its feet, it was hard to find people who could manage it, get good teaching, satisfy parents, and be able to make it go with the money required. So that the notion that in some way private schools are going to take over all education seems very improbable. Private schools are going to be hanging in there, but they are not going to expand very much.

Ridings: I've got a few phrases, and I thought we would end with them.

Tyler: Clichés, I hope?

Ridings: Yes, your favorite clichés; clichés that will make me vulnerable to all your one-liners. I thought if you would give a couple of sentences, whatever comes to mind. First, the most promising development in educational evaluation.

Tyler: I always believe the most promising developments are people with vision and dedication to education who get some additional technical skills to handle it. Developments in human things are the persons— the ideas are only guiding persons.

Ridings: Okay. How about the major problem in American education K–12?

Tyler: The most obvious one that we are still struggling with is reaching the proportion of the population that is now here. The civil rights movement has made us conscious of a lack of adequate service for the minority groups of various sorts, and that's still with us. And it is likely to be with us for some time because of the increased number of illegitimate children born to teenage mothers who won't be able to provide a background for their children unless their grandparents bring them up. We're going to have a lot of children coming in that do not have the background in the home that we've been accustomed to teaching, so that's certainly a problem that we must keep working on—the so-called education of disadvantaged children.

The second problem that we've got to work on more effectively is the transition of youth into constructive adult life—which means being able to move easily from school to work, being able to accept and carry on effectively the responsibilities of citizenship, of adults in all aspects of life. We have continually tried to keep youth off the labor market and we've continually tried to lengthen their period of childhood without allowing them to gradually assume more responsibilities. Kids have to learn to take responsibility and take the consequences when they make a mistake; that's the way they learn. The transition to adult life is terrible now, and we've become so concerned with it that there have been four commissions publishing reports on the importance of that transition. I think we're going to work more on that.

And the third problem, greatly related to it, is the problem of rebuilding the total education environment for children. What's happened with the changes in the home, with mother's employment? What's happened with television taking the place of recreational things in which there's more constructive activity for the child? We've got to rebuild that environment because the demands of education are far greater than the school time of five or six hours a day for five days a week for perhaps nine or ten months a year. There is far too little to do, and that's a big problem.

Why don't we stop with those three? I could add some more if you wish; there's enough to keep us busy and happy for some time.

Ridings: You've put in more than your share of time on this; why don't we conclude now? Let me thank you, I've enjoyed it.

Tyler: Now, fine, can we make a date for a later time.

Ridings: Sure.

Tyler: And a different place . . .

Interviews with Ralph W. Tyler

MARY LOUISE MICKLER

Educational Forum, Fall 1985, pp. 23–46.

In the first of two interviews, Tyler addresses the larger issues facing educators today. He comments on the purpose of education and provides a historical perspective on the current controversies concerning American public school curricula. He also discusses basic education and general education, and offers his own personal definition of what it means to be an educated person. Tyler describes the teacher as a professional by considering questions related to such timely and controversial topics as teacher competence, evaluation, stress, the increased emphasis on research and publication, and the growing attention given to the computer as an educational resource.

Mickler: The results of recent Gallup polls have shown an increase in dissatisfaction with the public schools. Do you interpret this to mean that Americans also lack confidence in the current educational process?

Tyler: Since the schools were first established in this nation, there have always been critics, parents who wanted their children to get a somewhat different education, community members who were concerned about the support or the usefulness of what was being taught, and others. Criticism is not something that just suddenly developed, although some writers today, who know very little about our history, talk as though this were a new phenomenon. In times of difficult financial circumstances, the criticisms rise. During the Great Depression, for example, when many families who had been planning to buy a second car, or get a larger house, or send their children to more expensive colleges found themselves caught with lower incomes, there was a great outcry against most of the social institutions—for example, the government or the banks. But the schools were most heavily criticized because they were viewed as the most vital of our social institutions. In 1935, there was a big national conference on the crisis in our schools, and in the excitement of that attack, a United States senator from New York maintained that the schools had gotten so bad that probably by 1940 they would collapse, and we would have no public education. We must realize that this is not something new, this is common, and it is right for our schools to be examined and criticized by the public because they are *public* schools.

We should then look at another phenomenon of the Gallup Poll, which shows that although the average public rating of the schools in general in this country is below a B, the rating of their own school—the school their children attend—is much better. It is a good B+. That suggests to me that when parents and community members have contact with the schools, they think the schools are doing pretty well. This verifies a well-known principle of communication that when people have direct contact with something, they make their judgments from their own experience. When they do not have contact, they depend upon the impressions they get from others, especially the mass media. Parents who know about their own schools think, on the whole, that these schools are pretty good. But not knowing about other schools, they depend on what they read in the newspaper or see on the TV, and they think that the other schools must be terrible. This suggests the need for a procedure by which we could emphasize communication and cooperation within the community, where the school is, so that local people could get to know the school. After all, that is where the action is, where the people are who vote to support education.

Mickler: The concept of basic education is another serious concern of most educators. What do you see as the major differences between what is described as basic education today and the movement of the 1950s and 1960s which called for greater emphasis on subject matter and a corresponding increase in intellectual stimulation?

Tyler: One, there is dissatisfaction and fear about our social institutions today. When they are in danger, some people have a tendency to say, "Let us go back to where we used to be. That was safe; things seemed to be going well then." On the other hand, the same people are looking at the society and saying "My, computers are becoming important. We should have computer literacy in the school." Or, "We are having greater problems with drug addiction. We should do something about drug addiction in the school." There is then the ambivalence between believing, on the one hand, that if we could only go back to the older things we could be better off in education, and realizing, on the other hand, that the society has changed. The only proper answer to that is a continuing re-examination of both what it is that our young people need to learn and which of those things the school can do well.

There is always a danger, of course, that we will try to do too much in responding to all these things. Everything cannot be done in the five hours a day that most schools provide. There is also the danger that we will go back to minimum things like just teaching reading and arithmetic, when we well know that our society cannot get along with people who only know how to read and write, and who do not understand the scientific world, who do not understand the social world in which they live, or who do not appreciate other things that are a necessary part of their intellectual equipment.

Mickler: What do you think is the most important part of education in the school as opposed to education that can take place elsewhere?

Tyler: The school's special responsibility is to help young people discover the resources that there are in scholarship. By that I mean carefully developed knowledge and skills like reading, writing, speaking, computing, and a view of the world obtained from literature, history, science, and philosophy. These are the kinds of things that children are not going to get from direct contact with the community. If they depend only on what the community can teach, it is going to be provincial, and there is going to be bias rather than a more objective examination of our social institutions. So the special role of the school is to help free our young people from the limitations and provincialism of direct experience, and to give to them all that they can get from the resources of scholarship. In that sense, subject matter has to be seen as a vital resource to be drawn upon, rather than something that is bottled up and put on a shelf as soon as an examination has been passed.

Mickler: Many of us in the teaching profession do see as our primary responsibility the creation of an intellectual atmosphere that will motivate our students to expand their knowledge beyond the horizons of their immediate environment. However, this concept of teaching is not practiced in all schools today, partly because of the emphasis on minimum competencies in basic skills. How do you feel about this problem? What action would you propose to resolve it?

Tyler: Right now about 20% of children in the United States do not learn to read well and do not learn to compute well, and the public has become so concerned about the 20% that they have impressed many educators and teachers with the idea that we just have to concentrate on those 20%. My view is that every child should have a chance to keep learning as much as he can, but it is more important to see that the 80% have a challenge and keep moving than it is to concentrate upon the minimum competencies. As a matter of fact, I was a member of the National Education Association committee that studied the minimum competency program in Florida. We were distressed to find that many teachers had given up attention to science and social studies in order to drill upon mathematics and reading, even though less than 20% of the students in that state had any difficulty with minimum competency. We must not let little distortions get in the way.

Mickler: There is increasing public concern that general education programs in American high schools, and in institutions of higher education as well, do not reflect the kinds of knowledge that students will need for life in the 21st century. Therefore, as you know, there is currently a movement underway, the goal of which is to redefine general education. Would you comment on this movement or trend?

Tyler: As societies change, one must continuously re-examine what young people need to learn and look again to our resources, what we have in the sciences and arts and other areas that are helpful to teach people. Historically, that was the question Plato and Socrates were discussing at some length, and it was the question that Aristotle and the great philosophers at Athens discussed in the days before Christ, namely what is worth learning? In the English tradition, Spencer, in the last century, wrote the famous book on what knowledge is of most worth. We must make a continuing search to find out what it is, and we must draw upon our intellectual heritage to help us as we face new problems. What is good general education is a continuing problem. It is not answered easily by somebody's panacea. We have got to look at all the possibilities and realize that many things we have been teaching for generations are still important, and that some other things may be less important. There are no easy answers. We must thoughtfully raise the question: Is this something that our young people should learn? Will it be helpful to them? Does it have permanent value, or is it largely peripheral? These kinds of questions must be dealt with in every generation.

Of course, this has been true in our history. For example, I was director of the Cooperative Study in General Education that began in 1939 under the support of the American Council on Education. At that time, with the development of the Depression, there was great concern over what general education should be. It was believed that too much attention was given to specialized occupational education. Hence, 22 colleges and universities undertook a pilot study to try to formulate what good general education should be, and to work out programs in their own institutions. As soon as the war came, there was no unemployment and there was a good deal of money available to support the war, people forgot about general education. Now they are coming back to it again. This has happened over the years.

Mickler: Ernest Boyer advocates seeing the "connectedness" of things as a rationale for emphasis on general education, and he has promoted his ideas on this topic extensively in his writings, including the Carnegie Foundation for the Advancement of Teaching report, *High School.* How would you react to this concept?

Tyler: The problem resides in what is called integration, one's own personal integration. If your learning is compartmentalized, what you learn on Sunday has nothing to do with how you behave on Monday. If what you think about science has nothing to do with how you are developing in literature, there is a lack of connectedness. One of the most important functions of education is to help the person develop some integration—some unity of understanding, belief, and practice—so that the person uses his knowledge and ideas in all appropriate walks of life and makes them consistent with one another.

Mickler: As you see it, then, connectedness in one's thinking is an essential part of an educated person. Would you expand further upon this concept?

Tyler: Education is the means of becoming increasingly more humane, the means of achieving the potential of what we hope a human being can be—so, as we continue to redefine our notions about what a utopia is and what a good life can be, we must continue to redefine our notions of what constitutes an educated person. It would never be as though this were the final thing set in concrete. It is ever changing.

Mickler: The image of an educated person changes, in part, from one age to another, right? Do you see particular characteristics of an educated person that have remained the same throughout time?

Tyler: Well, on that question we could spend a whole course on the philosophy of education. But let me comment on a few generalizations that I could spell out in more detail. One of them is that an educated person is continually seeking to understand more fully oneself, other human beings, and the world in which one lives in order to live more intelligently. Second, the person is open to continuous learning. The mind stays open, looks for ideas, and tries to expand one's learning just as science is continually trying to get more and more knowledge in certain areas. Third, the educated one recognizes that her or his own existence as a person depends upon the stability and openness of the social system in which one lives, and thus is concerned about other people, not only the face-to-face relationships but also the kind of society in which one lives. The person tries to make it a more unselfish and a more open society, one where people trust and communicate with each other, and are accordingly able to be free to develop.

Mickler: Would you discuss the distinction between education and training, and the relationship of both to the total educational process?

Tyler: Until the founders of our nation had the vision of a free democratic society, there had always been a distinction between education and training. The ruling classes got education; that is, they were taught what the leaders of that society believed necessary for them to know in order to rule the people and to understand the wider world. The common people, who represented the vast majority, were trained to carry on their working life. This separation still prevails in secondary and higher education in most countries, and especially in Europe. But here, the common view is that everybody should become educated. This view was also expressed by Jefferson when he said that we are forming a country where everybody is both a worker and a ruler. In this country, where we are developing freedom, all people are created free and equal, as is stated in the Declaration of Independence. We must see that everyone is both educated and able to carry on the work of life. That has been our ideal. We have not achieved it fully, but we probably have more educated people than most countries, judging from the results of the international evaluation. We still have many young people who only get training that prepares them for an occupation, and they do not continue their education beyond that point. This is one of our problems, and we must try to increase education so that eventually 100% of our population is educated.

Mickler: Now, let us move further into the educational process and take a look at the teacher as a professional. Teacher competence has become a major public issue. Some educators contend that teachers have been made scapegoats for an ineffective evaluation process. That is to say, there appears to be little or no reliable basis for evaluating teacher competency effectively. Would you express your ideas about this?

Tyler: First, I think that we often have a wrong conception of what is involved in the development of a professional. There is a common belief that the administration should decide what is needed, and should evaluate the teachers and reward them accordingly. This is a mistaken view. Professional people should share in the business of deciding what it is they are trying to do, what skills are needed to do it, and how well they are measuring up. We should start out with the view that every teacher is a professional, and that everyone wants to learn. We can usually assume that everyone wants to improve, and that everyone can be a growing person and can cooperate with other professionals. It becomes a matter, then, not of measuring each person against a single standard, as though everybody is to be the same, but a matter of looking at outcomes. Where are the classrooms that are having difficulty? What is needed there to help make them better? In my 61 years of teaching and in working with teachers, I have never found anyone who objected to help. But when teacher evaluation is viewed simply as the application of my standards as a principal or a school board member, then the principal and the school board are seen to be measuring you in terms of what they want you to be. That is an undignified way to treat a professional. We are all responsible for a mission, and we all need to look at what we are doing now to accomplish that mission. Then we need to determine what it is we need to learn in order to do it better.

Mickler: I certainly agree with that. But we continue to hear the criticism that one of the major difficulties in evaluation is measuring with confidence how much a particular instructor has taught someone. I think this is an expectation that has grown out of the accountability movement.

Tyler: Probably a negative one. In any organization there is usually a very small percentage of persons, who for some reasons that may vary, do not make constructive contributions and who eventually need to be removed from the organization. Fortunately, they are few in number. Instead of concentrating on the business of making fine distinctions among all the staff, we need to identify those few who are found to be continuously hindering children's learning and get them somewhere else. We should concentrate our major efforts on the growth and development of all staff members. This seems to me a better way of carrying on a professional development program.

Mickler: How do you feel about student evaluation of teachers? Should it be used as the basis for assigning teacher rewards and penalties?

Tyler: Let me pretend that I am a professor in this institution. I need information about how I am perceived by the people I come in contact with, my students, colleagues, and others. I need to know how these people react to me because that information can be very helpful, just as consumer surveys are very helpful to companies selling retail goods. Now, of course, you cannot view that information as though it were the only information because it is silly to think that any one source is the basis for rewards or something of that sort. It is *one* kind of information, and it helps me in improving. I might find, for example, that the good students think that I do not challenge them enough—the stuff is Mickey Mouse to them. The poor students, the students who have difficulty, may feel that I am very helpful and that they have been able to understand something. Now, that kind of information is useful to me in planning for the future. But the notion that you are going to weigh these different perceptions of me against some criteria of rewards is a silly business. Certainly,

I would again take the view that one should look at the kinds of evidence we have that will help us discover where some of our difficulties lie and where our effectiveness lies. Typically, student evaluations are a good source if they are used in connection with other sources for evaluation.

Micker: Would you clarify the difference between evaluation and testing? For many people the distinction between the two is not clear.

Tyler: There is no dictionary or ruling body that determines the meaning of many of the words we use. "Testing" at one time was meant by many people to be simply a written examination. Then, after 1920, it came to mean an objective test that could be scored in terms of the number of right or wrong answers. In order to focus attention away from that view of testing, I developed, in 1929, the term "evaluation" to refer to the process of finding out the kinds of things the student was learning and the things of value he or she was getting from it. Then in 1963, when I was asked to develop a different kind of appraisal, namely, one that would summarize the learning of whole groups of children of different ages and backgrounds, I coined the term "assessment" for the National Assessment of Educational Progress. But these different terms are used only to be sure that people do not confuse the particular kind of appraisal with some other notions they have about testing or about evaluation. Right now, the term "assessment" has become popular and is being used to refer to almost any kind of testing. One cannot control people's use of words. To understand what is meant, one must find out how the terms are being used in a particular case.

Mickler: The concept of professional development has been generally well received by teachers. The practice of requiring teachers to participate in these programs, however, bothers some people in education. What is your reaction to this development?

Tyler: Any of these universal panaceas are like using big axes to try to cut down a little sapling. The particular needs for development vary among people and situations. For example, the needs for further education on the part of a high school science teacher in this nation, where society experiences rapid changes, may be quite different from the needs of a kindergarten or primary teacher. The use of a single law to mandate these things is an example of the mistaken notion that you can make laws that will improve human relations. If teachers can be convinced of the need for professional development, it is likely that they will participate in such activities and experience growth. But professional people tend to resent mandates or laws that specify how they should become—these laws really do not work. You could find a good many examples of states that have tried such laws and then have given them up after a while. The important point is that the employers of school personnel must become knowledgeable about what kind of persons they need, and they must encourage their teachers to get the necessary additional knowledge, skills, or other things that may be involved. But just as you cannot guarantee that unhealthy people will become healthy if they are forced to visit the doctor regularly, you cannot guarantee that people suddenly will become able if they are forced to take a course or two.

Professional development has to become a conceptual, philosophic basis for the development of professionals in a social institution, such as a school, or a hospital, or other kind of social agency. In the first place, the professionals who are there are employed because they were thought to have the competence to carry on the mission of that institution, or school. Now, as they begin to work there, the need for further development on their part may be identified. For example, if a school has some problems that are quite serious, it must help some teachers gain additional skills that will enable them to deal with those problems.

Mickler: Yes, and there are some teachers who have problems of a personal nature as well. Many educators are currently afflicted by stress, and "teacher burnout" often results in absenteeism and in the loss to the profession of many caring people. Would you comment on this problem?

Tyler: There are ongoing studies on teacher burnout, and I am told, in general, that burnout does not arise from the difficulty of the job. Many teachers like difficult jobs. It is when the teacher develops a sense of frustration that burnout often ensues.

Mickler: What are the conditions under which this sense of frustration develops?

Tyler: One is when they are unprepared to deal with a situation they find. For example, teachers who come from middle-class backgrounds are quite unprepared to meet the situation in the school in the slums, where they find poor children; nobody has ever read to them, some do not even have the language, and so on. Teachers are unprepared for it. They struggle without any way of deciding how to deal with it, and they become frustrated, and finally the tension becomes too much. On the other hand, researchers find that some of the highest morale is in schools where the principal provides leadership, helps teachers see the real problems, and works out a plan of attack. The teachers recognize that the kids come from difficult backgrounds, where the families have not had an education. They realize that they must begin with the children where children are—so the teachers develop a plan, go ahead, see they are making progress, and encourage the kids. In such schools morale can be very high.

Mickler: It is difficult to develop high morale, though, when problems are so complex.

Tyler: I think one of the problems is that as we get new groups into the school, such as children from disadvantaged backgrounds, we are also getting teachers in there who have never had any notion of how to deal with such children, as well as principals who apparently have not, either. Instead of creating a plan of action that would help them deal with a difficult problem, they are left to become frustrated. Back in the 1890s, when there were more immigrants in Chicago than there were people who were born there, the schools had a very difficult time educating the immigrant children. Jane Addams established Hull House, where volunteers worked with these children, tutoring them, giving them friendly counsel and encouragement. This helped build morale in the Chicago schools. I think that burnout, in a majority of cases, is due to the lack of a sense of mission, the lack of a plan to attack it, and the lack of any evidence showing they are making progress. So teachers develop a sense of frustration. They feel worse and worse until they finally get out.

Mickler: Also, it appears that some of these elements of burnout are evident in higher education today. The dictum of publish or perish, which appears to be gaining momentum in spite of financial austerity and declining enrollments, tends to create such frustration.

Tyler: In the first place, I question the notion that during periods of austerity, the publish-or-perish rule will be the dominant mode of rewarding people. I am chairman of the Educational Advisory Committee for the School of Education at the University of Massachusetts, which is concerned with the attitude of the legislature toward the university. There we find the emphasis is going to be on encouraging the university to work more effectively with the schools of the state in order to help improve education. Some faculty members will do research, but more will be asked to help the schools make use of relevant knowledge from whatever source it may come, from their own research or from the research of others. In times of depression in the past, there was less emphasis upon the notion that every institution ought to be a research institution.

Statistics show very clearly that no more than 15% of the faculty members in the United States who are engaged in research are able to produce new knowledge. But we all can help to improve the use of knowledge and of inquiry into the particular local situations. We can all try to understand what is going on in our institution and how to bring more generalized knowledge to help it. The message for most of us is to seek to find and use relevant knowledge as a base for action. This is much more important than the notion that everybody must in some way produce new knowledge. Producing new knowledge is as difficult a business as being a great surgeon. We must realize that not everybody can produce new knowledge, but educational institutions do have a role of seeing that knowledge is used effectively.

Mickler: Often the need for action research to solve practical classroom problems takes precedence over basic research, especially in the human services fields, does it not?

Tyler: There are two pulls that need to be well balanced in institutions of higher education, and they are often not well balanced. On the one hand, you have got the pull for practicability. The legislature wants to know what the state is getting for its money, what the faculty is doing. In fact, during the 1930s at the Ohio State, the legislature voted not to support any faculty research because they thought it was not appropriate. They were in difficult times. Why should they be supporting this business of getting new knowledge? So there is the danger, on the one hand, that leadership or the legislature or other groups will mandate practicality, as though knowledge were not a basis for making things more practical. We should want to get new knowledge in order to deal, in some way, with such diseases as heart attacks and so on.

On the other hand, you have the other extreme position that maintains that all a university is supposed to do is get new knowledge. That, too, is a mistake, because the value of knowledge to society requires that the knowledge be utilized effectively. Hence, the university has an important role in interpreting knowledge, in understanding it, in seeing how it applies to particular situations, and in the case of education the university's job is to help the local area study its problems and put all of these things together. That is a tremendously important role, and it is unwise for an institution to overlook that part of its responsibility.

Mickler: The computer as an educational resource has received considerable attention recently. As we move into the age of high technology and as the use of microcomputers increases both in schools and in homes, what changes do you anticipate in instruction?

Tyler: First, let us look at some of the facts. Actually, few school districts have microcomputers. Of course, even 5% would be a large number, because there are approximately 26,000 school districts. In the second place, the percentage of homes with microcomputers is even less. Third, we need to understand that the computer is a very rapid adding machine with a capacity for storage and retrieval. It is not magic. We must remember that it is a tool for people to use, and that in some respects it is like the typewriter. When we discovered we could handle writing much more rapidly if we learned to use a typewriter, more and more schools obtained them. From 1910 to 1914, the typewriter companies supported a research project to see whether children in the primary grades could learn to write more easily and quickly with a typewriter than by learning to write manually. The research showed that children could learn to write more quickly with a typewriter. Why, then, did typewriters not become common in all the schools? Because the cost of providing typewriters to every child was far more than the schools could afford, and the noise in the classroom when all children were typing was a serious handicap. So the typewriter, although it has educational potential, never became the primary means of instruction in the elementary school. It is, of course, used in the high school as a tool for occupations and for secretarial work.

I suspect something like that will happen with computers. It is a very useful tool, but it is expensive. They say it is cheap and will be cheaper, but what is cheap, $500 to $600? That is not cheap to most families. Furthermore, if the schools are going to use them, they can use them most economically for managing instruction. In fact, many schools are doing that—when there is just one microcomputer per classroom it is usually used for pupil testing and diagnosis. It is not yet widely used for computer-assisted instruction. I think we need a continuing study of how this interesting and helpful tool can be useful to teachers. Instead of going all out and suddenly saying we are in the computer age—as we said about the typewriter age, or the age of educational movies, or the educational radio age and the television age—we need to study the advantages, the limitations and the possible uses of computers in education. We need to remember that teaching is a human enterprise.

* * *

The public expectation for schools to assist with moral education and to teach the fundamental values of the democratic political system are the primary issues considered in this interview. Tyler briefly addresses non-academic additions to the curriculum and the resultant criticism from the public. He concludes with a discussion of several current and critical issues that have future implications, e.g., teacher supply and demand, the future role of the federal government in education, and training programs for business and industry.

Mickler: Currently the whole area of values education is generating a great deal of controversy. Perhaps this is due to the confusion and the disagreement over whether values should be taught, or even whether they could be taught. What are your thoughts on this issue?

Tyler: Every human being develops things that he or she believes in, cherishes, and uses to guide his or her life. These are the things one values, and people value many sorts of things. Some values, however, are cherished in all societies. One of these is honesty. If people cannot trust most other people to tell the truth, there cannot be a real society, for a society involves interdependence—we work together, we accomplish things together, we are therefore a society. So, there is a functional basis for saying that every society should emphasize telling the truth. The same thing can be said with reference to the security of one's property. Nobody really, except those who have nothing and want to take something from somebody else, has the view that one should not teach children not to steal. Another essential value in all societies is the belief in the importance of contributing to others, the belief that you are not alone in the world and that you need to help others. People in a democratic society profess the belief that we should respect and help other people, all other people. This is one of our values, and certainly respect for the individual and concern about helping others are essential to the operation of our society. In addition to these most basic values, there is one that is essential to peace and order, namely, respect for constituted authority. When there are difficulties, we need laws and rules and some people who can adjudicate them. Otherwise, groups will be fighting each other all the time.

Mickler: How do children learn to value these things?

Tyler: The development of these values ought to begin in the home with parents who are concerned about honesty, about not stealing, about helping others, and about respecting authority. Unfortunately, that is not always the case. The school certainly has the responsibility to do two things. Its first responsibility is to operate the school community on a moral basis, where everybody is respected, where unselfishness is shown, where lying is not permitted, and where people who do lie are punished. If students are stealing from others, they must be stopped. These are important values, which the school must uphold in its operation.

The school's second responsibility—and this is one that homes often do not have—is the responsibility to provide an intellectual basis for these values, so students understand that the values are not arbitrary. For example, one of the things that is hard for adolescents to understand is why they should obey constituted authority, why they are not permitted to do something they want to do. As children get older, the school should help them understand why these values are important to them and their society. The school should not answer adolescents' questions by replying, "This is what you must do because we say so," which is often what they are told in the home. The school should help the student understand that societies have found these values necessary, that without them societies perish.

Mickler: Why is there such a controversy over values education in schools?

Tyler: The debates over the responsibility of the public school to teach values often seems to be due to a notion of values other than those that are fundamental to our society. The fundamental ones are central in public education. Supreme courts have ruled in several states, for example, that it is incumbent upon a public school to help children develop values that are essential to our society, such as those values indicated by the Constitution, the Declaration of Independence, Lincoln's Gettysburg Address, and other basic documents. In addition to helping children develop moral values, the school has responsibility for helping children extend their range of enjoyment. Human beings can value things that are beyond the basic needs. We can learn to appreciate good behavior, learn to appreciate the process of learning itself, learn to appreciate a person who has sacrificed and made something of himself. It is important for the school to help children to develop these values. Life is not very meaningful if one cherishes only material values. Hence, part of the task of the school is to help children find many other things that are enjoyable and can give deeper meaning to life.

Mickler: What is your opinion of the attacks sometimes made on the teaching of values in the school?

Tyler: I have observed three kinds of attacks. One is made by those who have read a little about the study of primitive societies and have discovered many quaint customs. They mistake these customs for basic values and say, "All values are relative to particular societies and circumstances." But this is not true of basic values; the societies that survive have a number of common basic values. The second attack occurs where there is a particular sectarian interpretation. Public schools, they say, have no right to take the sectarian way, a point, they argue, that is made perfectly clear in our Constitution. But the basic values mentioned earlier are *not* sectarian; they are accepted as important in all modern religions. Then there is still another attack that is really anarchist. It maintains that all values should be individualistic, and that there are no common values that should be taught. However, this position is in conflict with the school's basic responsibility to educate children for constructive citizenship. Citizenship requires commitment to certain social-civic values.

Mickler: Another facet of the debate concerns "values clarification."

Tyler: Now values clarification involves helping people understand that when they make a choice of action they ought to consider how desirable it is to attain what they value highly. When you choose, for example, to go out with a bunch and drink a lot of beer, you may enjoy the fun of being with your companions, but you have a headache the next day and cannot get much done. In such a case, you should make it clear to yourself what values you cherish. That was what was meant by values clarification as it was originally developed by one of my former doctoral students, Louis Raths. But there are other people who interpret values education as the process of merely helping students to clarify their values;

whether their values are bad or not is of no concern. I believe this to be the notion that is in the minds of the Moral Majority when they attack values clarification. Because of this confusion, I would not use the term. I would just say there are important values that we all agree on.

Mickler: How can educators help students to clarify their own values?

Tyler: The role of the school is to help children understand values and to use them to guide their actions, rather than just talking about them on Sunday and then doing nothing the next day. Children as well as adults often make decisions and take actions without thinking of the consequences in terms of the things important to their values. We are not always clear about the values that we have in mind. We have to learn to ask ourselves, "Now why do I want to do this? Is this really something I want to do? What will I get in return for it?" Clarifying values is an essential part of being an intelligent person. It is simply a sensible way of helping children as they go through life, a way to think about the things they do and to ask questions about the values involved in their actions.

Mickler: Would you make a distinction between moral education and values education?

Tyler: The term "morals" has to do with not only one's thinking and one's planning but with one's actions. For instance, Lawrence Kohlberg is especially interested in the intellectual level of moral decisions. You may remember some of the episodes that he uses. In one episode, the person's wife is suffering from a fatal disease, and the doctors tell her that there is a particular medicine that will cure it. The man goes to the pharmacy to get the medicine and discovers that it costs far more than he has. The question is, should he steal it? The medicine is there right in the window. Discussion of this dilemma brings out the conflict among moral principles. You cannot possibly be both kind to your wife and avoid stealing, but in some way you have to deal with those conflicting values or moral principles, if you want to refer to it that way. The intellectual problem is to justify what should finally be done. This is only part of moral education. Moral education has occurred when you not only decide wisely what you should do, but you have the courage to do it and you actually do it.

Mickler: Do you see Kohlberg's conceptual framework for moral development as a useful tool in the school?

Tyler: He is trying to identify stages in moral reasoning like those Piaget has talked about in intellectual development. Kohlberg has identified and classified moral reasoning into six levels, like the Piaget levels. At the highest level, one understands the moral principles and the consequences, and one decides what is the right thing to do in terms of the consequences for others. However, Kohlberg finds very few people reason that way.

They are more likely to say, "Well, it is the law," or "Well, everybody else does it," or something like that.

Just in designing a program for reading, you have to find out where your students are and seek to help them move intellectually, but do not stop there. The courage to operate and practice is essential to moral behavior. The danger is that school activities will be only discussion matters rather than practical matters. Now one method that I used when I was teaching in the school was to talk about their own decisions, things they had done last week, and review them in terms of what happened. Is that really the principle that you wanted to follow? Begin to use moral reasoning as a guide to your own actions.

Mickler: Why has there not been as much controversy surrounding civic education as there has been recently in terms of moral and values education? How do you account for this?

Tyler: Well, that is because the term "moral" tends to be associated with religion, and the general sectarian view is so common in America, with different sects having different views about religious matters. Everybody is willing to believe in civic education so long as they can interpret it. In the primary grades, for example, the civic community is the community of the school and the home, the community children know about. There the question is how to behave so that the community becomes a better place, a place where one has greater freedom to do the right things. The child's understanding of the civic arena, of course, should include the economic part of it. Who produces the goods and services? Is your mother going to do everything or are you going to help? Are you going to do the dishes? The child's society includes a whole series of things, and the teacher should keep building on them. However, if civic education means, as it does to some social studies teachers, just reading books but not really understanding something, then that, I think, is one of the defects of civic education.

Mickler: Was not there a drop in political civic knowledge of the 9-, 13-, and 17-year-olds between the first and the second National Assessments? To what do you attribute this drop?

Tyler: It was not a very big drop. One really ought to look at each school in order to determine what accounted for it, but there were some generally publicized matters in America at that time, such as an increasing attack upon government and other parts of our civic society, the talk of loss of confidence in our social institutions. These may have caused changes in the civic achievement of children. There has also been a general emphasis upon freedom, an emphasis upon rights rather than responsibilities. Both have to be nicely balanced in the society. You cannot have the right to do something without also having the responsibility to use that right well. From the time the Civil Rights Movement began, we have had a heavy emphasis upon the rights of minorities, the rights of women, the rights of workers, the rights of children, and so on. These are all fine if they are balanced with the responsibilities that accompany them. But we find in looking at the National Assessment that many students do not even believe in the things that are in the first ten amendments of the Constitution, the Bill of Rights, and that many do not even know about them. They are not familiar with what our society guarantees its citizens.

Mickler: Why do you think this is true? What is happening? Is civic education being neglected in the schools or not?

Tyler: Again, you have to look at the particular schools in order to answer that question, but my guess is that many social studies books during the 1960s and 1970s were devoted to complex studies of social issues, issues that were beyond the experience of the students, and dealt with few of the things they were experiencing in their own contact with the civic world. What do you think?

Mickler: I think that is probably true. Are there other considerations?

Tyler: Yes, of course. In reviewing the reports of the International Evaluation of Educational Achievement, I have noted that students in the top 5 percent in any area are deeply interested in that subject, and that students do equally well on the tests in every one of the countries where they have opportunity to learn. We do not have to worry in our country about producing the top 5% of scientists. We already do, and they are winning Nobel Prizes and other awards. Other countries also produce great scholars and scientists. But in the United States, the bottom 25% of our children achieve at about the middle level of the students in other countries. The middle of the student distribution tends to be affected primarily by public opinion. As Alfred Kroeber, an anthropologist who has now passed away, very nicely expressed it: "Young people in every culture will learn the things that are considered important by the adults they respect." When our adult society in general greatly respects science, you will find the scores of the middle group will go up. If they greatly respect civic knowledge and responsibility, I think scores in these areas will go up again. But we must not think the school can accomplish much in moving the average kid against the view of the majority in our society. He tends to be like the adults he respects.

Mickler: Do you believe, then, that the haphazard additions to the curriculum we have had in recent years have been due, at least in part, to the fact that society has expressed interest in different kinds of learning and has then promoted the inclusion of related topics in the schools?

Tyler: I think that is quite true. Many schools have accepted many more tasks than they can possibly accomplish. They felt flattered by being asked to do it. But we miss today the admonitions of some of the great educational leaders, like Robert Hutchins, in my time. He was continually reminding the public what the schools are for. Schools must not forget the basic important job of education and become overly interested in peripheral things like driver education. School administrators must not simply listen to what people say, as though they were responding to public opinion polls. Instead, educational leaders must help shape that public opinion by helping the public understand what the schools can and cannot do. By being so subservient to public opinion, our leadership is missing a point. If you are going to be subservient, you should not be surprised to learn that people do not respect the schools. Educational leaders should go out there and help parents and others understand what schools can do, help them understand what the home responsibilities are, and remind them that when 60% of the mothers of school-age children are in the labor force, many children have fewer opportunities for learning at home. In such cases, parents must make arrangements to provide supervision and constructive learning opportunities for their children.

Mickler: By taking on all of these responsibilities we may have created a lot of problems for the schools, and the task has become almost insurmountable. Do you feel that this situation has led to some of the criticism and the public's lack of confidence in the schools that we talked about earlier?

Tyler: Sure, we are taking on much more than we can accomplish. Education takes time. Of course, through research on "time on task," we have rediscovered what is only common sense, that time is very important in determining how much children learn.

Mickler: I would like to move now to some questions about the future of education. What do you believe will occur regarding teacher supply and demand?

Tyler: In 1960, or thereabouts, George Stigler, a distinguished labor economist for the National Bureau of Economic Research, studied the supply and demand for professional people, including engineers and scientists as well as others. He found that over the years in these various ups and downs in the economy, the demand and supply followed pretty well the signals that the young people got. When they saw engineering was becoming popular, they enrolled in engineering. When there was a demand for teachers, more people enrolled in teaching. I think this trend is going to continue in teaching as well as in other fields. Right now, for example, there seems to be a surplus of lawyers, and fewer people are enrolling in law schools. Unless you want to make this a totalitarian society, where officers of the government, rather than students and parents, make the decisions, young people are going to select those occupations in which they think they will have a chance to succeed. I think this practice will continue, as it has over the last 200 years.

Another relevant research finding is that people who prepare for teaching find that teacher training is a very useful preparation for some other occupations. Several years ago, the National Center for Educational Statistics supported a study of teacher supply and demand. This investigation found not only that fewer students enrolled in teacher education programs when they thought there was not much opportunity for employment, but they also found that when teacher education graduates could not find jobs in teaching, many found other good jobs. They were not unemployed. A good education for teaching gives the graduate a degree of flexibility. It does not narrow the graduate so that he can operate only as a teacher. He or she can do a good many other things that involve human relations.

Furthermore, the career for graduates of colleges and universities is not limited to the locality of their training. In the southern states, the market area is largely regional because of the close connections of people. In the north, the market area tends to be more national. But in any event, people usually get their promotions by moving, if necessary, from one institution to another. In my own case, I started as a teacher in the high school. Then I taught at the University of Nebraska, then the University of North Carolina, then the Ohio State University, then the University of Chicago, and then continued my career as Director of the Center for Advanced Study in the Behavioral Sciences in Stanford, California. Because chances for advancement within the same institution are limited, many of my students also moved from one institution to another as opportunities opened up. This means that faculty members who cannot move because of circumstances such as family responsibilities will find it more difficult to become increasingly recognized in their field because they do not have the same degree of physical mobility. But by and large, I see no reason to believe that the physical mobility in the faculties will not continue as it has over the last 50 years.

Mickler: Would you talk some more about career mobility, moving from education into other areas?

Tyler: If you are talking about college professors, the percentage of those who move into positions that are not professorial is small but important. For example, most of the people who are recruited into the "think tanks" and other agencies that do intellectual planning for various organizations and institutions have been college professors. In the political arena, the current Secretary of State was a professor at the University of Chicago in Business Administration, George Schultz. Although there is a wide range of opportunities for professors to move into other intellectual agencies, the percentage who move out of college or university teaching is less than 10% or 15%.

Mickler: Do you expect the percentage of college faculty moving out of education to increase over the next decade or so?

Tyler: The question is whether they move out, or whether there are fewer moving in. Faculties generally have some degree of tenure, so what happens in periods of decline is usually not that more people move out, but that fewer people move in. There will be a period in which there will be fewer young people of college age, but the question is how many more older people will enroll in universities or other institutions. Right now, more than half the people in community colleges are over the usual college age. They are over 25, and a good number of them are over 35.

Mickler: In one of the recent Association for Supervision and Curriculum Development *Updates*, the following question was presented: "With large cuts in federal programs and with the apparent demise of the Department of Education, what do you see as the future role of the federal government in education?" What would your answer be to this question?

Tyler: One could approach this in two ways. One could look at the Constitution and the view there, a view I thoroughly endorse, that education is a function of the state and the local community and not a function of the federal government. We view the schools as the means by which our children become more human and become the kinds of persons we would like to have them become. This view is in contrast to that held by totalitarian states, where education is viewed as a function of the state, and the individual's happiness and interests are of no great concern. With these considerations in mind, we might say then that the federal government should not do what it has been doing. Often, it seems that the schools are enticed to do things the pressure groups think are important. Probably, the federal government should stay away from this kind of enticement, and let the schools focus on what the district and the states identify as important.

On the other hand, the federal government should do certain things. For example, in line with the 1954 decision of the Supreme Court, where it is found that schools are disregarding the rights that are guaranteed by our Constitution, the government has the responsibility to protect these rights. Furthermore, the federal government can provide, without interfering with the schools, funds for research to try to deal with society's critical problems, to get more knowledge of these problems. However, the federal government should not try to persuade schools to do what some person conducting research believes would be a good thing to do. Knowledge should be available, and persons should use it, but they should not be forced to do so by the government. Third, I believe that the federal government should undertake the role that was envisioned for it when the original Bureau of Education was established. That is, the commissioner should study education throughout the nation and should inform the public about the status of education on at least an annual basis. The rediscovery of that early law in 1963 prompted Francis Keppel, the then Commissioner of Education, to ask me on July 5, 1963, to design a national assessment. He found that we had no data on the progress of education; we had only data on the input. That is, we knew how many teachers there were and what expenditures were made by the schools of the nation, and other things like that, but we had no indications as to who was learning what, or how much they were learning. Yet, the reporting of things of that sort was envisioned in 1868, when the Office of Education was established. I believe the federal government should support the collection and reporting of information on the progress of education and that the emphasis of that study should be on what young people are learning.

Mickler: How do you view the increasing number of personnel training programs in industry? What implications does this trend have for education?

Tyler: Well, as industry becomes more technical, employees need more training, and much of this training certainly ought to be the job of the industries that are going to use the skills, rather than the job of the schools. How can you know that John Smith is going to get a job in electronics? When he gets the job in electronics, then is the time for him to obtain the specialized skills required for it.

Mickler: How do you think this trend will affect the job market for graduates of teacher preparation programs?

Tyler: The demand for teachers outside of the traditional elementary and secondary schools and colleges is increasing. A person at Teachers College of Columbia tells me that about 20% of their graduates are going into teaching in industry. The institution that I know best, the IBM, employs a large number of persons who teach not only training for particular jobs but a whole variety of other educational programs, executive training, management training, and other things of that sort. That is one source of demand for teachers. So we can no longer look just at the elementary and secondary schools and the usual college level to find out where teachers are to be employed. Furthermore, as our population gets older, more teachers are going to be employed in teaching the older people. The development of education for generations has been aimed at making it more of a human enterprise, an enterprise that helps young people and older people meet their needs in a human society. Do you not agree that you are more thoughtful of your students than your professors were when you were in college?

Mickler: Even this notion is criticized today.

Tyler: There is always criticism. There are always people who want to be harsh. There are always people who look down upon others and want to throw them out, and that has been true probably forever. But do not take these critics too seriously. Your mission is to help education be increasingly more effective in helping young people become human, in helping them become deeply concerned about the well being of others.

Mickler: That is quite a challenge for anybody. I think that much of what you have said in these interviews will help all of us understand our mission better and come closer to achieving our goals.

Ralph W. Tyler: An Interview Conducted by Malca Chall (Excerpts)

Bancroft Library, Regional Oral History Office, University of California at Berkeley, 1985–1987.

TYLER REJECTS PLACING LABELS ON HIMSELF OR OTHERS

Chall: This morning when I came in you were discussing putting labels on others. How do you view yourself?

Tyler: I don't view myself as a label. I view myself as a person.

Chall: People have, I guess, in the past put labels on you as a humanist or a behaviorist.

Tyler: They still do, but the effort of some of the best behavioral scientists I know is to remind people that you can't do that. It's a limited view of persons. If you want to understand them, don't try to label them because it's some particular aspect they pick out. Why should one call, we'll say, Arthur Combs—I think he's often labeled as a humanist? Most people that I know are humane. What does it mean? It's just a way that somebody picks out. They see some side of a person and say, "That's what I'm going to talk about," but it denigrates the importance of being a human being, which is that you're many-sided, not one-sided. You can't catalogue a person accurately. Do you want to be catalogued?

Chall: No, I don't think I do. Of course, cataloguing people as humanists is now something that people do, with respect to education, whom we consider to be a little right of center. You were quoting a little while ago the Bible in saying that you can't label others. Do you want to tell me about that one again?

Tyler: Just, "What is man is beyond"—as I recall—"beyond measure."

Chall: So you don't like being labeled even though people do label you?

Tyler: Well, I don't mind if they want to, but it shows their inadequate conception of humanity, of human beings.

Chall: Does it show an inadequate understanding of what you have been striving to do and what you've been writing about?

Tyler: Probably so. Nobody would ever have a full understanding of what anybody else was striving to do.

Chall: You have a body of literature that you're leaving in the library; does it—

Tyler: I hope it will be the ideas rather than me that they get interested in.

Chall: Is it possible to take all of that writing and focus it and say, "This man was a behaviorist"?

Tyler: If they wanted to define "behaviorist" in a way to accomplish this, but usually it isn't. I don't understand why they want it except to be lazy and not to try to understand somebody fully.

THE TYLER RATIONALE: BUILDING A CURRICULUM IS AN ACTIVE, NOT A PASSIVE, PURSUIT

Chall: Now there's been a body, I understand, of critical literature about your rationale, the so-called Tyler "rationale," which I'm sure you probably know about more than I do. In fact, I think Dr. Goodlad told me that there are some people who seem to spend their careers criticizing the rationale. I just wondered how this has affected you over the years? Did it early-on have any influence on you or affect you?

Tyler: No. Mostly they're people who think of the curriculum as something out there that they're looking at, rather than being involved in developing an educational program for a school. In the latter case one asks: "How am I going to develop one? I've got to have kids learning something. What is it they'll learn, and how would I select it to be sure that what they're learning is worth learning?" Then there's the question of how we're going to help them learn it. "What do I know about learning?" How should I set up an instructional program? And, "How am I going to organize it so that they can build each year on what they've learned last year? Finally, how can I evaluate the effectiveness of this educational program?"

Those are the questions for people who are going to have to make a curriculum or use a curriculum. They're the action people. Now in a sense it's like the person you're going to train to be an architect. He has to build a building. But if you have people who only want to look at the building from the standpoint of "Is it Georgian or is it Old Colonial something?" that's what most of the people in curriculum do. They don't go out and help people build curriculum, they want to look at it as an object rather than an action program.

So the answer is I'm sorry that more people don't want to work on curriculum with the schools. My little book has been widely translated. In fact, I didn't notice it was in Portuguese until I got a letter from a Portuguese woman yesterday saying that she had been impressed with it and was working on it. She studied it in Portuguese. But the reason for the popularity of my little book is because most people that are really concerned with the curriculum, other than those that are dilettantes sitting around wanting to talk about it, are people who have to make one or deal with one. There are very few books that help them that way.

I have a manuscript chapter by an acquaintance which he sent me. "What do you think of this chapter?" Well, he makes distinctions and classifies. I'm trying to figure out what to say to him without hurting his feelings. I can say to him, "Who are you writing this for? Are these students going to be teachers having to deal with the curriculum? Let's talk about it as an active document." Because he classifies curriculum workers as to "humanist," "managerial," and so on, which has nothing to do with the question "How can the curriculum be improved?" If you go out to get an effective program of health, you don't ask, "Is that managerial, or is it something else?" [Laughs]

The first time curriculum making was viewed as a profession was in the twenty-sixth Year Book of the National Society for the Study of Education. Both parts one and two, in 1927, were devoted to curriculum-making theory and practice. That's where it first became a recognized specialization. But then, because it became so popular, a lot of people got on the bandwagon who had no interest in working with the schools or making a curriculum; they just wanted to talk about it. It's like people who have no interest in being architects, but they want to talk about "Shall we call this Colonial? Would you rather have this one over here?" or something else.

So the answer to your question is that it hasn't influenced me except to wonder why we can't get more people wanting help for the curriculum. John Goodlad, for example, is successful because he works with these partnerships helping them build curricula. So does Bob Sinclair, with whom I'm working in Massachusetts, and so did Hilda Taba, and so did those others that I've mentioned. They saw the curriculum as a vital means by which kids are being educated, not something that you sit back and talk about. "What is the philosophy this person has?" or something else isn't the question.

Chall: Are you saying that most of the critical literature about the rationale is—?

Tyler: —misconceives what it's about.

Chall: Are these people who are not out there working with the schools primarily?

Tyler: Not a one of them is. In fact, the ASCD about three years ago asked me to appear on the same program with a professor of curriculum then at the University of Rochester. I didn't want to attack him—I'm much older than he, I wouldn't want to humiliate him—but some of the people in the audience said, "Mr. So-and-So," whose name I've forgotten, "How would you . . . ?" He said, "I don't want to work with the curriculum. I want to think about it."

Chall: Is that right?

Tyler: That's what he actually said. He sees the curriculum only as an object; he just likes to think about houses, he doesn't want to be an architect.

Chall: Are there a lot of those people out there?

Tyler: In the universities. They like to be in ivory towers; they don't like to go out where the action is. I don't know one who goes out where the action is except in the subject matter areas. You've got in Berkeley, you've got people in English who are going out with the Bay Area Writing Project. You had, when you had Abraham Fishler there, a very good person to go out for science. I don't know who does that now. But, by and large, these professors of education, not connected with subject matter, are just talking about things, rarely going out to work with the schools.

Chall: There are those who say that you moved into consulting rather than staying in research and scholarship where you had started. Was there any reason why you went in that direction?

Tyler: When you're in a university, you have graduate students who work with you. You can conduct research and you also have a library to serve you. But when you're not there, your opportunity is consulting. That's what happens to most people when they retire.

ALWAYS A TEACHER

Chall: In terms of your career, was there any facet of it that you might have enjoyed more? I'm thinking of your work as a teacher, which you said you really like to do. You said once that you were "hooked on teaching." You taught in college for many years. I mean, many, many years you were a college teacher working with graduate students and influencing them, sending them out into the world. Then, as you say, you went into consulting.

Tyler: But I also teach.

Chall: You are teaching as well, in a different setup?

Tyler: Yes, indeed. I've been a visiting professor at many different institutions since I've retired. And I teach when I'm consulting. For example, on Tuesday morning I was in the Shutesbury, Massachusetts, Elementary School. The teachers were concerned about their elementary social studies program, the topics that would be relevant to the students. So I visited a first-grade class and talked about division of labor. What do you do in the home and so on? I said, "Now you can begin to understand economics starting with the division of labor." I talked to the kids and they were interested and they wanted to know what school was like when I was in school. Then we went on to the second, and third, and fourth, and fifth grades—they only have up until the fifth grades. I think they have a middle school in that district.

Then in the afternoon I was in a very different district, in West Springfield, Massachusetts. There the fifth graders had already wanted to discuss immigration with me. They were studying immigration—the values and the difficulties and so on of immigration. So we had quite a session. There I was working with kids as well as with the teachers, talking to them at the same time.

So I'm not for giving up teaching.

Chall: No. I see. You find a way no matter where you are to do some teaching. In terms of your favorite kind of teaching, has there been a favorite area?

Tyler: It has to be something that I know something about. But mostly teaching, as I conceive it, is raising the questions that cause the students to have to inquire and find out for themselves. The teacher's the stimulator and guider of their learning, but he is not the one who tells them everything, in our kind of society. Now, when I go to a totalitarian society, it's quite different, because there the thing is to get the kids to be conformists. The real knowledge is up at the central committee of the Communist Party. Or in Hitler's case, there with Der Führer himself.

Chall: In other words, at whatever stage of career you've been in, you've managed to find a way to teach?

Tyler: Yes. When I was a dean at Chicago I had a full-time teaching load. In the morning I would be in the dean's office, in the afternoon at the board of examinations, and then from 4 o'clock until 9 o'clock in the evening I would be teaching.

Chall: Was there any area of your career in teaching that you liked better than any other?

Tyler: I don't think so. All people are very interesting. I've never found a person who wasn't interesting, have you?

Chall: I haven't thought about it. So wherever you were in your career, you've just enjoyed it?

Tyler: Sure.

Chall: Well, that's important.

Tyler: And every day now, I wake up and I'm still alive; I'm so happy that I'm still alive at my age. I just passed the age at which my father passed away. I'm happy to live longer than he did.

Chall: Yes, and in good health. That's what counts. You're able to enjoy your years.

INFLUENCING THE CAREERS OF OTHERS:
RESPONSIBILITY VS. POWER

Chall: All right, now, the next question that I had, as you see [on the outline], is about your influence on the careers of many persons in the field of education and social sciences. I wondered if you've ever considered how many people have received appointments or might not have received appointments as a result of your influence. Does that weigh heavily on you in any way?

Tyler: I conceive my role is, of course, to do what I can to help improve education. That means a sense of what kind of faculty members should be in universities, what kind of graduate students there should be. So when I find a person who seems to be able to make an important contribution to education or the improvement of education, I make note of it, as I did about Ernie Boyer, and think about him. I question, "What is he down there? Couldn't he do something better?" Then somebody calls me up and says, "Do you know of anybody?" Immediately I think of Ernie Boyer as worth finding.

But this happens right along. I was down at the predominantly black institution at Pine Bluff, Arkansas—the University of Arkansas, Pine Bluff. The dean of education there, George Antonelli, was doing an amazing job of helping those black young people become more intellectual. Instead of just trying to turn to athletics or something, helping them, and together with the teachers, getting them interested and excited about real learning. I noted that and kept in touch with him. Then the chancellor, a black man, left that institution, and another black man came in, who did not give George freedom to work as he had been doing. So I helped George move to Chapel Hill, where he is a vice-president in the University of North Carolina system.

He is the equivalent of dean of students in the University of North Carolina. But that's an illustration of trying to help people who have talents find a place where their talents can be used. If he's going to have a president who tries to get rid of him rather than trying to help him, he'd better get to some other institution.

No, I don't know the number, but I imagine I do something to help people at least once a month.

Chall: People come to you. Now there might be people who have been considered for appointments that you have not thought worthy.

Tyler: I never wrote anything against anybody. Why would I do that?

Chall: Oh, I don't know, but there might be people that you would not consider worthy of a particular appointment, about whom you are asked.

Tyler: I don't think in terms of worthy. When I last wrote—Let's see if I've got some illustrations here of some recent letters [looks through his file of letters].

Chall: Worthy may be the wrong word. Perhaps I should say capable of serving in the particular position.

Tyler: I try to write what I know about them. Let's see if I can find one here. Here's one in March. Let's find one in February. What I'm trying to bring out is that the effort is to try to describe what I've learned about them as best I can. I'm not going to make the judgment whether they should be taken or not. That's up to the institution. They'd be happier in making their own decisions rather than being able to blame somebody else for a decision they've made.

Here's one about Antonelli. He applied for a position at the San Jose State [University] [reading]: "Dear Dr. Spaulding—(the chairman of the search committee). I've known Dr. Antonelli for more than fifteen years and have gained increasing respect for his understanding of education, his effectiveness in working with students, his devotion to improving educational programs, his energy in attacking professional problems, and his courage and integrity. He is a prolific writer and his publications are clearly written and deal with important educational issues.

"His plan for guaranteeing the quality effectiveness of graduates who take teaching positions in the public schools is an innovative solution to the alleged incompetence of many graduates of teacher education programs.

"His development at Pine Bluff of an advocacy center for equity and excellence has received national attention. Much of this is due to his heavy commitment of time and thought. He's an outstanding educational leader."

You know, that's simply trying to describe the person. But don't try to tell somebody who should be appointed because, in the first place, you don't know enough about the situation to know what they need to do. In the second place, you don't want them to come back and say, "I appointed him just because you asked me to." I wouldn't think of it.

Chall: It's the way in which you analyze their qualities and capabilities.

Tyler: It's what I've tried to learn about them. It's just what I [was] saying, why I don't say, "He's a humanist" or "a right-wing person." I tried to write what I had observed about him, what he'd done.

Chall: And if that's what they want, that's what they'll take.

Tyler: That's why some of your questions here seem to me to imply a kind of political relationship rather than an effort to help improve education by finding people with talents and helping them to use their talents constructively.

Chall: They may seem a little political, but there are people out in this world that think that way. If we're going to get the answer to some of the questions they pose, I think we need to pose them to you so that people will in the future understand exactly what it is you're doing and why you do it.

Tyler: The problem of many people is that they think of social situations as giving power rather than responsibility. I find that as I read some of the American histories. I'm quite sure that people like Jefferson, for example, considered the responsibility of trying to make this nation work rather than the question "I've now got power!"

When I worked with Mr. Truman I found a man who had not intended to be president. He didn't even intend to be vice-president. They just chose him because it turned out that [Henry] Wallace had become a communist and so they selected him quickly from the Senate to be the vice-president. Then Roosevelt died and he was left as president. But I found him always asking the question, "How can I exercise this responsibility? What can I do about it?"

During the Second World War, scientists and engineers produced the atomic bomb and Truman was asked to approve its being dropped on targets in Japan. In focusing his response, Truman asked the Joint Chiefs: "Should I or should I not?" Well, they said, "You'll save millions of lives because the Japanese are killing off so many of us and we're killing many of them." The mindless notion that the bomb shouldn't have been used because a lot of people were killed at Hiroshima doesn't get around the fact that a lot of people were saved because they didn't have to continue the fighting that was going on to try to get into Tokyo with maniacal defenses that they had. It would have cost probably another million lives at that point. But this is the kind of thing that Truman had to think about. He didn't talk about power or anything like that.

I think that too many people, never having had to take responsibility, don't know how important responsibility is to people who have been educated with character. The responsibility that they bear and how they discharge it are the important tests of their character, not the power they have.

Chall: That's how you look at it. Well, that's worth our knowing.

Tyler: Yes? [Laughs] I keep telling that to Joe O'Shea, who wrote these articles like "Journey to the Midway."

Professional people should have a sense of responsibility. Is a doctor trying to ask, "What's my power?" rather than "How can I save this life?" I can't imagine how the public gets these notions that treat education as a power struggle.

Chall: But they do.

Tyler: Well, they do. Of course, I understand with uneducated people. I told you about the time they had this school board in East Chicago, didn't I?

Chall: Yes.

Now, the *Phi Delta Kappan,* as you know, in January 1981, had an article based on a poll of professors of curriculum who rated the influence of significant writings issued since 1906. You were there on the top, practically tied with John Dewey. Among others at the top were students of yours, Ben Bloom, and Mr. Havighurst; the Eight-Year Study itself. Hilda Taba was among the nominees. How did you feel when you read this article?

Tyler: Well, I'm glad that they found what I've written useful. I've always been impressed by the number of different languages in which it's been translated. That is another implication it must be useful. But, as I say, I'm afraid it's just because almost nobody else writes about how you try to build a curriculum.

MAJOR INFLUENCES IN RALPH TYLER'S LIFE AND CAREER

Chall: If you were asked to list those people or literature which had a major influence in your life, whom or what would you list?

Tyler: In looking down at your list I certainly would put my father and my mother as very important in the notion of responsibility. The fact that they gave up what they thought was income that might make them worship material things rather than helping others has always been a great influence in my life. I must tell you that when I accept a different position I've never asked what my salary's going to be until after I got there and discovered what it was, because to me the important thing is not salary but doing things that are important to be done.

This I got certainly from the influence of my father and mother, who never worried about income. About every year in three the farmers would have a drought; they didn't have irrigation in Nebraska. They could not contribute to our church in those years. We had to go out and shoot rabbits and other things for our meat because we didn't have enough money to buy meat, but nobody ever complained about it. That was the nature of life. You did the things that you thought were important. That was what was important to do. I think that influence of my father and mother has been very, very important to me.

Chall: Yes. Were there differences in the influences of your father and your mother? Did they each influence you differently?

Tyler: No, they did things together. They always would. The decision to give up medicine was done jointly, the two of them praying about it. They came from a very different background. Dad was born two years after the end of the Civil War in Illinois. Then the next year the family moved to Nebraska to homestead, to get a farm of their own. He was raised on a farm. Mother's father, who had been active in the Civil War, became a lawyer and was made judge of the city of Washington by President Grant. So she was raised in a different kind of environment, graduate of some of the best of the New England finishing schools, Abbott Academy of Andover.

But they were both deeply religious and both jointly led the family. I never heard of them doing anything except by planning it together.

Chall: Has religion remained a potent force in your own life?

Tyler: Yes. If by the sense of religion you mean the view that the purpose of life is to help improve the nature of humankind and make them more and more civilized, that every individual is worth preserving as a person himself. Things of that sort which are part of the deep religious beliefs held by most of the modern religions—Judaism, Christianity, the best of some of the other religions. The religious question is how to explain the world and what is the purpose of living?

Chall: But in your own life, going to church regularly is not a purpose in your religion?

Tyler: Going to church regularly I did until my wife died and I moved back to Chicago. Then I came back here, where I had no access to transportation. I'm still a member of the First Congregational Church at Palo Alto, and I pay contributions to them, but I haven't been there for a long time.

Chall: All right. Now, in your career, were there others who had influence on you?

Tyler: The next in terms of chronology was Joseph Taylor, a professor at Doane College. He would meet us students, boys and girls, young men and young women, in the college post office and say, "You know, I've got a new book." I remember, for example, "I've got a new book by MacDougall which gives quite a different view of abnormal psychology and why people get pathological. When I finish reading it, you can pass it around and then come out to my house and let's talk about it." So that we were always—about once a month—we'd be out there discussing things with him and his ideas. He was not only a fine example for us but also for his children. One of his sons became the head of the Eastman School of Music. Another one is a professor at Yale, a Congregational college in New Haven. He was a great influence in college.

Then, when I came back after my first year of teaching at Pierre, during the summer to get some work in education, the person who was head of the department of secondary education at the University of Nebraska, and also responsible in methods in the teaching of science, was Herbert Brownell, Sr. He had lived next door to us when we lived in Peru when he was at the Peru State Normal. He was a man who had graduated from the Oswego State Normal, which was headed by Sheldon back in the nineties. Sheldon had gone to Germany and studied with Herbart. The Herbartian notion of teaching was to build on the background of the student.

Professor Brownell emphasized the need for students to learn inductively, observe what goes on and then try to explain it. Never be deductive, never start with a principle and have them deduce the answers, unless there's no way they can do it inductively. But normally you start with the observations and experience as a basis, begin to try to explain it. That was a very great influence. And he influenced me further when in 1926 his son decided to go on to obtain a Ph.D. Sam later became U.S. Commissioner of Education and superintendent of the Detroit schools. He was my age and we started kindergarten together. In 1926 he was a superintendent of schools in a small town about forty miles east of Lincoln. Sam decided he wanted to go ahead and get a doctorate; we both had masters. His father said to me, "I think of you as one of my boys. I think you should get a doctorate, too, and I'll loan you the money to go ahead and get a doctorate degree, but I advise you to go to Chicago to work with Charles Judd, who is a real scientist. Don't go to Yale, although that's the best place for Sam. He's a born administrator, and Frank Spaulding, who had been superintendent at Cleveland, is a professor of administration at Yale and he'll get good training there, but I think you should go to Chicago." So Brownell had a good deal of influence on my life.

Then when I got to Chicago I worked with Charles Judd, who taught me, again, about this labeling, namely that there's no substitute for going to *observe* social phenomena. He was a Ph.D. under Wilhelm Wundt in

Leipzig. The substance of education is going to come from the observation and work with persons learning, not from books. You can write books about what you learn but the substance comes from the observation and experiment with people learning.

Judd had every one of us in every course go out and do a study, working with kids to discover how they learned and the ways they learned. So his great influence was that view that one learned about education from being in the classroom and being on the playground with kids and not from just reading books about it. He had a low opinion of students who tried to just stay in the library and never went out to learn something directly.

I was a graduate student at Chicago for only twelve months. I got there September first and the session didn't start until the end of September. In that month I passed both the foreign language examinations, the French and German, and took the qualifying examination to be admitted to candidacy. I was ready to go ahead to work on my dissertation by the time school started.

Judd explained to me. He said, "Tyler, we at Chicago don't count units and things, we count what you know and what you can do. You go ahead. Take those exams if you want to." So I did.

Then at Chicago, of course, I needed some extra money since I had a wife and two children to support. W. W. Charters was conducting the Commonwealth Teacher Training Study. They had collected about two million cards from teachers all over the country on their activities to get a notion of what teachers really did and what they should be prepared to do. They needed some way to classify and to treat those cards so I became a statistical assistant and my dissertation was: "Statistical Methods for Utilizing Personal Judgments to Evaluate Activities for Teacher-Training Curricula." We reduced these two million cards to what were called in the book "a thousand and one activities of teachers."

So that's where I first got to know Charters; I was his assistant on that project.

Chall: What was his influence? I mean, aside from your having worked with him or for him, what was his influence on your future?

Tyler: Well, after I received my Ph.D., I went to the University of North Carolina as an associate professor. While I was there at the end of the second year, Charters had moved to the Ohio State University to head its Bureau of Educational Research. He asked me to join him there and to head a division of the bureau. So I worked under him for nine years and learned many things from him. For example, every other Monday evening we met at his home, all the heads of divisions in the Bureau of Educational Research reporting on what we had done, what problems we had found, how we proposed to attack them, and then there was a discussion of the reports. That taught me a great deal. I followed this with the Eight-Year Study from 1934–42. Always the staff would return from our visits to the cooperating schools with, What had we done? What problems had we found? What ways were there to deal with those problems? These were matters discussed by the group as a whole.

Many other things I learned from Charters. He was a Scotsman who was raised in Canada, graduated from McMaster University, then came to the University of Chicago. The school of education was then headed by John Dewey and he was number four in the list of those earning the Ph.D. in Education. The first Ph.D. in education at the University of Chicago was Ella Flag Young, the superintendent of schools of Chicago. In those days, many superintendents were women. She was number one; he was number four, the fourth of Dewey's students.

Then, of course, when I moved to Chicago in 1938 to join the faculty, I was influenced by Robert Hutchins and his sense of mission. He kept asking: What is a university for? I couldn't go in with any suggestion about money or anything without knowing what my proposal had to do with the mission of the university? How will it strengthen it? Is this person the kind of person who understands and can help pursue this, and so forth? Hutchins was another one who greatly influenced me.

So I think the answers to your question would be those persons I've named. George Counts was helpful as a professor in one course in which I did the studies of the immigrants, in this case the Polish coming to Chicago and their education. James Conant was influential in some ways, but nothing compared with those others that I worked with for a long length of time.

Chall: What about John Dewey? I knew you had worked with him—

Tyler: Oh, yes. I should have—I marked him here, too. I met with him several times to discuss the Eight-Year Study, and his writings have been profoundly influential in my thinking about education.

Chall: How was the meeting? Did you enjoy meeting him?

Tyler: He was a very thoughtful person. As you know, his wife ran his life because he couldn't make practical decisions very easily, but he would say, "Well, Tyler, that sounds—Let me think about that a moment. Yes, yes, I think so. Have you ever thought of this?" This is the way he would talk.

For students who knew what they were after he was a great teacher, but most of the students at Columbia thought him dull and uninteresting and didn't attend his classes because they were expecting somebody to tell them rather than somebody to start reflecting, so that they could begin reflecting too, as I did.

Chall: That's a method that you use when you're working with others, too, is to reflect, to bring out their own ideas rather than telling them.

Tyler: Oh, yes.

Chall: Is that a Dewey—?

Tyler: Yes, I followed that practice, being influenced not only by Dewey but by several others of my teachers, but I got most of it from Dewey. The purpose of education is to help them become inquirers and not to tell them what I have learned.

Chall: And that was Dewey's method, the inquiry? The Socratic method, is that how you would define it?

Tyler: Well, much of the discussion of Socrates was of the same sort. You remember, in the *Meno,* for example, he says, "Can virtue be taught?" Then he has people commenting on this. Then he brings in a young slave boy to show them that somehow, although the slave boy hasn't had the benefits of their education, he is more virtuous than they are in some ways [laughs]. That dialogue I find useful in my teaching. "How much of virtue is learned in early upbringing of children, how much of it is a conscious effort to understand?" Of course, that became then the problems of Plato when he talks about the philosopher kings.

Chall: So Dewey had considerable influence?

Tyler: I still read Dewey very often. He left in the dean's office the logs he made of school experiences. When I was at Chicago, responsible for the laboratory schools, I liked to go over the logs and see some of the things he commented about that he'd learned from children in that connection.

Chall: Have there been any other influences? I listed some but I didn't list them all, and you may have others.

Tyler: No, I mentioned Brownell and Taylor, you remember.

Chall: Yes.

Tyler: Since Hutchins passed away, I do not know of anyone who has profoundly influenced me in the way that these older ones imply. Of course, in actual fact, one is influenced in the conversations that go on with other people. The give and take of a good interaction is one where you learn from them as I learn from children when I talk to them about things. They suddenly raise questions that I haven't thought about before. In that sense, there's no way of limiting the number of persons who may influence you. But in the way we're talking about it, a kind of person that you get ideas from and seek to emulate, I think those are the ones that have been important to me.

Chall: And now there are people whom you are probably influencing in the same way that these people influenced you.

Tyler: Perhaps so.

Chall: It probably has a relationship to one's age, too, an age when one can be influenced.

Tyler: Yes. It's hard to feel that a younger person is influencing you in that way. Although, in fact, the interaction with them may cause you to gain more than you realize.

Chall: Have any of your students influenced you?

Tyler: Well, the ones that I've had a chance to be in contact with. During the Eight-Year Study, of course, many of them were there and we were influencing each other back and forth. The ones that occur most readily are Hilda Taba, Benjamin Bloom, Lee Cronbach, John Goodlad, Christine McGuire, Louis Raths, and Fred Frutchey.

Chall: Have there been negative influences on your life as well as positive?

Tyler: What is a negative—?

Chall: I don't know what I mean by that.

Tyler: I was going to say, I don't know what you mean, either. What do you mean by a negative influence?

Chall: Well, I guess I mean influences—

Tyler: That lead you in a bad, and what would be unfortunate, directions, limiting your operations? Getting you into a blind alley, getting you into bad habits and so on?

Chall: Something of this kind, or maybe influences that did not move you ahead. I mean, you'd be the kind of person who would say, "That's no good, and I'm not going to accept it." These people that we've talked about were very positive influences. Could there have been influences which came along that you might have accepted for a short while and then dropped?

Tyler: I don't recall any. I think that the early training tends to shut out what seem to you to be a waste of time or not valuable or even evil in some respect. But tell me what would be a case of a negative influence in your life and maybe I can find a similar one.

Chall: Well, I don't know. The idea came to me as I was thinking of positive influences.

Tyler: One can always think of negative, but there are some things you can't be negative about. Like, in the real world you can't have less than no water [laughs].

Chall: Well, I think we'll skip that because neither one of us knows what I mean [laughter].

Tyler: Well, I think of the way in which you can define a negative in mathematics as a potential if there were that, for example, in dimensional mathematics. If you could have that many dimensions then you could think of a matrix that would be all this way. But it's not characteristic of the real world [laughs].

Chall: What do you think to have been your greatest satisfactions in your long, good life?

Tyler: Probably just living a long time [laughs].

Chall: Well, that's one. That's a major one, of course, and in good health [laughs]. Any others as you look back, some of the major ones?

Tyler: I find every day satisfying. I'm sure that there are key points—that is, that one has peak satisfactions with some special things but I can't recall one recently. But I'm sure there must be. I'm sure, for example, that when a study comes out and it turns out you've learned something that you didn't know before that that's a peak satisfaction for a researcher or for me. But, offhand, I can't think of what those unusual satisfactions are. But tell me some in your life; have you thought of some in that way?

Chall: I haven't thought about them but I mean I'm not reflecting on my life quite so much. I guess then that all stages of your life in your career have generally been satisfying to you—each step that you moved into has been satisfying?

Tyler: I find myself, ever since a small child when I was carrying newspapers when it would be freezing and my nose and eyes would be running and so on, to say, "Well, this has to be done. The world is like this. You can't change it so let's go ahead and do something with it." I find myself not bemoaning if an airplane doesn't fly. Well, that's that. There's something else I can do with my time while waiting for another plane. That avoids a lot of the senses of dissatisfaction. So long as you can think about things important. If the thing I'm doing is stopped for some reason, I start to think about a paper I want to write or something else and keep my mind occupied so it isn't just wasting time.

Chall: Have there been disappointments along the way?

Tyler: No, I've been able to think about the things I want to, write about the things I want to, and asked to do things that I didn't anticipate, so that there's usually more opportunity than I wanted [laughs]. Like this business of writing another paper at the moment.

Chall: Yes. Do you enjoy writing? You write clearly. I've enjoyed reading what I've read but I wondered how you like it.

Tyler: Well, like people often do about jobs. I know it's going to be hard so I try to put it off awhile, then when I no longer can put it off any further, I get down to work. When I once get into it, and get the first transition, "This will be the way, this will be the leading statement," then it begins to move easier. But thinking about that, how to get into this, to move naturally from it, is something that I think about a good deal before I start to write.

Chall: I've noticed in your writing that you are apt to provide a certain amount of background and research. To what extent have you had to review the works of others in order to write? Are you going back over people's writings? Are you reviewing them?

Tyler: Fortunately I've got a very good memory and I read a great deal and have occasion to read when coming in on a bus every morning. I get a good hour of reading then, as well as here in the office. But the answer is when I need more precise things, I have to go and look them up.

Chall: Are you still reading a great deal in the literature of education?

Tyler: Yes.

Chall: There's quite a bit.

Tyler: That's right. Sometimes I read more. For example, right now—the Kappa Delta Phi is giving a prize to a Ph.D. dissertation that has the most merit. I had to read the abstracts of twenty. Then we agreed on four that looked good enough to read, so now I'm reading the four dissertations. So I keep reading all the time, including people's writings and dissertations.

Chall: You have told me that you don't see well, but you don't have any trouble reading, do you?

Tyler: I don't see at a distance. No, I can see this nicely [gestures at the paper].

Chall: Oh, I see. So you can read print without any difficulty.

Tyler: Well, I may get tired after a while, but I can read it.

Chall: That's very good.

You mentioned to me just a little while ago something out of *Ms.* magazine. I wondered to what extent your reading goes beyond the field of education?

Tyler: When I'm in a position where the only reading material around is something else—I don't subscribe to—

Chall: [laughs]—not to *Ms.* But you read the daily press, I assume, or some—?

Tyler: The most dependable daily press is the *Wall Street Journal*. Dolores takes the *Chronicle*.

Chall: Get a balance there. At the moment, I can't think of any other questions to ask you. Is there anything that you'd like to say and put on to the record?

Tyler: Well, I'm going to miss you when you're not here. You're a nice companion. I've learned a great deal from you.

Chall: Oh, I think I've learned more from you. It's been a pleasure to work with you.

EDUCATION AS A PROFESSION

Chall: There were some questions that I guess you and Mr. Tjerandsen thought were left out that we might focus on in this final interview. That's what we're going to do today. I have a couple of questions that I think we can manage in this hour.

First. Apparently you have been concerned with education as a profession. What do you mean by education as a profession, or professionals in education?

Tyler: Professions historically were separated from commercial activities or farming and so on, as being guided by an effort to serve humanity; guided by an ethical principle rather than by the desire to make money; and trying to understand underlying principles rather than just rule of thumb procedure. If you look at the development of professions in those ways, beginning with the priesthood or the ministry, you'll find that there was that continuing effort. Now, it seems to me, by calling anybody a professional who does it [his work] for money, like the professional football player, we've lost the sense of what a profession is.

I have an article prepared for the Association of Social Workers on social work as a profession, in which I try to emphasize the nature of being guided by an unselfish desire to improve society in some way or other by having ethical principles that guide what is proper to do by attempting to derive principles of procedure rather than simply patterns that could be used as models afterwards.

Chall: How do you look at this in terms of education?

Tyler: Well, in education you'd be guided not by the notion which it seems too many people are suggesting—that you'd get better teachers by paying them higher salaries—but by the concept that the professional teacher has the desire to help children learn, to contribute to society in that way. That desire to do those things should be his or her primary incentive. Then the teachers would try to understand teaching not as a simple rule of thumb like carpentry, but rather to try to understand principles that would enable them to use their own special talents without the restrictions imposed upon them if they simply tried to follow a pattern designed by somebody else.

Chall: Do you think the teachers and others in the field of education have lost that—?

Tyler: I don't know that all of them ever had it. I'm sure there were some, but as you get a larger and larger group it's very necessary to help them understand and be guided by the notion that they're in a profession rather than just a job.

Chall: So you think that this isn't even taught in the schools of education?

Tyler: Again, you have a number of institutions that established teacher education just because they thought of it as the same sort of occupation as establishing a business management program or engineering or something. That's a mistake. How to get more understanding of a profession is one of the roles, I think, that people who really care about education ought to make, rather than talking too much about higher or greater prestige or something like that to attract teachers.

Chall: Is what you are advocating being done anywhere? Is it being written in any of the journals, is it coming out of the school system?

Tyler: It's being done in places that have people with understanding and themselves are professionals. So, you'll find them scattered around. You'll find some of them in the state institutions, but they're more likely to be found in the private ones since most of the private institutions have more of a sense of dedication; they're not supported by the state; they have to go out and make something for themselves.

Doane College, for example, where I graduated, attracts a great many young people because it talks about the tremendous service rendered by education. It doesn't talk about the jobs open. And it sees to it that graduates are followed. Doane has a contract with the employers that they will follow graduates for several years to help—if they need additional instruction—to help them gain that.

Chall: Is that still being practiced at Doane?

Tyler: Oh, yes. And there are certain other places. When George Antonelli was dean at the predominantly black institution at the University of Arkansas at Pine Bluff, he developed that program there in which they followed their students through. They have a tremendous dedication to helping those students become good teachers.

When I get about and talk to the teachers I try to help them realize that this is the most important occupation to help our civilization to become civilized. Because there's no other institution that tries to help individuals become understanding and helpful and so on. Teachers see much greater meaning to their lives when they see teaching as a profession rather than just another job.

Chall: Does the average parent or person on the street understand teaching as a profession?

Tyler: The average parent I don't think understands. But why are you so concerned with the average parent? The object is to help *more* parents understand, not to talk about the average. This concern about the average I think sets a low goal for people.

Chall: How do you think we could go about helping parents understand?

Tyler: Who are "you"? You have to say who you are talking about. If it's another parent, I can suggest ways of organizing parents' groups; if it's a teacher, then you have to get them interested; if it's a public-spirited citizen who is not himself a parent, then there's another way. There's not a single formula; it depends on your position, what you are able to do.

Chall: Who are the leaders that you can think of, in terms of providing understanding about teaching as a profession? You're one of them; who else is out there?

Tyler: Certainly at the national level you have people like Ernie Boyer, the president of the Carnegie Foundation for the Advancement of Teaching. Thinking of other people who have this great respect for teaching, I think of people at my age level who tend to be more and more retiring. Fanny Shaftel, who used to be at Stanford in elementary education, was one who inspired her students that way. Charles Judd, who was my mentor for my Ph.D., had this view of teaching. He was, of course, a missionary's son, born in India, so he had the conception of the role of missions in this connection. Frank Freeman, another missionary's son, who was dean at Berkeley, had that sense of mission of teaching.

Chall: Do you know any of the younger people?

Tyler: I don't know the younger people well enough to answer that question, but I'm sure there are some. For example, Robert Sinclair, with whom I work in University of Massachusetts, has that sense.

THE RIGIDITY OF THE BUREAUCRACY IN EDUCATION

Chall: I understand that you are concerned with overcoming the rigidity of the bureaucracy in the field of education in the schools. What forms the bureaucracy? Who are the bureaucrats?

Tyler: The problem of all bureaucracies is that they become an institution which protects itself, so that you rarely get members of a bureaucracy admitting errors or talking about anything that needs improvement; they're already there. It's the problem that is due to our being, as human beings, gregarious. We want to be with others, our group needs to be protected. It's common in all groups. There's likely to become a sense of protection that guides their energies rather than the sense of improvement.

Chall: How do you try to overcome this rigidity in the bureaucracy? What can be done about it?

Tyler: They should try to set goals for themselves that move ahead, and then ask themselves as they move along what is interfering with the goal. They need to set an outside goal; otherwise the goal is to protect our institution. You'll find the alumni talking about "dear old Siwash." They're much more concerned about keeping the famous institution than the question of whether it could be improved and what could they do about it. But if you set a general agenda each year of trying to identify problems that need to be solved, improvements that could be made, and set goals for that, then you have something else to look forward to rather than being proud of maintaining old Siwash just as she was.

Chall: The most effective work in teaching, I would guess, would be at the school level. Does the bureaucracy hamper the work at the school building level?

Tyler: It can, if they think of themselves as *the* ways in which kids get educated, that they've got to go through *our* system, rather than understanding that they have to share with parents, and that they have to discuss with parents the problems of individual children and what responsibilities each can take in connection with their education.

Chall: Can the teachers who might be interested in trying out new ways and setting goals be stopped at some point by their principals?

Tyler: One of the problems in a bureaucracy is the hierarchy, in which somebody is thought to control the whole group. The principal's role is to open communication and to chair whatever is needed to get discussion going, and so on, but not to operate the group.

Chall: But do they? Is part of the rigidity right there?

Tyler: Often it is. That's why when I work with principals—In fact, I've got a paper which was developed for the New England area on the role of the principal in promoting student learning, which has been adopted by the Western Massachusetts Association of School Principals.

Chall: Principals have beyond them not only a number of administrators, but at the top is the superintendent and the board. Are they rigid as well?

Tyler: Well, they can be. The tendency toward bureaucracy is part of the tendency toward routine. You try to move your experience so you get to the point where you can handle it without thinking. That's the great disaster. When you handle things without thinking, then you keep everything the way it is. My effort is to continually stimulate you and to look for problems and not ever to get to the point where you feel you've got the problem solved and you don't have to consider it any longer.

We found, for example, in a study made in Connecticut in the 1950s that physicians got to the point in about seven years. They got to be worse physicians after seven years because they got into a rut. The value of having clinics like the Palo Alto Clinic is that it stimulates them; they have to discuss with each other and they can't begin to say, "Now I know everything," because somebody will say, "Have you learned about this new thing?" Suddenly you discover that you've got to keep learning.

Chall: The medical profession requires doctors in their fields to upgrade their knowledge—

Tyler: Where? Where is it required?

Chall: I don't know for certain that the law requires it—perhaps it's the medical profession itself—but many doctors do take classes periodically to upgrade their skills.

Tyler: There are requirements just like there are with teachers. But it is by no means common. You go out into the rural areas and you find physicians who have never had a new idea for a long time. And some of the big city physicians who get a great deal of money are satisfied with the money. Usually they're working with patients who need their hands held and aren't really in trouble, but they've got money so they want to feel they're in a bad way in health. No, the temptations to become relaxed and not to study any further are great in all professions.

Chall: You've been working mostly with teachers—

Tyler: Teachers, principals, superintendents.

Chall: Are you working with superintendents in any of your projects now?

Tyler: They must think so; they honored me for distinguished contributions to the Association for School Administrators, and so did the State Superintendents of Public Instruction.

Chall: Do you find other people doing what you are doing, trying to open up the process?

Tyler: There are people who are really trying to improve education—like Ernie Boyer at the foundation level; like John Goodlad at the university level, through the partnerships and other things he's trying to develop to get this going on. The leadership of education right now is in that direction of trying to improve. Sometimes they miss because they conceive it at a national level, without realizing that you have to work at the lower levels.

TEACHER STANDARDS AND CERTIFICATION

Tyler: For example, the new board for certifying teachers at the national level is, I think, going to have very little influence because teaching is not a national market. Most teachers, 86 percent of them, teach within two hundred miles of where they were raised and where they were educated. So the market for teachers and what is expected of them in western Massachusetts is not the same as in Montana; nor in Denver is it the same as in Los Angeles. The effort to try to set uniform standards nationally is likely to fail because it doesn't meet the needs of a large number of teachers who have to consider what would be expected in their communities.

But people do love to jump to a state or national scale. I suggest to them that, really, education begins with human beings individually; it's the individual who learns, not the group. You may learn in a group, and a group is a very helpful way of stimulating, but the individual has to learn. This desire to be national, you have a whole cohort. They're not educated; the big cohorts are obedient soldiers [laughs] who don't know what they're doing necessarily, but they go along with the mob.

Chall: Where are the national teacher tests being worked out—in the departments of education?

Tyler: They're sponsored, I think, by the Carnegie Foundation for the Advancement of Teaching. The director of it is Jim Kelley, who is now the head of the art center in Detroit and who used to be at one time the head of the conference center noted for the excellence of the intellectual conferences carried on in a community just outside of Minneapolis.

Chall: Do you think he's going along with the general big idea?

Tyler: People love to feel they've got a national program. In fact, a lot of them want to be international, as though in some way it added a great strength, rather than being a question of what they are doing.

Chall: There have been some state teaching tests set up. I think there was one in Texas, and there have been some others at the state level.

Tyler: Remember, that when you certify, it's got to be a low enough standard so that most people can pass it or you wouldn't have enough teachers to operate. So that represents no standard; that represents just trying to keep out those who might be thought likely to cause damage rather than help. That's the problem with all of these minimum competency devices, that they don't understand that the stimulation is to have a higher standard.

There's a beautiful article in the last issue of the *Educational Researcher*, by a person studying the effect of the minimum standard testing of teachers in Texas, showing that it reduced the morale because it was so simple. It was no standard to set high goals; it just represented the notion that in some way teachers are pretty bad—they ought to be able to spell and do things. It was not a way to inspire teachers to be good teachers. The result was that it got a lot of people out of teaching. It lost the morale and it got people to believe that teaching was really at a very low level. The whole thing was disastrous. That was sponsored by the governor of Texas, you know.

Wherever we've done that—in Florida they did that with kids—minimum competency—and that lowered their achievement a good deal. Because they thought, well, if that's all you have to do—if that's the standard everybody was looking at—when they reached it they rested on their oars and didn't try to learn more. This idea that you set low standards rather than high standards is unwise. You want to set high enough standards so that they really require a great effort, and not so high that they think they are impossible.

Chall: That must take a bit of work, to figure out where that lies.

Tyler: You have to try it. Don't be afraid to try something. If it's too high, lower it; if it's too low, raise it. No decision is irrevocable. We've had cycles going around and around ever since I've been alive.

Chall: You know them all by now.

Tyler: I've seen most of them happening [laughs]. But some things keep moving toward the hopes of our forefathers, that we would have a literate society. We are getting more and more people who are literate. Judging literacy by the standards of the past, we've got 82 percent of our seventeen-year-olds who are literate. But, of course, at the same time the complex society demands a higher level of literacy, much more than just reading and understanding what you are reading. Being able to analyze it, evaluate it, and so on, is required, and increasingly we have to set more and more standards for us to reach.

RALPH TYLER'S OPTIMISM ABOUT EDUCATION

Chall: Do you feel optimistic about education in this country today?

Tyler: Why would one be pessimistic? We're moving ahead with it. Look at the tremendous problems we've had with all this immigration. We've reached it bit by bit; they're learning. Of course I'm optimistic. We accomplish more, especially at the lower end. Our lowest 25 percent is at the 50 percent level of other countries. We focus on everybody.

Great Britain, for example, has two classes, as you know. The working class doesn't get much education. They take tests at eleven years of age and then they don't get into higher education; only 18 percent get into secondary education. So, we have taken the democratic ideal; we haven't achieved it but we've been working on it and are making great progress toward it. Wouldn't you be happy about it? Look at the society we have compared to what you find when you go somewhere else.

Chall: Yet there are people, as there have been right along during the last decade or so, who have been decrying the state of education and literacy in this country. They are writing books that are on the best-seller lists.

Tyler: Sure. The way you get attention is to show how terrible things are. People don't want to read about good things; they want to read about the things they've got to avoid. Every mass media expert would tell you that.

Chall: So you don't really take to heart these latest books that have been coming out by Allan Bloom [*Closing of the American Mind*] and another one by [E. D.] Hirsch [*Cultural Literacy*].

Tyler: If it resulted in our saying let's find the reason why kids don't understand some of these things and pointed out that it's because you don't understand things and you don't remember things that have little meaning, that might have some merit. The point is that we have been teaching children the way *they* have advocated, as items rather than seeing the nation as a whole trying to move toward more and more democracy, or whatever view you want to take of the nation—seeing the role of different historical events. Seeing the effort, for example, to get rid of slavery, the movement that took place; or the efforts to get greater literacy, the movement that took place; the effort to get away from an established religion. If you could see things moving that way, then kids would understand it. But if you're going to teach them the way Hirsch and others talk, as though they were separate and isolated items, they'll get nowhere. So, most of this stuff represents people who haven't really thought about education.

Chall: Have you ever written any articles to answer the charges?

Tyler: Why would I? You don't operate at that level. People who are in education at the local level will not be influenced by the books. They'll sell books, but they won't result in anything. Have you ever heard of anything changing by the result of those books? You get people excited about things, and then they buy the books, and then they don't do anything about it.

THE ROLES OF THE STATE AND FEDERAL GOVERNMENT IN EDUCATION

Chall: Sometimes Congress gets excited about some of these things.

Tyler: What can Congress do? Tell me one thing that Congress has done that has influenced education seriously, except to establish programs like the Smith-Hughes Program, which provided a notion of an idea and support for it.

Chall: Has there been any recent move on the part of Congress to assist education that you are aware of?

Tyler: Well, no. Have you heard of any? [Laughs] You *don't get* education affected much by the federal government. You talk about it, but what goes on in your local schools hasn't been affected by it.

Chall: What does affect what goes on in the local schools, just the local school board?

Tyler: And the ideas they get and the teachers and parents. If they get ideas and translate them into what needs to be done. But the action has to take place there.

Chall: What about the role of state government?

Tyler: They can provide funds.

Chall: In the state of California they provide textbooks.

Tyler: Good teachers use textbooks as aids; they aren't guided by them. When I was teaching science in South Dakota we had terrible textbooks. I'd have the kids find out what errors there were, show how the textbooks were wrong and try to demonstrate what the real facts were. So you could use a textbook as a stimulation to show that textbooks are not very helpful if they're not good ones.

Chall: The State of California has been setting up guidelines—curriculum, standards for graduation, and things of this kind. Is that a proper role?

Tyler: You can set up general standards, that is, what it is you want to try to attain. But beyond that the actual curriculum has to be developed by the teachers who have to carry it through. So, much of the work that goes on at the state level doesn't affect what goes on in the classroom.

Chall: Should it?

Tyler: I don't believe that the state has the judgment and the understanding of the local situation. They can set some general guidelines. They can say we ought to reach the Hispanic population effectively and emphasize that, and if necessary provide, as we did with disadvantaged children, special funds to help. These are things they can do. But the responsibility of how you are going to do it and what curriculum is needed has to be worked out at the local level. The state could provide, which it doesn't, people who go out to work with the individual schools, helping them in developing curriculum. You can't do it by inspection because it still has to be done by the people whose information and beliefs have to be considered.

Chall: Do you feel that our emphasis on state and federal government in terms of education is misplaced?

Tyler: It doesn't do any good. You can talk about it.

In a totalitarian state, what the children are to learn—they're not to be independent thinkers—is decided from above and transferred down there. They memorize it and repeat it. You visit a Chinese classroom and they go again and again, repeating what was said. In contrast to that, a democracy is trying to help individual young people become self-directive, to learn to make their own decisions, to be intelligent citizens. Now, that's not a thing that can be pushed by the state. You've got to help teachers with it.

If you had a good state leadership—but in our political climate it's likely not to happen. You could have the state go out and help local schools in a helping situation, in a stimulating teaching situation. But there are no effective results from any legislation. The American Bar Association two years ago published a study they'd made of the statutes in states affecting curriculum. None of them ever were followed, because teachers can't teach what they don't understand. They're not going to teach something they don't believe in, and you can't force a professional. You can force a ditch digger because you can see what he is doing; but you can't force a teacher.

Notes

CHAPTER 1: INTRODUCTION

1. "Tyler for Judd," *Time,* February 28, 1938, 44.
2. Ralph W. Tyler [hereafter RWT] to Finder, September 11, 1990.
3. RWT to Morris Finder, December 12, 1988.

CHAPTER 2: THE MAKING OF AN EDUCATOR

1. RWT to Finder, January 16, 1987.
2. RWT to Finder, December 14, 1990.
3. RWT to Finder, December 19, 1986.
4. On August 1, 1947, Tyler married a former student, Louise M. Lingenfelder, now Louise M. Tyler, professor emeritus, University of California at Los Angeles, School of Education. They were divorced about the time Tyler left the University of Chicago.
5. RWT to Finder, May 31, 1992.
6. James Philip Echols, "The Rise of the Evaluation Movement, 1920–1942" (Ph.D. dissertation, Stanford University, 1973), 171.
7. "Tyler for Judd."
8. RWT to Finder, July 3, 1989.
9. RWT to Finder, December 19, 1986.
10. RWT to Finder, May 19, 1987.
11. George S. Counts, "The Subject Matter of the Curriculum and Sociology," *Journal of Educational Sociology* 1, no. 1 (September 1927): 11–17.
12. "The phrase was common during the twenties among those with an unqualified faith in science." Lawrence A. Cremin, *The Transformation of the School: Progressivism in American Education, 1876–1957* (New York: Vintage Books, 1961), 199.

13. Herbert M. Kliebard, *The Struggle for the American Curriculum 1893–1858* (New York: Routledge and Kegan Paul, 1987), 119.

14. Ibid.

15. RWT to Finder, May 19, 1987.

16. RWT to Finder, August 28, 1989.

17. *Ohio State University Research Bulletin,* February 11, 1953. Cited in RWT to Finder, March 2, 1991.

18. RWT to Finder, December 21, 1987.

19. Echols, 179.

20. Ibid.

21. RWT to Finder, December 30, 1988.

22. RWT to Finder, September 30, 1989.

CHAPTER 3: DEMOCRATIZING HIGH SCHOOLS AND COLLEGE ADMISSIONS

1. Kliebard, 191.

2. RWT to Finder, January 16, 1988.

3. RWT to Finder, February 18, 1989.

4. RWT to Finder, June 28, 1989.

5. RWT to Finder, May 30, 1990.

6. RWT to Finder, July 8, 1989.

7. RWT to Finder, May 30, 1990.

8. The evaluation staff included such luminaries as Maurice L. Hartung, Bruno Bettelheim, Paul B. Diederich, Wifred Eberhart, Louis M. Heil, George Sheviakov, Hilda Taba, and Harold Trimble. Among the assistants were Fred P. Frutchey, Chester William Harris, Carleton C. Jones, and Christine McGuire. "When the project was over, the following became U. of Chicago examiners: Diederich, McGuire, Abraham, Heil. Maurice Hartung became the faculty member at U of C on the teaching of Math" (RWT to Finder, June 12, 1989).

CHAPTER 4: THE TYLER RATIONALE

1. John I. Goodlad to Joseph Finder, April 4, 2003. Although Tyler mentioned dictating the syllabus over a single weekend, John Goodlad recalled, "His graduate assistant, Louise, who later became his wife and who became one of our good friends, told me that Ralph dictated it over a series of weekends. Indeed, it was she who persuaded him to do this so that he could get it out. When I took Ralph's course in winter 1948, we received each week mimeographed copies of chunks of the manuscript hot off the press. The distribution of the whole spread out over a good deal of the quarter, and that would seem to confirm what Louise told me."

2. In a telephone call to the University of Chicago Press in July 1991, the author learned that 187,687 copies had been sold. Tyler has received no royalties. Royalties are submitted to an account called the College Publication Fund.

An e-mail from the University of Chicago press on May 13, 2003, stated that the Press sells between four and six thousand copies a year.

3. The author used Tyler's *Basic Principles,* which had been translated into Afghani Persian, when he taught teachers at Kabul University from 1960 to 1962.

4. Echols, 183.

5. RWT to Finder, April 10, 1992.

6. RWT to Finder, February 2, 1991.

CHAPTER 5: APPRAISING THE NATION'S SCHOOLS

1. Francis Keppel to Finder, August 26, 1988. Francis Keppel followed Sterling M. McMurrin, who had served as Kennedy's first commissioner of education from 1961 to 1962. McMurrin was later at the University of Utah.

2. Reprinted in "History of the National Assessment of Educational Progress" (n.d.), sent by Tyler to Finder, December 19, 1986.

3. Frank Stanton to Finder, December 23, 1987. Frank Stanton, president emeritus of CBS in 1987, recalled selecting Ralph Tyler to be director of the Center for the Advanced Study of the Behavioral Sciences. In 1953 Stanton was chairman of the Ford Foundation board of trustees responsible for the project. Stanton wrote: "About Ralph Tyler, I have only the highest regard. When the history of the social sciences for this period is written, Ralph's name will hold a special place of honor. If any one individual is responsible for the success of the Center it is he. When I sought him out to become Director back in 1953 it was a great day for the Center and all those who came to know him."

4. John W. Gardner to Finder, March 13, 1998: "In the early 1960s, when Frank Keppel was Commissioner of Education, and I was still at Carnegie, he came to me with the idea of a national assessment. We both agreed that Ralph Tyler would be a valuable ally. . . . We had agreed that Carnegie Corporation should do the groundwork in shaking the idea down. This included the bringing together of a group of qualified people to discuss the idea. As I remember it, Ralph was part of that group."

5. John W. Gardner to RWT, January 3, 1964. Also, RWT to Finder, updated conversation.

6. RWT to Finder, September 18, 1992. "The design of NAEP identified the objectives of public schooling that were accepted by the general public. We held meetings of representative samples of the public in four areas of the nation, discussing the desired objectives for public schooling. We did not identify the objectives particular teachers had in mind."

7. RWT to Finder, November 18, 1990.

8. RWT to Finder, August 7, 1989.

9. Francis Keppel to Finder, October 11, 1990.

10. Ralph W. Tyler, "National Assessment: A History and Sociology," *School and Society* 98, no. 2329 (December 1970): 477.

11. Ibid.

12. John I. Goodlad, "Assessment of Educational Performance," in *White House Conference on Education: A Milestone for Educational Progress,* prepared for the Subcommittee on Education of the Committee on Labor and Public Welfare, U.S. Senate, August 1965 (Washington, D.C.: U.S. Government Printing Office, 1965).

13. John Goodlad to Finder, July 10, 2000.

14. RWT to Finder, December 19, 1986. "The assessment was fought by the American Association of School Administrators for fear it would show up their schools in a bad light."

15. Ibid. "To gain acceptance of NAEP, I had to meet with many different groups of teachers, administrators, school boards, state and local parent organizations and business and industrial organizations. I wrote articles for several journals and magazines. It was hard work, but fun, and the eventual success was very rewarding."

16. Carmen J. Finley and Frances S. Berdie, *The National Assessment Approach to Exercise Development* (Ann Arbor, Mich.: National Assessment of Educational Progress, 1970), 3. "The term 'exercise' is used throughout to distinguish National Assessment materials from standardized test items."

17. RWT, undated conversation with Finder.

18. RWT to Finder, November 1, 1987.

19. RWT to Finder, June 28, 1989.

20. National Center for Educational Statistics on "The Nation's Report Card," at nces. ed. gov/nationsreportcard [accessed April 19, 2003].

CHAPTER 6: CONTRARIAN VIEWS

1. Ralph W. Tyler, "Emphasize Tasks Appropriate for the School," *Phi Delta Kappan* 40 (November 1958): 72–74.

2. RWT to Finder, March 21, 1988: "Psychometric tests, which standardized tests became after World War I, were sorting and selecting tests."

3. RWT to Finder, June 9, 1987.

4. Ibid.

5. Ibid.

6. Ibid.

7. RWT to Finder, December 13, 1987.

8. Ibid.

9. Ibid.

10. RWT to Finder, August 3, 1988.

11. RWT to Finder, May 25, 1987.

12. RWT to Finder, May 5, 1990.

13. RWT to Finder, March 16, 1991.

CHAPTER 7: THE MENTOR

1. Jeri Ridings Nowakowski, interview with Ralph Tyler, November 1981,

in *Educational Evaluation: Classic Works of Ralph W. Tyler,* ed. George F. Madaus and Daniel L. Stufflebeam (Boston: Kluwer Academic, 1989), 257.

2. Lee Cronbach, "Tyler's Contribution to Measurement and Evaluation," *Journal of Thought* 11, no. 1 (Spring 1986), 47.

3. RWT to Finder, March 21, 1989.

4. James A. Michener to Finder, December 29, 1987.

5. RWT to Finder, March 21, 1989.

6. Robert Gottlieb, "The Strange Case of Dr. B," *New York Review of Books,* February 27, 2003, 44.

7. Tyler enlarged upon this in an exchange with the author in March 1990. In a letter to Tyler dated March 20, 1990, Finder pointed out that the obituary of Bruno Bettelheim in that day's *New York Times* discussed the role of Eleanor Roosevelt and Governor Herbert Lehman of New York in securing Tyler's release from the concentration camp but did not mention any part played by the Rockefeller Foundation. Finder also spoke with Bettelheim in Albany, New York, and asked about his release from the camps; Bettelheim credited an unnamed "family" who intervened with ransom money. Tyler's response to this explanation came in a letter dated March 24, 1990: "The statement is not plausible to me. Hitler hated Eleanor Roosevelt and despised Jews like Lehman. When some situation gains great publicity many people think about it and their thoughts become realities to them. I believe my recollections are likely to be more accurate because I had to do a number of things in order to get Bruno admitted to the U.S. as a resident scholar."

8. RWT, undated private conversation with Finder. Tyler's letter of May 25, 1987, discusses the ransom, but only in private conversation did he mention the amount. The author found no record of such a ransom in the Rockefeller Archives in North Tarrytown, New York. Told this, Tyler speculated that the foundation may have attempted to conceal its payment to the Hitler regime, adding that "a clever tax lawyer" could easily have devised a method to hide the ransom. In any case, however, Tyler felt that the main issue about the controversy was the moral dilemma faced by the Rockefeller Foundation's board of directors (RWT to Finder, February 28, 1991).

9. RWT to Finder, May 25, 1987.

10. RWT to Finder, April 9, 1990.

11. Ibid.

12. RWT to Finder, May 25, 1987.

13. Gottlieb, 43.

14. RWT to Finder, March 27, 1991: "I thought Bruno had an advanced degree in art; whether he did or not was not important for our purposes. Cooperating with Thomas Monroe, Curator of the Cleveland Museum of Art, he developed an excellent procedure for evaluating the student's development of appreciation of art objects."

15. RWT to Finder, March 2, 1991.

16. RWT to Finder, May 5, 1990. Tyler wrote that he participated on May 3, 1990, as second speaker, after Eric Bettelheim, Bruno's son, at a memorial service at the Rockefeller Chapel of the University of Chicago.

17. RWT to Finder, June 28, 1991.

18. RWT to Finder, September 22, 1988.

19. T. W. Schultz to Finder, November 18, 1987.

20. Schultz to President Charles E. Friley, September 15, 1943. A copy of the letter was sent to Finder on November 18, 1987.

21. Raymond R. Beneke, "T. W. Schultz and Pamphlet 5: The Oleo Margarine War and Academic Freedom," Iowa State University *Choices* (Second Quarter 1998).

22. RWT to Finder, June 18, 1988.

23. Allison Davis in interview published as "Profile—Allison Davis: The Man and His Research," *Education at Chicago* (Autumn 1972): 23.

24. Ibid.

25. David Riesman with Nathan Glazer and Reuel Denney, *The Lonely Crowd: A Study of the Changing American Character* (abridged by the authors) (New Haven, Conn.: Yale University Press, 1950; repr. Garden City, N.Y.: Doubleday, 1953), 145.

26. RWT to Finder, August 23, 1991.

27. Edwin R. Embree to Edgar B. Stern, February 24, 1942.

28. Allison Davis in an undated conversation with Finder.

29. Davis, "Profile," 22.

30. In conversation with Finder. Ralph Tyler had replaced L. L. Thurstone as examiner at the University of Chicago. Thurstone had returned to the psychology department. Both Thurstone and his wife, Thelma Gwinn Thurstone, were working on a theory of multiple intelligence and factor analysis. The Chicago Test of Primary Mental Abilities, based on their research, was published by SRA.

31. Allison Davis, *Social-Class Influences upon Learning* (Cambridge, Mass.: Harvard University Press, 1950), 95–96.

32. David Riesman, telephone interview with Finder, February 12, 1999.

33. Larissa Swartwout of the Yale University Press in a conversation with Finder, February 19, 1999.

34. RWT to Finder, August 12, 1989.

35. Benjamin S. Bloom, ed., *Taxonomy of Educational Objectives: The Classification of Educational Goals,* handbook 1: *Cognitive Domain* (New York: David McKay, 1956); David R. Krathwohl, Benjamin S. Bloom, and Bertram B. Masia, *Taxonomy of Educational Objectives: The Classification of Educational Goals,* handbook 2: *Affective Domain* (New York: David McKay, 1964).

36. The author is indebted to Sophie Bloom, widow of Benjamin S. Bloom, for this biographical information.

37. RWT in conversations with Finder, n.d.

38. Ernest Boyer to Finder, April 19, 1991.

39. Boyer to Finder, December 21, 1987.

40. RWT to Finder, May 10, 1989.

41. RWT to Finder, June 18, 1988.

42. RWT to Finder, May 10, 1989.

43. RWT to Finder, November 3, 1989.

44. Thelma Gwinn Thurstone, the author's colleague in Kabul in 1961 said that Lyle Spencer relied heavily on Ralph Tyler's advice.

45. RWT to Finder, November 8, 1989.

46. RWT to Finder, August 12, 1989.

47. Ibid.

48. Patricia Albjerg Graham, *Twenty-five Years of Grantmaking*, 1996 Annual Report (Chicago: Spencer Foundation, 1996), 6.

49. RWT to Finder, November 3, 1989.

50. Goodlad to Finder, March 28, 1991.

51. Ibid.

52. Nowakowski, 261.

53. RWT to Finder, December 12, 1988.

54. Nowakowski, 267.

A Chronological Bibliography of Tyler's Works: 1930–1985

Excerpts from Helen M. Kolodziey, Compiler. *Ralph W. Tyler, a Bibliography, 1929–1986.* Washington, D.C.: Ralph W. Tyler Project, National Foundation for the Improvement of Education, 1986. [Included by Lisa N. Finder]

1930

Tyler, Ralph W., and Douglas Waples. *Research Methods and Teachers' Problems: A Manual for Systematic Studies of Classroom Procedure.* New York: Macmillan, 1930. 653 pp.

1931

"The Development of Examinations at Ohio State University." In *Recent Trends in American College Education*, edited by William S. Gray, pp. 228–38. Proceedings of the Institute for Administrative Officers of Higher Institutions, vol. 3. Chicago: University of Chicago Press, 1931.

"Ohio State University." In *Practices of American Universities in Granting Higher Degrees in Education*, pp. 37–40. Studies in Education, Yearbook 19 of the National Society of College Teachers of Education. Chicago: University of Chicago Press, 1931.

Tyler, Ralph W., and Douglas Waples. *What People Want to Read About: A Study of Group Interests and a Survey of Problems in Adult Reading.* Chicago: American Library Association and University of Chicago Press, 1931. 312 pp.

1932

"Certain Administrative Procedures in Botany and Zoology." In *Service Studies in Higher Education*, edited by Ralph W. Tyler et al., pp. 109–22. Bureau of Educational Research Monographs 15. Columbus: Bureau of Educational Research, Ohio State University, 1932. Also published in *Constructing Achievement Tests* (1934).

"Construction of Examinations in Botany and Zoology." In *Service Studies in Higher Education*, edited by Ralph W. Tyler et al., pp. 43–51. Bureau of Educational Research Monographs 15. Columbus: Bureau of Educational Research, Ohio State University, 1932.

"A Survey of Present Training Courses for Research Workers." In *Proceedings of the Seventieth Annual Meeting of the National Education Association*, vol. 70, pp. 368–69. Washington, D.C.: National Education Association, 1932.

1934

Constructing Achievement Tests. Columbus: Bureau of Educational Research, Ohio State University, 1934. 102 pp. (This monograph, a collection of writings on the development of the Tyler Rationale for educational evaluation activities, appeared in the *Educational Research Bulletin* and other publications of the Ohio State University Bureau of Educational Research. The writings are identified in notes added to their main entries.)

"Cooperation of Teachers of Liberal Arts with Teachers of Education." In *Abstracts of Papers at the Cleveland M*eeting, *1934*, pp. 14–15. Studies in Education, Yearbook Number 22 of the National Society of College Teachers of Education. Chicago: University of Chicago Press, 1934.

"Discussion of a Theory of Selection of College Students." In *Transactions of the Sixty-second and Sixty-third Annual Meetings of the Ohio College Association*, pp. 21–23. Columbus, April 6–7, 1933, and April 5–6, 1934. [Ohio College Association, n.d.]

"Measuring the Effectiveness of Instruction." In *Proceedings of the Forty-seventh Annual Convention of the Association of Land-Grant Colleges and Universities*, edited by Charles A. McCue, pp. 130–33. Chicago, November 13–15, 1933. Washington, D.C.: Association of Land-Grant Colleges and Universities, 1934.

1935

"Characteristics of a Satisfactory Diagnosis." In *Educational Diagnosis*, edited by Guy M. Whipple, pp. 95–111. Thirty-fourth Yearbook of the National Society for the Study of Education. Bloomington, Ill.: Public School, 1935.

"Elements of Diagnosis." In *Educational Diagnosis*, edited by Guy M. Whipple, pp. 113–29. Thirty-fourth Yearbook of the National Society for the Study of Education. Bloomington, Ill.: Public School, 1935.

"Techniques for Evaluating Behavior." In *Educational Responsibilities of Today and Tomorrow*, pp. 348–57. Twenty-second Annual Schoolmen's Week Proceedings, April 3–6, 1935. University of Pennsylvania Bulletin 35, no. 29. Philadelphia: University of Pennsylvania, 1935.

1936

"Evaluating the Outcomes of the Social Studies Curriculum." In *The Social Studies Curriculum*, pp. 312–43. Fourteenth Yearbook, Department of Superintendence of the National Education Association. Washington, D.C.: Department of Superintendence, National Education Association, 1936.

"Identification and Definition of the Objectives to Be Measured." In *The Construction and Use of Achievement Examinations*, edited by Herbert E. Hawkes, E. F. Lindquist, and C. R. Mann, pp. 3–16. Prepared under the auspices of a Committee of the American Council on Education, Herbert E. Hawkes, Chairman. Boston: Houghton Mifflin, 1936.

"Methods Used in Improving Tests and Examinations at the Ohio State University." In *Tests and Measurements in Higher Education,* compiled and edited by William S. Gray, pp. 146–54. Proceedings of the Institute for Administrative Officers of Higher Institutions, vol. 8. Chicago: University of Chicago Press, 1936.

"Needed Research in the Field of Tests and Examinations." In *Tests and Measurements in Higher Education*, compiled and edited by William S. Gray, pp. 230–37. Proceedings of the Institute for Administrative Officers of Higher Institutions, vol. 8. Chicago: University of Chicago Press, 1936.

"The Relation Between Recall and Higher Mental Processes." In *Education as Cultivation of the Higher Mental Processes*, edited by Charles Hubbard Judd, with the cooperation of Ernst R. Breslich, J. M. McCallister, and Ralph W. Tyler, pp. 6–17. New York: Macmillan, 1936.

"To What Degree Can the Content of the Social Studies Be Selected on an Objective Basis?" In *Proceedings of the Seventy-fourth Annual Meeting of the National Education Association*, vol. 74, pp. 453–54. Washington, D.C.: National Education Association, 1936.

Tyler, Ralph W., and Fred P. Frutchey. "Examinations in the Natural Sciences." In *The Construction and Use of Achievement Examinations*, edited by Herbert E. Hawkes, E. F. Lindquist, and C. R. Mann, pp. 214–63. Prepared under the auspices of a Committee of the American Council on Education, Herbert E. Hawkes, Chairman. Boston: Houghton Mifflin, 1936.

1937

"The Evaluation of Professional Training." In *Sixteenth Yearbook, 1937*, pp. 75–82. Washington, D.C.: American Association of Teachers Colleges, a department of the National Education Association, 1937.

"The Study of Adolescent Reading by the Progressive Education Association." In *Library Trends*, edited by Louis R. Wilson, pp. 269–85. Papers presented before the Library Institute at the University of Chicago, August 3–15, 1936. Chicago: University of Chicago Press, 1937.

1938

"Evaluating 4-H Club Work." In *Proceedings: Seventeenth National 4-H Club Congress*, pp. 1–11. Chicago, November 25–December 3, 1938. Chicago: National 4-H Club Congress, n.d.

"The Specific Techniques of Investigation: Examining and Testing Acquired Knowledge, Skill, and Ability." In *The Scientific Movement in Education*, edited by Guy M. Whipple, pp. 341–55. Thirty-seventh Yearbook of the National Society for the Study of Education, part 2. Bloomington, Ill.: Public School, 1938.

1939

"Basic Assumptions Which Guide My Work in Educational Measurement." In *Research on the Foundations of American Education*, pp. 139–41. Official Report, American Educational Research Association, a Department of the National Education Association, Cleveland, Ohio, February 25–March 1, 1939. Washington, D.C.: American Educational Research Association, 1939.

"Co-operation in the Study of Institutional Problems." In *The Outlook for Higher Education*, compiled and edited by John Dale Russell, pp. 230–43. Proceedings of the Institute for Administrative Officers of Higher Institutions, vol. 11. Chicago: University of Chicago Press, 1939.

"Evaluation in Teacher Education Programs." In *Bennington Planning Conference for the Cooperative Study of Teacher Education*, pp. 194–99. Reports and Addresses, August 21–September 1, 1939. Washington, D.C.: Commission on Teacher Education, American Council on Education, 1939.

"Evaluation of Business-Education Criteria." In *Business Education in School Situations*, pp. 13–18. Proceedings of the University of Chicago Conference on Business Education, 1939. Chicago: University of Chicago Press, 1939.

"Training Administrative Officers for Democratic Leadership." In Democratic Practices in School Administration, compiled and edited by William C. Reavis, pp. –72. Proceedings of the Eighth Annual Conference for Administrative Officers of Public and Private Schools, vol. 2. Chicago: University of Chicago Press, 1939.

Tyler, Ralph W., and W. Carson Ryan. *Summer Workshops in Secondary Education: An Experiment in the In-Service Training of Teachers and Other Educational Workers*. New York: Progressive Education Association, 1939. 46 pp.

1940

"An Appraisal of Technics of Evaluation: A Critique." In *Official Report of 1940 Meeting*, pp. 72–77. American Educational Research Association, a department of the National Education Association, St. Louis, Missouri,

February 24–27, 1940. Washington, D.C.: American Educational Research Association, 1940.

"The Future of the Liberal Arts College." In *Thirty-sixth Annual Meeting of the Federation of Illinois Colleges*, pp. 20–21. Bradley Polytechnic Institute, Peoria, February 16, 1940. [Federation of Illinois Colleges, n.d.]

"Newer Techniques in Evaluating Growth." In *Reading and Pupil Development*, compiled and edited by William S. Gray, pp. 275–81. Proceedings of the Conference on Reading held at the University of Chicago, vol. 2. Supplementary Educational Monographs 51. Chicago: University of Chicago, 1940.

"The Place of Evaluation in Modern Education." In *Evaluating the Work of the School*, compiled and edited by William C. Reavis, pp. 3–11. Proceedings of the Ninth Annual Conference for Administrative Officers of Public and Private Schools, vol. 3. Chicago: University of Chicago Press, 1940.

Tyler, Ralph W., et al. School and College Regional Conference, Commission on the Relation of School and College of the Progressive Education Association. University of Pennsylvania, April 18, 1940. [Commission on the Relation of School and College, Progressive Education Association, 1940.] 14 pp.

Tyler, Ralph W., et al. *What the High Schools Ought to Teach.* The Report of a Special Committee on the Secondary School Curriculum, Ben G. Graham, Chairman. Prepared for the American Youth Commission and Other Cooperating Organizations. Washington, D.C.: American Council on Education, 1940. 36 pp.

1941

"Contribution of Tests to Research in the Field of Student Personnel Work." In *Report of the Eighteenth Annual Meeting of the American College Personnel Association*, edited by Gwendolen G. Schneidler, pp. 98–105. Conference at Atlantic City, New Jersey, February 18–22, 1941. [American College Personnel Association, 1941.] Reprinted in *Educational and Psychological* Measurement 1 (April 1941):133–42.

"Educational Adjustments Necessitated by Changing Ideological Concepts." In *Administrative Adjustments Required by Socio-Economic Change*, compiled and edited by William C. Reavis, pp. 3–13. Proceedings of the Tenth Annual Conference of Administrative Officers of Public and Private Schools, vol. 4. Chicago: University of Chicago Press, 1941.

"Evaluation of Guidance." In *Proceedings of the Sixth Annual Guidance Conference held at Purdue University*, pp. 37–44. November 29–30, 1940. Division of Educational Reference, Studies in Higher Education 40. Lafayette, Ind.: Purdue University, 1941.

"The Interpretation of Evaluation Results." In *Proceedings of the Workshop in General Education*. Vol. 4: *Educational Administration*, pp. 137–42. University of Chicago, 1940. Chicago: Cooperative Study in General Education, American Council on Education, 1941.

Introduction to and "Use of the Survey Report." In *Survey of Hinsdale Schools*, by Committee on Field Services, Department of Education, University of Chicago, pp. 1–2, 115–16. Hinsdale, Illinois, Boards of Education Districts 55 and 86. Chicago: Department of Education, University of Chicago, 1941.

"Principles Involved in Evaluating Student Personnel Services." In *Student Personnel Services in Colleges and Universities*, compiled and edited by John Dale Russell, pp. 291–300. Proceedings of the Institute for Administrative Officers of Higher Institutions, vol. 12. Chicago: University of Chicago Press, 1941.

"The Relation of the Curriculum to American Democratic Ideals." In *Education in a Democracy*, compiled and edited by Newton Edwards, pp. 80–93. Chicago: University of Chicago Press, 1941.

Review of *Cooperative Biology Test* (High School, Form P). In *The Nineteen Forty Mental Measurements Yearbook*, edited by Oscar K. Buros, p. 380. Highland Park, N.J.: Mental Measurements Yearbook, 1941.

Review of *Cooperative Contemporary Affairs Test for College Students* (Form 1939). In *The Nineteen-Forty Mental Measurements Yearbook*, edited by Oscar K. Buros, pp. 19–20. Highland Park, N.J.: Mental Measurements Yearbook, 1941.

"A Summary of Trends in the Attack on College Instructional Problems." In *New Frontiers in Collegiate Instruction*, compiled and edited by John Dale Russell, pp. 237–48. Proceedings of the Institute for Administrative Officers of Higher Institutions, vol. 13. Chicago: University of Chicago Press, 1941.

1942

"Cooperation in Teacher Education as Related to Our War Effort." In *National Institutional Teacher Placement Association: Proceedings of the Ninth Annual Autumn Conference*, pp. 15–21. Chicago, November 27–28, 1942. [National Institutional Teacher Placement Association, n.d.]

"Evaluation Must Be Continual and Flexible." In General Education in the American High School, edited by Paul B. Jacobson et al., pp. 290–308, 315. Subcommittee of the General Education Committee, Commission on Curricula of Secondary Schools and Institutions of Higher Education of the North Central Association of Colleges and Secondary Schools. Chicago: Scott, Foresman, 1942.

"Implications of Communications Research for the Public Schools." In *Print, Radio, and Film in a Democracy*, edited by Douglas Waples, pp. 149–58. Papers on the Administration of Mass Communications in the Public Interest, Sixth Annual Institute, Graduate Library School, University of Chicago, August 4–9, 1941. Chicago: University of Chicago Press, 1942.

"Purposes and Procedures of the Evaluation Staff." In *Appraising and Recording Student Progress: Evaluation, Records and Reports in the Thirty Schools*, by Eugene R. Smith, Ralph W. Tyler, and the Evaluation Staff, pp. 3–34.

Progressive Education Association Publications, Commission on the Re-
lation of School and College, Adventure in American Education, vol. 3.
New York: Harper and Brothers, 1942. (Four other volumes recording
the eight-year study published by Harper and Brothers are: Vol. 1: Wilford
M. Aikin, *The Story of the Eight-Year Study* [1942]; Vol. 2: H. H. Giles,
S. P. McCutchen, and A. N. Zechiel, *Exploring the Curriculum* [1942];
Vol. 4: Dean Chamberlin et al., *Did They Succeed in College?* [1942]; and
Vol. 5: Each of the Participating Schools, *Thirty Schools Tell Their Story*
[1943].)

"Putting Life Values into Science Education." *In The Science Teacher Yearbook
Supplement*, pp. 1–2. Washington, D.C.: American Council of Science
Teachers, department of the National Education Association, 1942.

"Relations of the Urban Community and the Modern School." In *The School
and the Urban Community*, compiled and edited by William C. Reavis,
pp. 3–13. Proceedings of the Eleventh Annual Conference of Administrative Officers of Public and Private Schools, vol. 5. Chicago: University
of Chicago Press, 1942. Reprinted in *Elementary School Journal* 43 (September 1942):14–22.

"Trends in the Preparation of Teachers." In *Annual Report and Proceedings of
the Forty-eighth Annual Convention of the National League of Nursing
Education*, pp. 185–90. Chicago, May 17–22, 1942. New York: National
League of Nursing Education, 1942.

Tyler, Ralph W., and , J. B. Edmonson. Foreword to *Community Workshops for
Teachers in the Michigan Community Health Project*, by Henry J. Otto et
al., pp. v–vii. Ann Arbor: University of Michigan Press, 1942.

1943

"Acceptance of Military Experience toward College Credit." In *Higher Education under War Conditions*, compiled and edited by John Dale Russell,
pp. 107–16. Proceedings of the Institute for Administrative Officers of
Higher Institutions, vol. 15. Chicago: University of Chicago Press, 1943.

"Appraisal of Military Training and Experience." In *Challenges to Education, War
and Post-War*, pp. 346–52. Thirtieth Annual Schoolmen's Week Proceedings, March 24–27, 1943. University of Pennsylvania Bulletin 43,
no. 32. Philadelphia: University of Pennsylvania, 1943.

"Eight-Year Study of the Progressive Education Association." In *Encyclopedia
of Modern Education*, edited by Harry N. Rivlin and Herbert Schueler,
pp. 258–59. New York: Philosophical Library, 1943; reissued, Port Washington, N.Y.: Kennikat, 1969.

Eurich, Alvin C., and Richard P. McKeon. *Education for Freedom.* University of
Chicago Round Table Radio Discussion (Pamphlet) 261. In cooperation
with the National Broadcasting Company, March 21, 1943. Chicago:
University of Chicago, 1943. 19 pp.

"Evaluation as a Function of Supervision." In *Challenges to Education, War and
Post-War*, pp. 104–16. Thirtieth Annual Schoolmen's Week Proceedings,

March 24–27, 1943. University of Pennsylvania Bulletin 43, no. 32. Philadelphia: University of Pennsylvania, 1943.

Foreword to and "Introduction to Subsequent Chapters." In *Survey Report, Waukegan Township High School District 119, Waukegan, Illinois,* by Committee on Field Services, Department of Education, University of Chicago, pp. iii–iv, 97–98. Chicago: Department of Education, University of Chicago, 1943.

"Function of the Graduate School in the Education of Teachers." In *Proceedings of the Association of Land-Grant Colleges and Universities,* edited by W. L. Slate, pp. 186–88. Fifty-sixth Annual Convention, Chicago, October 28–30, 1942. Washington, D.C.: Association of Land-Grant Colleges and Universities, 1943.

Introduction to *Survey of Elementary Schools, Highland Park, Illinois, Boards of Education Districts 107 and 108,* by Committee on Field Services, Department of Education, University of Chicago, p. iii. Chicago: Department of Education, University of Chicago, 1943.

Nerlove, S. H., and Floyd Reeves. *When Johnny Comes Marching Home.* University of Chicago Round Table Radio Discussion (Pamphlet) 285. In cooperation with the National Broadcasting Company, September 5, 1943. Chicago: University of Chicago, 1943. 16 pp.

"The Role of the Schools in the Nation's War Efforts." In *War and Post-War Responsibilities of American Schools,* compiled and edited by William C. Reavis, pp. 2–12. Proceedings of the Twelfth Annual Conference for Administrative Officers of Public and Private Schools, vol. 6. Chicago: University of Chicago Press, 1943.

"Summary of the Conference." In *The Colleges in Wartime: New Responsibilities,* edited by John Dale Russell, pp. 69–77. Proceedings of a Conference of Invited College Representatives held at the University of Chicago, December 29–30, 1942. Chicago: University of Chicago, 1943.

"Wartime Interests and Needs and Their Relation to Reading Programs." *In Adapting Reading Programs to Wartime Needs,* compiled and edited by William S. Gray, pp. 14–19. Proceedings of the Conference on Reading held at the University of Chicago, vol. 5. Supplementary Educational Monographs 57. Chicago: University of Chicago, 1943.

Tyler, Ralph W., and Virgil E. Herrick. "The School Curriculum." In *Survey of Elementary Schools, Highland Park, Illinois, Boards of Education Districts 107 and 108,* by Committee on Field Services, Department of Education, University of Chicago, pp. 44–52. Chicago: Department of Education, University of Chicago, 1943.

1944

"Admission and Articulation Based on Study of the Individual." In *New Directions for Measurement and Guidance,* pp. 1–15. American Council on Education Studies, Series 1, Reports of Committees and Conferences 8, no. 20. Washington, D.C.: American Council on Education, 1944.

"Responsibility of the School for the Improvement of American Life." In *Significant Aspects of American Life and Postwar Education*, compiled and edited by William C. Reavis, pp. 1–7. Proceedings of the Thirteenth Annual Conference for Administrative Officers of Public and Private Schools, vol. 7. Chicago: University of Chicago Press, 1944. Reprinted in *School Review* 52 (September 1944): 400–405.

1945

Foreword to *Summary of Survey Report, Battle Creek Public Schools, Battle Creek, Michigan*, by Committee on Field Services, Department of Education, University of Chicago, pp. iii–iv. Chicago: Department of Education, University of Chicago, 1945.

Foreword to *Survey of Public Schools, Battle Creek, Michigan*, by Committee on Field Services, Department of Education, University of Chicago, pp. iii–iv. Chicago: Department of Education, University of Chicago, 1945.

Foreword to *Survey Report, The Shattuck School, Faribault, Minnesota*, by Committee on Field Services, Department of Education, University of Chicago, pp. iii–iv. Chicago: Department of Education, University of Chicago, 1945.

Introduction to *American Education in the Postwar Period: Curriculum Reconstruction*, edited by Nelson B. Henry, pp. 1–4. Forty-fourth Yearbook of the National Society for the Study of Education, Part 1. Chicago: University of Chicago Press, 1945.

"What Rural Schools Can Learn from the Training Programs of the Armed Forces." In *Education for Rural America*, edited by Floyd W. Reeves, pp. 107–18. Chicago: University of Chicago Press, 1945. Retitled and reprinted in "What the Schools Can Learn from the Training Programs of the Armed Forces." *Elementary School Journal* 45 (May 1945): 495–502.

"Workshop to Study Methods of Evaluating Extension Education." In *Report of Workshop to Study Methods of Evaluating Extension Programs*, pp. 1–2. University of Chicago, March 12–24, 1945. Washington, D.C.: Extension Service, War Food Administration, 1945.

1946

"The Evaluation of Faculty Services." In *Problems of Faculty Personnel*, compiled and edited by John Dale Russell, pp. 124–33. Proceedings of the Institute for Administrative Officers of Higher Institutions, vol. 18. Chicago: University of Chicago Press, 1946.

Faust, Clarence, and Henry Heald. *Education and the G.I.'s*. University of Chicago Round Table Radio Discussion (Pamphlet) 432. In cooperation with the National Broadcasting Company, June 30, 1946. Chicago: University of Chicago, 1946. 21 pp.

Hostetler, C. E., and Floyd Reeves. *G.I. Education*. University of Chicago Round Table Radio Discussion (Pamphlet) 410. In cooperation with the National

Broadcasting Company, January 27, 1946. Chicago: University of Chicago, 1946. 21 pp.

"The Role of University Departments of Education in the Preparation of School Administrators." In *Educational Administration: A Survey of Progress, Problems, and Needs*, compiled and edited by William C. Reavis, pp. 31–45. Proceedings of the Fifteenth Annual Conference for Administrative Officers of Public and Private Schools, vol. 9. Chicago: University of Chicago Press, 1946. Reprinted in *School Review* 54 (October 1946): 451–61.

"Situations Requiring an Extension of Institutional Responsibilities for Counseling and Guidance." In *Emergent Responsibilities in Higher Education*, compiled and edited by John Dale Russell with the assistance of Donald M. Mackenzie, pp. 1–14. Proceedings of the Institute for Administrative Officers of Higher Institutions, vol. 17. Chicago: University of Chicago Press, 1946. Retitled and reprinted in "Extension of Responsibilities for Counseling and Guidance in Higher Institutions." *School Review* 53 (September 1945): 391–400.

"Summary of Criteria for Appraising a School's Reading Program." In *The Appraisal of Current Practices in Reading*, compiled and edited by William S. Gray, pp. 222–30. Proceedings of the Annual Conference on Reading held at the University of Chicago, vol. 7. Supplementary Educational Monographs 61. Chicago: University of Chicago Press, 1946.

"What Is Supervision?" In *North Central States Extension Supervision Workshop Report*, pp. 12–14. Ohio State University, Columbus, September 16–27, 1946. [Ohio State University, n.d.]

1947

"Discussion." [Aptitude testing.] In *Third Congress on Dental Education and Licensure, 1947*, pp. 65–68. Chicago: Council on Dental Education, American Dental Association, 1947.

"Evaluation of Extension Supervision." In *Western Regional Workshop for Extension Supervisors*, pp. 39–43. State College of Washington, Pullman, March 12–21, 1947. Pullman: Extension Service, Institute of Agricultural Sciences, State College of Washington, 1947.

Foreword to *Cooperation in General Education: A Final Report of the Executive Committee of the Cooperative Study in General Education*, pp. v–xi. Ralph W. Tyler, Director; William P. Tolley, Chairman. Washington, D.C.: American Council on Education, 1947. (The Foreword also appeared in three other study reports published by the American Council on Education: *General Education in the Humanities*, by Harold B. Dunkel [1947]; *General Education in the Social Studies*, by Albert W. Levi [1948]; and *Student Personnel Services in General Education*, by Paul J. Brouwer [1949].)

"Proposals for Adults." In *Administrative Planning for School Programs and Plants*, compiled and edited by Dan H. Cooper, pp. 14–24. Proceedings of the Sixteenth Annual Conference for Administrative Officers of Public and Private Schools, vol. 10. Chicago: University of Chicago Press, 1947. Reprinted in *Elementary School Journal* 48 (November 1947): 127–36.

1948

"The Accomplishments and the Promise of Educational Research in Sharpening the Tools of Educational Science." In *Improving Educational Research*, pp. 84–89. Official Report, American Educational Research Association, Atlantic City, February 21–24, 1948. Washington, D.C.: American Educational Research Association, 1948.

[Presentations on objectives, evaluation, extension program building.] In *Report of Home Demonstration Leaders' Workshop*, pp. 25–32. Purdue University, Lafayette, Indiana, March 3–16, 1948. [Purdue University, 1948.]

"The School Curriculum in General." In *Report of the Directed Self Survey, Winnipeg Public Schools*, by Committee on Field Services, Department of Education, University of Chicago, pp. 123–42. Chicago: Department of Education, University of Chicago, 1948.

"The Significance of This Investigation to School Administrators, to Teachers and to Students of Education." In *How Well Are Indian Children Educated?* by Shailer Peterson, pp. 113–17. Washington, D.C.: U.S. Indian Service, Department of the Interior, 1948.

Stoddard, George; and Louis Wirth. *Equality of Educational Opportunity*. University of Chicago Round Table Radio Discussion (Pamphlet) 562. In cooperation with the National Broadcasting Company, December 26, 1948. Chicago: University of Chicago, 1948. 17 pp.

1949

"Achievement Testing and Curriculum Construction." In *Trends in Student Personnel Work*, edited by E. G. Williamson, pp. 391–407. Minneapolis: University of Minnesota Press, 1949.

Basic Principles of Curriculum and Instruction. Syllabus for Education 360. Chicago: University of Chicago Press, 1949. 128 pp. (The University of Chicago Press has authorized translation of the syllabus into Danish, Dutch, German, Japanese, Portuguese, and Spanish, and publication of an edition in English in Nigeria.)

Bell, Laird, and Arthur H. Compton. *What Should Society Expect from a University?* University of Chicago Round Table Radio Discussion (Pamphlet) 574. In cooperation with the National Broadcasting Company, March 20, 1949. Chicago: University of Chicago, 1949. 11 pp.

"Educational Problems in Other Professions." In *Education for Librarianship*, edited by Bernard Berelson, pp. 22–38. Papers presented at the Library Conference, University of Chicago, August 16–21, 1948. University of

Chicago Studies in Library Science. Chicago: American Library Association, 1949; reissued, Freeport, N.Y.: Books for Libraries, 1970.

Preface to *Adolescent Character and Personality*, by Robert J. Havighurst and Hilda Taba et al., in collaboration with the Committee on Human Development, the University of Chicago, pp. vii–viii. New York: John Wiley and Sons, 1949.

Review of *Cooperative Test on Recent Social and Scientific Developments* (Grades 9–12, 1946–47). In *The Third Mental Measurements Yearbook*, edited by Oscar K. Buros, pp. 11–12. Highland Park, N.J.: Gryphon, 1949.

"The School Curriculum in General." In *Grand Rapids School Survey, Grand Rapids, Michigan*, by Committee on Field Services, Department of Education, University of Chicago, pp. 183–91. Chicago: Department of Education, University of Chicago, 1949.

1950

"The Curriculum and Instruction" and "The Elementary Schools." In *School Survey, Taylorville, Illinois, Community Unit District No. 3*, by Committee on Field Services, Department of Education, University of Chicago, pp. 66–74, 75–79. Chicago: Department of Education, University of Chicago, 1950.

"Discussion by Ralph W. Tyler." In *A Forum on the Public Library Inquiry*, edited by Lester Asheim, pp. 242–52. Conference at the University of Chicago Graduate Library School, August 8–13, 1949. New York: Columbia University Press, 1950; reissued, Westport, Conn.: Greenwood, 1970.

"The Organization of Learning Experiences." In *Toward Improved Curriculum Theory*, compiled and edited by Virgil E. Herrick and Ralph W. Tyler, pp. 59–67. Papers presented at the Conference on Curriculum Theory held at the University of Chicago, October 16 and 17, 1947. Supplementary Educational Monographs 71. Chicago: University of Chicago Press, 1950.

Tyler, Ralph W., and Herrick, Virgil E. "Next Steps in the Development of a More Adequate Curriculum Theory." In *Toward Improved Curriculum Theory*, compiled and edited by Virgil E. Herrick and Ralph W. Tyler, pp. 118–24. Papers presented at the Conference on Curriculum Theory held at the University of Chicago, October 16 and 17, 1947. Supplementary Educational Monographs 71. Chicago: University of Chicago Press, 1950.

Tyler, Ralph W., and William C. Reavis. Foreword to *Milwaukee-Downer College, Milwaukee, Wisconsin, Survey Report*, by Committee on Field Services, Department of Education, University of Chicago, pp. iv–v. Chicago: Department of Education, University of Chicago, 1950.

Tyler, Ralph W., and Herbert A. Thelen. "Implications for Improving Instruction in the High School." In *Learning and Instruction*, edited by Nelson B. Henry, pp. 304–35. Forty-ninth Yearbook of the National Society for the Study of Education, part 1. Chicago: University of Chicago Press, 1950.

Tyler, Ralph W., et al. "The Committee on Relations with Higher Institutions." Ralph W. Tyler, Chairman. In *New College Admission Requirements Recommended*, pp. 5–14. Circular Series A 51, Illinois Secondary School Curriculum Program, Bulletin no. 9. Springfield: Illinois Department of Public Instruction, 1950.

1951

Bettelheim, Bruno, and Ethel Verry. *Love Is Not Enough*. University of Chicago Round Table Radio Discussion (Pamphlet) 695. In cooperation with the National Broadcasting Company, July 22, 1951. Chicago: University of Chicago, 1951. 11 pp.

"Can Intelligence Tests Be Used to Predict Educability?" In *Intelligence and Cultural Differences: A Study of Cultural Learning and Problem-Solving*, by Kenneth Eells, Allison Davis, Robert J. Havighurst, Virgil E. Herrick, and Ralph W. Tyler, pp. 39–47, 375–81. Chicago: University of Chicago Press, 1951.

Durmas, Clifford; and Bertrand L. Smith. "Evaluation." In *The Schools and National Security: Recommendations for Elementary and Secondary Schools*, edited by Charles W. Sanford, Harold C. Hand, and Willard B. Spalding, pp. 247–49. [Illinois Secondary School Curriculum Program.] New York: McGraw-Hill, 1951.

"Evolving a Functional Curriculum." In *Annual Report of the National League of Nursing Education and Record of Proceedings of the Fifty-fifth Convention, 1951*, pp. 350–58. New York: National League of Nursing Education, 1951.

"The Functions of Graduate Departments and Schools of Education." In *Graduate Study in Education*, edited by Nelson B. Henry, pp. 10–21. Fiftieth Yearbook of the National Society for the Study of Education, part 1. Chicago: University of Chicago Press, 1951.

"The Functions of Measurement in Improving Instruction." In *Educational Measurement*, edited by E. F. Lindquist, pp. 47–67. Washington, D.C.: American Council on Education, 1951.

"Graduate Programs in Education at the University of Chicago." In *Graduate Study in Education*, edited by Nelson B. Henry, pp. 150–57. Fiftieth Yearbook of the National Society for the Study of Education, part 1. Chicago: University of Chicago Press, 1951.

1952

"Distinctive Attributes of Education for the Professions." In *Proceedings of the 1952 Annual Meeting, American Association of Schools of Social Work*, pp. 3–11. January 30, 1952. New York: American Association of Schools of Social Work, 1952.

1953

Anderson, G. Lester, and James Lewis. *What Makes a Good Public School?* University of Chicago Round Table Radio Discussion (Pamphlet) 815. In cooperation with the National Broadcasting Company, November 22, 1953. Chicago: University of Chicago, 1953. 17 pp.

"Clear Objectives in Supervision as a Means of Promoting Good Human Relations." In *Knowledge and Skill in Working with Others: Human Relations in the Organization, Supervision and Operation of Extension Work*, pp. 48–53. Chicago: Farm Foundation, 1953.

"How Do People Learn?" In *Increasing Understanding of Public Problems and Policies*, pp. 9–13. Group Study of Four Topics in the Field of Extension Education. Chicago: Farm Foundation, 1953.

"Translating Youth Needs into Teaching Goals." In *Adapting the Secondary-School Program to the Needs of Youth*, edited by Nelson B. Henry, pp. 215–29. Fifty-second Yearbook of the National Society for the Study of Education, part 1. Chicago: University of Chicago Press, 1953.

"What Research Shows about the Human Factors Involved in Organization of Staff and Personnel Management Procedures." In *Knowledge and Skill in Working with Others: Human Relations in the Organization, Supervision and Operation of Extension Work*, pp. 54–57. Chicago: Farm Foundation, 1953.

1954

"Brief Statement on Evaluation and the Construction of Examinations." In *The Teaching of Physiology, Biochemistry, Pharmacology*, pp. 163–65. Report of the First Teaching Institute, Association of American Medical Colleges, Atlantic City, October 19–23, 1953. Chicago: Association of American Medical Colleges, 1954.

Fact-Finding Study of the Testing Program of the United States Armed Forces Institute. Madison, Wisc.: U.S. Armed Forces Institute, 1954. 304 pp. + Analysis, 34 pp.

Foreword to *The Learner in Education for the Professions as Seen in Education for Social Work*, by Charlotte Towle, pp. v–viii. Chicago: University of Chicago Press, 1954.

Havighurst, Robert J., and Benjamin C. Willis. *The Teacher Crisis.* University of Chicago Round Table Radio Discussion (Pamphlet) 858. In cooperation with the National Broadcasting Company, September 19, 1954. Chicago: University of Chicago, 1954. 12 pp.

"Objective-Type Tests: Possibilities and Limitations for Graduate Schools." In *The New England Conference on Graduate Education*, pp. 11–18. Eleventh Annual Meeting, April 30–May 1, 1954, held at Massachusetts Institute of Technology, Cambridge. [New England Conference on Graduate Education, n.d.]

1955

Foreword to *Curriculum Study in Basic Nursing Education*, by Ole Sand, pp. ix–x. Basic Nursing Education Curriculum Study Series, vol. 1. New York: G. P. Putnam's Sons, 1955.

Tyler, Ralph W., et al. *Analysis of the Purpose, Pattern, Scope, and Structure of the Officer Education Program of Air University.* Technical Memorandum OERL-TM-55-6. Maxwell Air Force Base, Ala.: Officer Education Research Laboratory, Air Force Personnel and Training Research Center, Air Research and Development Command, 1955. 260 pp.

1956

"Clarifying the Role of the Elementary School." In *Education, 2000 A.D.*, edited by C. W. Hunnicut, pp. 221–34. Lectures Delivered at the Fiftieth Anniversary Celebrations of the School of Education, Syracuse University, Syracuse, N.Y.: Syracuse University Press, 1956. Published simultaneously in: *Elementary School Journal* 57 (November 1956): 74–82.

"Evaluation in Relation to Problem Solving." In *Science Teaching through Problem Solving*, edited by Hubert M. Evans, pp. 69–73. A Report of the Fourth National Convention, National Science Teachers Association, March 14–17, 1956. Washington, D.C.: National Science Teachers Association, 1956.

"Making the Most of a Scarce Resource." In *Expanding Resources for College Teaching*, edited by Charles G. Dobbins, pp. 96–102; "Discussion," pp. 102–30. Report of the Conference on College Teaching Sponsored by the American Council on Education, Washington, D.C., January 19–20, 1956. Series 1: Reports of Committees and Conferences 20, no. 60. Washington, D.C.: American Council on Education, 1956.

1957

"The Curriculum: Then and Now." In Proceedings of the 1956 Invitational Conference on Testing Problems, pp. 79–94. November 3, 1956. Princeton, N.J.: Educational Testing Service, 1957. ED 174 669.

"Educational Values of Cooperative Education." In *Highlights of the Conference on Cooperative Education and the Impending Educational Crisis*, pp. 35–38. Sponsored by the Thomas Alva Edison Foundation, Dayton, Ohio, May 23–24, 1957. New York: Thomas Alva Edison Foundation, 1957.

"Environmental Conditions for Effective Learning through Problem-Solving." In *Proceedings of the Summer Conferences and Institute*, vol. 10, compiled and edited by J. Alan Ross and Ralph H. Thompson, pp. 19–25. Western Washington College Bulletin 53, no. 3, December 1957. Bellingham: Western Washington College of Education, 1957.

"Evaluation of Learning through Problem-Solving." In *Proceedings of the Summer Conferences and Institute*, vol. 10, compiled and edited by J. Alan Ross and Ralph H. Thompson, pp. 12–18. Western Washington College Bulletin 53, no. 3, December 1957. Bellingham: Western Washington College of Education, 1957.

Facts about Practical Nurse Education in Michigan. Summary of the Evaluation Study of the Five-Year Experience with the Michigan State-Wide Program for the Education of Practical Nurses: 1947–1952. Condensed by Ralph W. Tyler from the full report prepared by Mary Schmitt. Lansing: Michigan Department of Public Instruction, 1957. 55 pp.

"Inter-Communication for Effective Learning through Problem-Solving." In *Proceedings of the Summer Conferences and Institute,* vol. 10, compiled and edited by J. Alan Ross and Ralph H. Thompson, pp. 3–11. Western Washington College Bulletin 53, no. 3, December 1957. Bellingham: Western Washington College of Education, 1957.

"Organizing a State Extension Research Program." In *Organizing for Using Research in Extension,* pp. 11–21. Summary of an Extension Research Workshop, Washington, D.C., May 6–10, 1957. Washington, D.C.: Division of Extension Research and Training, Federal Extension Service, U.S. Department of Agriculture, 1957.

"Scholarship and Education for the Professions." In *Education for Social Work,* pp. 13–22. Proceedings of the Fifth Annual Program Meeting, Council on Social Work Education, Los Angeles, January 23–26, 1957. New York: Council on Social Work Education, 1957.

"Summary of Answers to Work Group Questions on Organizing a State Extension Research Program." In *Organizing for Using Research in Extension,* pp. 22–26. Summary of an Extension Research Workshop, Washington, D.C., May 6–10, 1957. Washington, D.C.: Division of Extension Research and Training, Federal Extension Service, U.S. Department of Agriculture, 1957.

"Ways of Getting Findings from Extension and Other Social Science Research Used." In *Organizing for Using Research in Extension,* pp. 27–33. Summary of an Extension Research Workshop, Washington, D.C., May 6–10, 1957. Washington, D.C.: Division of Extension Research and Training, Federal Extension Service, U.S. Department of Agriculture, 1957.

"What Will Be the Emerging Curricular Implications for Colleges and Universities of the New Social and Technological Concepts?" In *Higher Education: A Bold New Look at the Not-Too-Distant Future,* edited by G. Kerry Smith, pp. 78–80. Current Issues in Higher Education, 1957: Proceedings of the Twelfth Annual National Conference on Higher Education, Association for Higher Education, Chicago, March 3–6, 1957. Washington, D.C.: National Education Association, 1957.

1958

"Changing Horizons in Nursing Education." In New *Dimensions of Learning in a Free Society,* pp. 177–86. Pittsburgh: University of Pittsburgh Press, 1958.

"Curriculum Organization." In *The Integration of Educational Experiences*, edited by Nelson B. Henry, pp. 105–25. Fifty-seventh Yearbook of the National Society for the Study of Education, part 3. Chicago: University of Chicago Press, 1958.

"The Education of Teachers: A Major Responsibility of Colleges and Universities." In *The Education of Teachers: New Perspectives*, pp. 233–41. Official Report of the Second Bowling Green Conference, Bowling Green State University, National Commission on Teacher Education and Professional Standards. Washington, D.C.: National Education Association, 1958. Reprinted from: *Educational Record* 39 (July 1958): 253–61.

["Emphasize Tasks Appropriate for the School." *Phi Delta Kappan* 40 (Nov. 1958): 72–74.]

"Essential Aspects of Evaluation: What Is Evaluation?" In *Evaluation of Reading*, compiled and edited by Helen M. Robinson, pp. 4–9. Proceedings of the Annual Conference on Reading held at the University of Chicago, vol. 20. Supplementary Educational Monographs 88. Chicago: University of Chicago Press, 1958.

"The Evaluation of Teaching." In *The Two Ends of the Log: Learning and Teaching in Today's College*, edited by Russell M. Cooper, pp. 164–76. Centennial Conference on College Teaching, Minneapolis, 1958. Minneapolis: University of Minnesota Press, 1958.

"Insights from the Behavioral Sciences." In *Faculty-Administration Relationships*, edited by Frank C. Abbott, pp. 33–43. Report of a Work Conference, May 7–9, 1957, sponsored by the Commission on Instruction and Evaluation of the American Council on Education. Washington, D.C.: American Council on Education, 1958.

"New Criteria for Curriculum Content and Method." In *The High School in a New Era*, edited by Francis S. Chase and Harold A. Anderson, pp. 170–82. Papers presented at the Conference on the American High School at the University of Chicago, October 28–30, 1957. Chicago: University of Chicago Press, 1958.

Tyler, Ralph W., and Lucile P. Leone. Foreword to *An Experience in Basic Nursing Education*, by Ole Sand and Helen C. Belcher, pp. vii–ix. Basic Nursing Education Curriculum Study Series, vol. 3. New York: G. P. Putnam's Sons, 1958.

Tyler, Ralph W., et al. "Recent Developments in Psychology and Their Application to Problems of Higher Education: Panel Discussion." In *The Carnegie Conference on Higher Education*, edited by Earl J. McGrath, pp. 5–18. Princeton, N.J., March 31–April 6, 1957. [Carnegie Conference on Higher Education, 1958.]

1959

"Background for Recent Curriculum Developments." In *Measurement Implications of Recent Curriculum Developments*, pp. 4–17. Eighth Annual Western Regional Conference on Testing Problems, Los Angeles, May 1, 1959. Princeton, N.J.: Educational Testing Service, n.d.

"A Behavioral Scientist Looks at Medicine." In *Report of the First Institute on Clinical Teaching*, edited by Helen H. Gee and Julius B. Richmond, pp. 136–43. Report of the Sixth Teaching Institute, Association of American Medical Colleges, Swampscott, Massachusetts, October 7–11, 1958. Evanston, Ill.: Association of American Medical Colleges, 1959. Published simultaneously in *Journal of Medical Education*, 34, part 2 (October 1959): 136–43.

Institutional Organization of the Behavioral Sciences. Voice of America Forum Lectures, Behavioral Science Series 2. Aired September 21 and 24, 1959; revised slightly and aired August 7 and 10, 1961, Washington, D.C.: Voice of America, 1959. 10 pp.

Introduction to *Objectives of the Social Work Curriculum of the Future*. Vol. 1: *The Comprehensive Report of the Curriculum Study*, by Werner W. Boehm, pp. xiii–xiv. New York: Council on Social Work Education, 1959.

Review of *College Entrance Examination Board Achievement Test in Social Studies* (Form FAC). In *The Fifth Mental Measurements Yearbook*, edited by Oscar K. Buros, p. 842. Highland Park, N.J.: Gryphon, 1959.

Review of *Sequential Tests of Educational Progress: Social Studies* (Grades 4–6, 7–9, 10–12, 13–14, 1956–57). In *The Fifth Mental Measurements Yearbook*, edited by Oscar K. Buros, pp. 847–48. Highland Park, N.J.: Gryphon, 1959.

"The School Librarian's Boss." In *The Climate of Book Selection: Social Influences on School and Public Libraries*, edited by J. Periam Danton, pp. 35–40. Papers presented at a symposium held at the University of California, July 10–12, 1958. Berkeley: University of California School of Librarianship, 1959.

"Science and Education in Today's World." In *Report of National Conference on Science in 4-H Club Work*, pp. 17–18. Sponsored by the Cooperative Extension Service and the National Science Foundation, Kellogg Center, Michigan State University, September 20–22, 1959. [Michigan State University, 1959.]

"Some Thoughts on Extension's Programs in the Years Ahead." In *Report of National Conference on Science in 4-H Club Work*, pp. 55–56. Sponsored by the Cooperative Extension Service and the National Science Foundation, Kellogg Center, Michigan State University, September 20–22, 1959. [Michigan State University, 1959.]

1960

"The Behavioral Scientist Looks at the Purposes of Science-Teaching." In *Rethinking Science Education*, edited by Nelson B. Henry, pp. 31–33. Fifty-ninth Yearbook of the National Society for the Study of Education, part 1. Chicago: University of Chicago Press, 1960. ED 012 233.

"Conclusion." [Summary remarks on trends and continuities in research on colleges and students.] In *The American College and Student Personality:*

A Survey of Research Progress and Problems, pp. 67–70. Report of a Conference on College Influences on Personality, Andover, Massachusetts, March 26–28, 1959. New York: Committee on Personality Development in Youth, Social Science Research Council, 1960.

"Conducting Classes to Optimize Learning." In *Achieve Learning Objectives*, pp. C1–C13. Papers prepared for a Summer Institute on Effective Teaching for Young Engineering Teachers, Pennsylvania State University, August 28–September 9, 1960. American Society for Engineering Education and the Engineers' Council for Professional Development. University Park: Pennsylvania State University, 1960. ED 011 861. (The Tyler paper was also published in 1961 and 1963 editions of the report.)

"The Contribution of the Behavioral Sciences to Educational Research." In *First Annual Phi Delta Kappa Symposium on Educational Research*, edited by Frank W. Banghart, pp. 55–70; "Symposium Discussions," pp. 85–112. Bloomington, Ind.: Phi Delta Kappa, 1960.

"Educational Objectives of American Democracy." In *The Nation's Children*. Vol. 2: *Development and Education*, edited by Eli Ginzberg, pp. 70–92. Golden Anniversary White House Conference on Children and Youth. New York: Columbia University Press, 1960.

Foreword to *Patterns of Professional Education*, by William J. McGlothlin, pp. ix–x. New York: G. P. Putnam's Sons, 1960.

Foreword to *Undergraduate Education for Social Welfare*, by Bernice Madison, p. vii. San Francisco: Frederic Burk Foundation for Education, 1960.

"How Can Research Help Public School Leaders Improve Education for Responsible Citizenship?" In *Education for World Leadership*, pp. 273–83. Yearbook of Addresses from the 1960 Convention of the National School Boards Association, Chicago, April 24–27. Danville, Ill.: Interstate, 1960.

"Implications of Research in the Behavioral Sciences for Group Life and Group Services." In *The Social Welfare Forum, 1960*, pp. 113–26. Official Proceedings, Eighty-seventh Annual Forum, National Conference on Social Welfare, Atlantic City, June 5–10, 1960. New York: Columbia University Press, 1960.

"The Importance of Sequence in Teaching Reading." In *Sequential Development of Reading Abilities*, compiled and edited by Helen M. Robinson, pp. 3–8. Proceedings of the Annual Conference on Reading held at the University of Chicago, vol. 22. Supplementary Educational Monographs 90. Chicago: University of Chicago Press, 1960.

"New Areas for Foundation Initiative." In *Proceedings of the Conference of Foundations*, pp. 14–22. Associated Colleges, Claremont, California, November 10, 1960. Claremont, Calif.: Associated Colleges, n.d.

"Psychological Knowledge and Needed Curriculum Research." In *Research Frontiers in the Study of Children's Learning*, compiled and edited by James B. Macdonald, pp. 36–45. Papers presented at a May 11, 1960, Conference at the University of Wisconsin-Milwaukee. Milwaukee: School of Education, University of Wisconsin, 1960.

"Social Trends, and Problems for Tomorrow's Schools." In *New Teaching Aids for the American Classroom*, pp. 3–9. A symposium on the State of Research in Instructional Television and Tutorial Machines, November 13–14, 1959, at the Center for Advanced Study in the Behavioral Sciences, under the auspices of the U.S. Office of Education and the Institute for Communication Research, Stanford University. Stanford, Calif.: Institute for Communication Research, Stanford University, 1960. ED 003 146.

"What Testing Does to Teachers and Students." In *Proceedings of the 1959 Invitational Conference on Testing Problems*, pp. 10–16. New York City, October 31, 1959. Princeton, N.J.: Educational Testing Service, 1960. ED 181 054.

"What We Think We Know about College Teaching and Learning." In *Proceedings of the American Association of Land-Grant Colleges and State Universities*, edited by Charles P. McCurdy, Jr., pp. 257–58. St. Louis, November 9–11, 1959. Washington, D.C.: American Association of Land-Grant Colleges and State Universities, 1960.

1961

"The Educational Potential of 4-H." In *Selected Readings and References in 4-H Club Work*, compiled and edited by G. L. Carter, Jr., and Robert C. Clark, pp. 12–16. Madison: National Agricultural Extension Center for Advanced Study, University of Wisconsin, 1961.

"The Impact of Students on Schools and Colleges." In *Social Forces Influencing American Education*, edited by Nelson B. Henry, pp. 171–81. Sixtieth Yearbook of the National Society for the Study of Education, part 2. Chicago: University of Chicago Press, 1961.

"Introduction to the Study: Conclusions and Recommendations." *In Work-Study College Programs: Appraisal and Report of the Study of Cooperative Education*, by James W. Wilson and Edward H. Lyons, pp. 1–14. New York: Harper and Brothers, 1961; reissued, Westport, Conn.: Greenwood, 1977.

"Mental Health and National Survival: Mr. Tyler's Analysis." In *Official Report, American Association of School Administrators for the Year 1960–61*, pp. 44–54. Washington, D.C.: American Association of School Administrators, 1961.

Preface to *Evaluating Liberal Adult Education*, by Harry L. Miller and Christine H. McGuire, pp. iii–iv. Chicago: Center for the Study of Liberal Education for Adults, 1961.

"The Purpose and Plan of This Yearbook." In *Social Forces Influencing American Education*, edited by Nelson B. Henry, pp. 1–7. Sixtieth Yearbook of the National Society for the Study of Education, part 2. Chicago: University of Chicago Press, 1961.

"The Role and Responsibility of the College to Public Education." In *Appropriate Directions for the Modern College in the Challenging New Educational Era*, pp. 3–15. The Fiftieth Anniversary Celebration of the North

Carolina College at Durham, November 9–12, 1960. [North Carolina College at Durham, 1961.]

"Social Forces Influencing American Education." In *Unity in Diversity*, pp. 42–52. Fourteenth Yearbook, American Association of Colleges for Teacher Education. Washington, D.C.: American Association of Colleges for Teacher Education, 1961.

"Some Guiding Principles for Decision-Making." In *Measurement and Research in Today's Schools*, edited by Arthur E. Traxler, pp. 20–31. A Report of the Twenty-fifth Educational Conference, New York City, October 27–28, 1960, held under the auspices of the Educational Records Bureau and the American Council on Education. Washington, D.C.: American Council on Education, 1961.

"Trends in Interdisciplinary Research." In *Trends in Social Science*, edited by Donald P. Ray, pp. 137–51. New York: Philosophical Library, 1961.

"Understanding Stability and Change in American Education." In *Social Forces Influencing American Education*, edited by Nelson B. Henry, pp. 230–46. Sixtieth Yearbook of the National Society for the Study of Education, part 2. Chicago: University of Chicago Press, 1961.

The Values of Cooperative Education. Address delivered at the Founder's Day Convocation, December 6, 1960, on the occasion of the observance of the fortieth anniversary of the inauguration of the Program of Cooperative Education at Drexel Institute of Technology. Philadelphia: Drexel Institute of Technology, 1961. 12 pp.

Tyler, Ralph W., and Annice L. Mills. *Report on Cooperative Education*. Summary of the Two-Year National Study of Cooperative Education. New York: Thomas Alva Edison Foundation, 1961. 32 pp.

Tyler, Ralph W., et al. *Building the Social Work Curriculum*. Report of the National Curriculum Workshop, Allerton, Illinois, June 13–18, 1960. New York: Council on Social Work Education, 1961. 85 pp.

1962

"Applications of the Behavioral Sciences." In *Teacher Education: A Reappraisal*, edited by Elmer R. Smith, pp. 41–50. Report of a Conference Sponsored by the Fund for the Advancement of Education. New York: Harper & Row, 1962.

"The Curriculum in Higher Education." In *Higher Education Tomorrow: Challenges and Opportunities for the University of Minnesota*, pp. 46–56. Report of the proceedings of a faculty conference jointly sponsored by the Graduate School Research Center, University of Minnesota, and the Louis W. and Maud Hill Family Foundation, March 18–21, 1962. Minneapolis: University of Minnesota, 1962.

"The Evaluation of General Extension in Land-Grant Institutions." In *Proceedings of the American Association of Land-Grant Colleges and State Universities*. Vol. 2: *75th Annual Convention, Centennial Convocation*, edited by Charles P. McCurdy, Jr., pp. 135–54. Kansas City, Missouri, November 12–16, 1961. Washington, D.C.: American Association of Land-Grant Colleges and State Universities, 1962.

Foreword to *The Scholars Look at the Schools*. A Report of the Disciplines Seminar, NEA Center, June 15–17, 1961. A working paper prepared for the Project on the Instructional Program of the Public Schools. Washington, D.C.: National Education Association, 1962.

Some Reflections on Soviet Education. Rochester, N.Y.: Rochester Institute of Technology, 1962. 31 pp.

"The Worth of a Small Christian College." In *Aurora College: A Dedication Record, the Charles B. Phillips Library*, pp. 5–10. Aurora, Ill.: Aurora College Library, 1962.

1963

"An Assessment: The Edge of the Future." In *The Social Studies: Curriculum Proposals for the Future*, edited by G. Wesley Sowards, pp. 119–32. Papers presented at the 1963 Cubberly Conference, School of Education, Stanford University. Chicago: Scott, Foresman, 1963.

"The Behavioral Sciences and Education." In *The 1963 Jennings Scholar Lectures*, pp. 113–28. Report on a program for outstanding teachers sponsored by the Martha Holden Jennings Foundation. Cleveland, Ohio: Educational Research Council of Greater Cleveland, 1963.

"The Impact of External Testing Programs." In *The Impact and Improvement of School Testing Programs*, edited by Warren G. Findley, pp. 193–210. Sixty-second Yearbook of the National Society for the Study of Education, part 2. Chicago: University of Chicago Press, 1963.

"Programming of Science and Technology within the Educational Structure." In *Science, Technology, and Development*. Vol. 11: *Human Resources: Training of Scientific and Technical Personnel*, pp. 133–43. U.S. papers prepared for the United Nations Conference on the Application of Science and Technology for the Benefit of the Less Developed Areas. [Geneva, February 4–20, 1963.] Washington, D.C.: U.S. Government Printing Office, 1963. ED 011 863.

"The Role of Machines in Educational Decision-Making." In *Proceedings of the 1962 Invitational Conference on Testing Problems*, pp. 102–13. New York City, November 3, 1962. Princeton, N.J.: Educational Testing Service, 1963. ED 173 437.

"Social Change and College Admissions." In *The Behavioral Sciences and Education*, pp. 1–8. Princeton, N.J.: College Entrance Examination Board, 1963.

"The Social or Behavioral Sciences." In *Science in the College Curriculum*, pp. 73–90 [comments on the Tyler paper and reply], pp. 91–98. Report of a conference sponsored by Oakland University and supported by a grant from the National Science Foundation, May 24–26, 1962. Rochester, Mich.: Oakland University, 1963.

"The Study of Campus Cultures." In *The Study of Campus Cultures*, edited by

Terry F. Lunsford, pp. 1–10. Papers presented at the Fourth Annual Institute on College Self Study, University of California, Berkeley, July 24–27, 1962. Boulder, Colo.: Western Interstate Commission for Higher Education, 1963.

1964

"Future Prospects of the Behavioral Sciences." In *The Behavioral Sciences: Problems and Prospects*, pp. 27–40. Boulder: Institute of Behavioral Science, University of Colorado, 1964.

"In-Service Training: Problems and Needs." In *Proceedings: Region Six Conference on Planning In-Service Training Programs for Mental Health*, edited by Joanna Nelle, pp. 3–10. Omaha, December 2–5, 1963. Omaha: Nebraska Psychiatric Institute, 1964.

"National Planning and Quality Control in Education." In *Modern Viewpoints in the Curriculum*, edited by Paul C. Rosenbloom with the assistance of Paul C. Hillestad, pp. 11–18. National Conference on Curriculum Experimentation, September 25–28, 1961. Institute of Curriculum Experimentation of the Center for Continuation Study, University of Minnesota. New York: McGraw-Hill, 1964.

"Research on Academic Curriculum Innovations." In *Research on Academic Curriculum Innovations*, pp. 3–4. Proceedings of the Sixteenth Annual State Conference on Educational Research. Conducted by the California Advisory Council on Educational Research for the California Teachers Association. Burlingame: California Teachers Association, 1964.

"Some Persistent Questions on the Defining of Objectives." In *Defining Educational Objectives*, edited by C. M. Lindvall, pp. 77–83. Report of the Regional Commission on Educational Coordination and the Learning Research and Development Center. Pittsburgh: University of Pittsburgh Press, 1964.

Tyler, Ralph W., et al. *The Foreign Student: Whom Shall We Welcome?* Report of the EWA Study Committee on Foreign Student Affairs, Ralph W. Tyler, Chairman. New York: Education and World Affairs, 1964. 35 pp.

1965

"A Behavioral Scientist's View of the Expanding Frontiers in Nursing." In *The Expanding Frontiers in Nursing*, pp. 1–10. Pittsburgh: University of Pittsburgh, 1965.

"The Center for Advanced Study in the Behavioral Sciences: An Experiment." In *The Creative Organization*, edited by Gary A. Steiner, pp. 246–54. Proceedings of a seminar sponsored by the Graduate School of Business. Chicago: University of Chicago Press, 1965.

"Criteria for Evaluating Research." In *Translating Research into Action*, pp. 1–23. Educational research symposium sponsored by District 1 and International Office, Phi Delta Kappa, October 22–23, 1965. Seattle: Office of Educational Research, College of Education, University of Washington, n.d.

"The Field of Educational Research." In *The Training and Nurture of Educational Researchers*, edited by Egon Guba and Stanley Elam, pp. 1–12; "Discussions," pp. 49–72, 111–37, 181–202. Sixth Annual Phi Delta Kappa Symposium on Educational Research. Bloomington, Ind.: Phi Delta Kappa, 1965.

"Innovations in Our Schools and Colleges." In *White House Conference on Education: A Milestone for Educational Progress*, pp. 185–90. Committee print, Subcommittee on Education of the Committee on Labor and Public Welfare, U.S. Senate, 89th Congress, 1st sess., 1965. Washington, D.C.: U.S. Government Printing Office, 1965.

[Report of Vice Chairman for Panels on Innovations in Education.] In *White House Conference on Education: A Milestone for Educational Progress*, pp. 201–203. Committee print, Subcommittee on Education of the Committee on Labor and Public Welfare, U.S. Senate, 89th Congress, 1st sess., 1965. Washington, D.C.: U.S. Government Printing Office, 1965.

"Sequences in Learning in Teacher Education." In *Eighteenth Teacher Education Conference*, pp. 1–6. University of Georgia, College of Education, Center for Continuing Education, January 20–22, 1965. Athens: College of Education, University of Georgia, 1965.

"Summary of Topic 6: What Is the Continuing Development of Occupation or Career after the Initial Commitment?" In *Summarizers' Reports of the Conference on Unexplored Aspects of the Development of Occupational Goals of Youth*, edited by Benton Johnson with the assistance of Joanne Kitchel, pp. 38–42. University of Oregon, August 9–13, 1965. Eugene: Center for Research in Occupational Planning, University of Oregon, 1965. ED 036 605.

1966

"Analysis of Strengths and Weaknesses in Current Research in Science Education." In *The Role of Centers for Science Education in the Production, Demonstration, and Dissemination of Research*, edited by John S. Richardson and Robert W. Howe, pp. 15–29. U.S. Department of Health, Education, and Welfare, Office of Education, Cooperative Research Project Y-002. Columbus: Research Foundation, Ohio State University, 1966. ED 013 220.

"Answers to Inquiries." In *National Educational Assessment: Pro and Con*, pp. 33–34. Washington, D.C.: National Education Association and American Association of School Administrators, 1966. ED 070 172.

"Assessing the Progress of Education." In *Education and Social Change*, pp. 82–85. Proceedings of the Fourth Annual Conference, National Committee for Support of the Public Schools, Washington, D.C., April 17–19, 1966.

Washington, D.C.: National Committee for Support of the Public Schools, 1966.

"The Behavioral Sciences and the Schools." In *The Changing American School*, edited by John I. Goodlad, pp. 200–14. Sixty-fifth Yearbook of the National Society for the Study of Education, part 2. Chicago: University of Chicago Press, 1966.

"Curriculum: Challenge for Experimentation." In *Nursing Education: Creative, Continuing, Experimental*, pp. 3–10. Papers presented at the Twentieth Conference of the Council of Member Agencies of the Department of Baccalaureate and Higher Degree Programs, Philadelphia, November 10–12, 1965. New York: National League for Nursing, 1966.

"The Development of Instruments for Assessing Educational Progress." In *Proceedings of the 1965 Invitational Conference on Testing Problems*, pp. 95–105. New York City, October 30, 1965. Princeton, N.J.: Educational Testing Service, 1966. Excerpts reprinted in "Assessing Educational Progress." *School Boards* 8 (December 1965): 6–8.

"Frontiers in Industrial Arts Education." In *Frontiers in Industrial Arts Education*, edited by Elisabeth MacDonnell and Floy Strosnider, pp. 15–22. Addresses and proceedings of the Twenty-eighth Annual Convention of the American Industrial Arts Association, San Francisco, 1966. Washington, D.C.: American Industrial Arts Association, 1966. ED 057 238. Published simultaneously in: *Journal of Industrial Arts Education* 25 (May–June 1966): 28–31.

"Resources, Models, and Theory in the Improvement of Research in Science Education." In *The Role of Centers for Science Education in the Production, Demonstration, and Dissemination of Research*, by John S. Richardson and Robert W. Howe, pp. 31–40. U.S. Department of Health, Education, and Welfare, Office of Education, Cooperative Research Project Y-002. Columbus: Research Foundation, Ohio State University, 1966. ED 013 220.

"The Social Sciences: Major Problems and Challenges of the Future." In *Expanding Horizons of Knowledge about* Man, pp. 25–33. New York: Yeshiva University, 1966.

"The Task Ahead." In *National Conference on Education of the Disadvantaged*, edited by Bernard Asbell, pp. 60–63. Report of a national conference held in Washington, D.C., July 18–20, 1966. Title I, Elementary and Secondary Education Act of 1965. U.S. Department of Health, Education, and Welfare, Office of Education. Washington, D.C.: U.S. Government Printing Office, 1966. ED 016 713.

"Values for a Changing America." In *Values for a Changing America*, edited by Helen Huus, pp. 28–42. Fifty-second Schoolmen's Week Proceedings, University of Pennsylvania, October 7–10, 1964. Philadelphia: University of Pennsylvania Press, 1966.

"What Is Evaluation?" In *Reading: Seventy-five years of Progress*, compiled and edited by H. Alan Robinson, pp. 190–98. Proceedings of the Annual

Conference on Reading held at the University of Chicago, vol. 28. Supplementary Educational Monographs 96. Chicago: University of Chicago Press, 1966.

Tyler, Ralph W., et al. *Dialogue on Out-of-Classroom Education.* A report on a consultation of educational experts on the role of the land grant university in informal youth education. Washington, D.C.: 4-H and Youth Development, Federal Extension Service, U.S. Department of Agriculture, 1966. 55 pp.

Tyler, Ralph W., et al. "A Program of National Assessment." Address and Panel Reactions. In *Official Report, American Association of School Administrators, 1965–66*, pp. 5–30. Washington, D.C.: American Association of School Administrators, 1966.

1967

"Changing Concepts of Educational Evaluation." In *Perspectives of Curriculum Evaluation*, by Ralph W. Tyler, Robert M. Gagne, and Michael Scriven, pp. 13–18. American Educational Research Association Monograph Series on Curriculum Evaluation. Chicago: Rand-McNally, 1967. ED 030 949.

"Development of the National Assessment Project." In *Improving Mathematics Education for Elementary School Teachers: A Conference Report*, edited by W. Robert Houston, pp. 76–83. Sponsored by the Science and Mathematics Teaching Center, Michigan State University and the National Science Foundation. East Lansing: Science and Mathematics Teaching Center, Michigan State University, 1967.

"The Educational Opportunity for the American College." In *Thoughts about the Private Colleges*, pp. 11–17. Delivered at the inauguration of the eleventh president of Blackburn College, Glenn Lowery McConagha, April 22, 1967. Carlinville, Ill.: Blackburn College, 1967.

"Hutchins, Robert Maynard." In *Encyclopaedia Britannica*, vol. 11, 1967, pp. 913–14.

"The National Assessment of American Education." In *Proceedings of the Summer Conference*, vol. 19, compiled and edited by J. Alan Ross and Ralph Thompson, pp. 1–7. Western Washington State College [Bulletin] 19, no. 3, January 1967. Bellingham: Western Washington State College, 1967.

"An Overview of American Higher Education." In *Higher Education in a Changing World*, pp. 62–68. Addresses selected from the 1965 Conferences for the Visiting Fulbright-Hays Scholars in the United States. Jointly sponsored by Stanford University, the George Washington University, Indiana University, and the Committee on International Exchange of Persons, Conference Board of Associated Research Councils, and Supported by the U.S. Department of State. [Washington, D.C., 1967.]

"Purposes, Scope and Organization of Education." In *Implications for Education of Prospective Changes in Society*, edited by Edgar L. Morphet and Charles O. Ryan, pp. 34–46. Reports Prepared for the Second Area Conference. Denver: Designing Education for the Future: An Eight-State Project, 1967; reissued, New York: Citation, 1967. ED 013 479. Condensed and reprinted in *Implications for Education of Prospective Changes in Society*, pp. 1–3. Summary of talks presented at the Salt Lake City Area Conference, October 24–26, 1966. Cheyenne: Wyoming State Department of Education, 1967.

Report of the Postdoctoral Educational Research Training Program of the Center for Advanced Study in the Behavioral Sciences. Stanford, Calif.: Center for Advanced Study in the Behavioral Sciences, 1967. 13 pp. ED 021 817.

Tyler, Ralph W., et al. *National Assessment of Educational Progress: Some Questions and Comments.* Department of Elementary School Principals in cooperation with NEA Center for the Study of Instruction. Washington, D.C.: Department of Elementary School Principals, National Education Association, 1967. 28 pp.

1968

The Challenge of National Assessment. The Virgil E. Herrick Memorial Lecture Series. [University of Wisconsin, July 1967.] Columbus, Ohio: Charles E. Merrill, 1968. 18 pp.

"Contributions of the Behavioral Sciences to Teacher Education." In *Vocational-Technical Teacher Education: National Seminar Proceedings*, compiled by Neal E. Vivian and Kenneth E. Hoffman, pp. 73–81. Held September 24–29, 1967. Columbus: Center for Vocational and Technical Education, Ohio State University, 1968. ED 020 431.

Foreword to *Picking Up the Options*, by Harold Howe II, pp. vii–viii. Washington, D.C.: Department of Elementary School Principals, National Education Association, 1968. ED 072 507.

"Human Behavior in a Humanistic Curriculum." In *Human Potential in a Dynamic Environment*, pp. 4–5. School Health Education Study, Airlie House Conference, June 9–11, 1968. Washington, D.C.: School Health Education Study, 1968.

"Investing in Better Schools." In *Agenda for the Nation*, edited by Kermit Gordon, pp. 207–36. Papers on Domestic and Foreign Policy Issues. Washington, D.C.: Brookings Institution, 1968.

"New Directions in Individualizing Instruction." In *The Abington Conference '67 on New Directions in Individualizing Instruction*, pp. 3–15. Willow Grove, Pennsylvania, April 23–25, 1967. Abington, Pa.: Abington Conference, 1968.

"The Rationale for Nationwide Assessment of Music Instruction." In *Music in American Society: Documentary Report of the Tanglewood Symposium*, edited by Robert A. Choate, pp. 78–80. Washington, D.C.: Music Educators National Conference, 1968.

"The Role of Music in Our Philosophy of Education." In *Music in American Society: Documentary Report of the Tanglewood Symposium*, edited by

Robert A. Choate, pp. 19–20. Washington, D.C.: Music Educators National Conference, 1968.

What Is an Ideal Assessment Program? Prepared at the Meeting of Special Consultants on the State Testing Program, Sacramento, July 19–21, 1968. Sacramento: Bureau of Reference Services, California State Department of Education, 1968. 9 pp.

"What Price Quality in Education?" In *The Unfinished Journey: Issues in American Education*, pp. 19–32. [Centennial volume, U.S. Office of Education.] New York: John Day, 1968.

Tyler, Ralph W., et al. *National Assessment of Educational Progress: Some Questions and Comments.* Revised edition. Edited by Dorothy Neubauer. Department of Elementary School Principals in Cooperation with NEA Center for the Study of Instruction. Washington, D.C.: Department of Elementary School Principals, National Education Association, 1968. 32 pp.

1969

"The Changing Structure of American Institutions of Higher Education." In *The Economics and Financing of Higher Education in the United States*, pp. 305–20. A compendium of papers submitted to the Joint Economic Committee, U.S. Congress. Joint Committee Print, 91st Congress, 1st sess. Washington, D.C.: U.S. Government Printing Office, 1969. ED 052 764.

"Charge to the Conference." In *Teaching Psychiatry in Medical School*, pp. 1–6. Working papers of the Conference on Psychiatry and Medical Education, held at Atlanta, March 6–10, 1967 under the auspices of the American Psychiatric Association and the Association of American Medical Colleges. Washington, D.C.: American Psychiatric Association, 1969.

"Education Must Relate to a Way of Life." In *Automation and Society*, edited by Ellis L. Scott and Roger W. Bolz, pp. 91–106. Athens, Ga.: Center for the Study of Automation and Society, 1969. ED 047 116.

"Educational Effects of Examinations in the United States." In *Examinations: The World Year Book of Education 1969*, edited by Joseph A. Lauwerys and David G. Scanlon, pp. 342–46. New York: Harcourt, Brace and World, 1969.

Foreword to *Evaluation and the Work of the Teacher*, by Enoch I. Sawin, p. v. Belmont, Calif.: Wadsworth, 1969.

Foreword to *A Guide to Curriculum Construction for the Religious School*, by Irving H. Skolnick, p. vi. Chicago: College of Jewish Studies Press, 1969.

Foreword to *Research for Tomorrow's Schools: Disciplined Inquiry for Education*, edited by Lee J. Cronbach and Patrick Suppes, pp. vii–ix. Report of the Committee on Educational Research of the National Academy of Education. New York: Macmillan, 1969.

"Impact of Testing on Student Development." In *Impact of Testing on Student Development* pp. 3–6. Addresses delivered at the Michigan School Testing Conference, University of Michigan, Ann Arbor, March 5, 1969. Sponsored by the University of Michigan, Bureau of School Services with the Cooperation of the University Extension Service. Ann Arbor: Michigan School Testing Service, 1969. ED 035 894.

Introduction to *Educational Evaluation: New Roles, New Means,* edited by Ralph W. Tyler, pp. 1–5. Sixty-eighth Yearbook of the National Society for the Study of Education, part 2. Chicago: University of Chicago Press, 1969.

Introduction to *National Assessment of Educational Progress: Citizenship Objectives,* pp. 1–3. Ann Arbor, Mich.: Committee on Assessing the Progress of Education, 1969. (The introduction or versions of it also appeared in nine other NAEP Objectives pamphlets on learning areas covered in the first assessment and in some on objectives covered in subsequent assessments. Other pamphlets in the initial assessment series published by the Committee on Assessing the Progress of Education were *Science Objectives* [1969] and *Writing Objectives* [1969]. The following pamphlets in the first assessment series, all entered into the ERIC data base, were published by the National Assessment of Educational Progress, which had become a project governed by the Education Commission of the States in mid-1969: *Literature Objectives* [1970], ED 041 009; *Reading Objectives* [1970], ED 041 010; *Social Studies Objectives* [1970], ED 049 111; *Mathematics Objectives* [1970], ED 063 140; *Music Objectives* [1970], ED 063 197; *Art Objectives* [1971], ED 051 255; and *Objectives for Career and Occupational Development* [1971], ED 059 119.)

"Keynote Address: Symposium on Medical Education and Practice." In *Medicine in the University and Community of the Future,* edited by I. E. Purkis and U. F. Matthews, pp. 1–4; "Round Table Discussion," pp. 73–78. Proceedings of the scientific sessions marking the centennial of the Faculty of Medicine, Dalhousie University, September 11–13, 1968. Halifax, Nova Scotia: Faculty of Medicine, Dalhousie University, 1969.

"The Learning Problems of the Young Adult." In *The Young Adult,* pp. 1–15. The 1967–68 Guest Lecture Series, Forest Hospital Foundation. Des Plaines, Ill.: Forest Hospital Foundation, 1969.

"Outlook for the Future." In *Educational Evaluation: New Roles, New Means,* edited by Ralph W. Tyler, pp. 391–400. Sixty-eighth Yearbook of the National Society for the Study of Education, part 2. Chicago: University of Chicago Press, 1969.

"The Problems and Possibilities of Educational Evaluation." In *The Schools and the Challenge of Innovation,* pp. 76–90. Committee for Economic Development, Supplementary Paper 28. New York: Committee for Economic Development, 1969; reissued, New York: McGraw-Hill, 1969.

"The Purposes of Assessment." In *Improving Educational Assessment and an Inventory of Measures of Affective Behavior,* edited by Walcott H. Beatty, pp. 2–13. Prepared by the ASCD Commission on Assessment of Educational Outcomes. Washington, D.C.: Association for Supervision and Curriculum Development, National Education Association, 1969. ED 034 730.

"Statement by Ralph W. Tyler and Discussion." In *Training Analysis: Report of the First Three-Institute Conference on Psychoanalytic Education*, by Charlotte G. Babcock, M.D., pp. 175–99. held at Western Psychiatric Institute and Clinic, Pittsburgh, April 1–4, 1965. Pittsburgh: Pittsburgh Psychoanalytic Institute, 1969.

1970

"Changing Responsibilities of Higher Education." In *Academic Change and the Library Function*, compiled by C. Walter Stone, pp. 5–26. Papers delivered at a meeting of the College and Research Division, Pennsylvania Library Association, October 1969. Pittsburgh: Pennsylvania Library Association, 1970. ED 047 707.

"Epilogue: Academic Excellence and Equal Opportunity." In Issues of the Seventies: The Future of Higher Education, edited by Fred F. Harcleroad, pp. 166–83. San Francisco: Jossey-Bass, 1970.

Introduction to *Every Kid a Winner: Accountability in Education*, by Leon M. Lessinger, p. xv. New York: Simon & Schuster, 1970.

"Schools for the 70's." In *Individualized Curriculum and Instruction*, edited by K. Allen Neufeld, pp. 7–16. Proceedings of the Third Invitational Conference on Elementary Education, Banff, Alberta, October 29–November 1, 1969. Edmonton: Department of Elementary Education, University of Alberta, 1970. ED 046 122.

1971

"Accountability in Education: The Shift in Criteria." In *Accountability in Education*, edited by Leon M. Lessinger and Ralph W. Tyler, pp. 75–79. National Society for the Study of Education Series on Contemporary Educational Issues. Worthington, Ohio: Charles A. Jones, 1971.

"Accountability in Perspective." In *Accountability in Education*, edited by Leon M. Lessinger and Ralph W. Tyler, pp. 1–6. National Society for the Study of Education Series on Contemporary Educational Issues. Worthington, Ohio: Charles A. Jones, 1971.

"The Concept of Functional Education." In *Functional Education for Disadvantaged Youth*, edited by Sterling M. McMurrin, pp. 3–23. Committee for Economic Development, Supplementary Paper 32. New York: Committee for Economic Development, 1971. ED 055 141.

"Concepts and the Teaching-Learning Process." In *Selected Concepts from Educational Psychology and Adult Education for Extension and Continuing Educators*, by J. Paul Leagans, Harlan G. Copeland, and Gertrude E. Kaiser, pp. 1–8. Syracuse University Publications in Continuing Education. Syracuse, N.Y.: Syracuse University Press, 1971.

"Curriculum Development in the Twenties and Thirties." In *The Curriculum: Retrospect and Prospect*, edited by Robert M. McClure, pp. 26–44. Seventieth Yearbook of the National Society for the Study of Education, part 1. Chicago: University of Chicago Press, 1971.

"Education: Balancing Conditioned Response and Responsible Claims." In *Environment and Society in Transition: Scientific Developments, Social Consequences, Policy Implications*, pp. 297–307. Annals of the New York Academy of Sciences, vol. 184. International Joint Conference of the American Geographical Society and the American Division of the World Academy of Art and Science, April 27–May 2, 1970. New York: New York Academy of Sciences, 1971.

Foreword to *Children Teach Children: Learning by Teaching*, by Alan Gartner, Mary Conway Kohler, and Frank Riessman, pp. ix–xii. New York: Harper & Row, 1971.

"In-Service Education of Teachers: A Look at the Past and Future." In *Improving In-Service Education: Proposals and Procedures for Change*, edited by Louis J. Rubin, pp. 5–17. Boston: Allyn & Bacon, 1971.

Introduction to *Discrepancy Evaluation for Educational Program Improvement and Assessment*, by Malcolm Provus, pp. 1–3; "Critique of the Model: Remarks by Ralph W. Tyler," pp. 120–25; discussion, pp. 140–41, 150, 152–53. Berkeley, Calif.: McCutchan, 1971.

"National Assessment: A History and Sociology." In *New Models for American Education*, edited by James W. Guthrie and Edward Wynne, pp. 20–34. Englewood Cliffs, N.J.: Prentice Hall, 1971. Reprinted in *School and Society* 98 (December 1970): 471–77.

"Report of the Ad hoc Committee on International Activities after the Granna Seminar." In *Report of the International Seminar for Advanced Training in Curriculum Development and Innovation*, pp. VI.7–VI.10. Granna, Sweden, July 5–August 14, 1971. Stockholm: International Association for the Evaluation of Educational Achievement, 1971.

"Testing and Assessment Programs, National." In The *Encyclopedia of Education*, edited by Lee C. Deighton, vol. 9, pp. 175–79. New York: Macmillan, 1971.

"Values and Objectives." In *Handbook of Cooperative Education*, by Asa S. Knowles and Associates, pp. 18–25. San Francisco: Jossey-Bass, 1971.

A Viable Model for a College of Education. Presentation at the inauguration of Dean Doi, University of Rochester, October 30, 1971. 14 pp. ED 059 961.

1972

"Annual Report of the Acting President." In *Social Science Research Council Annual Report, 1971–1972*, pp. 9–19. New York: Social Science Research Council, 1972.

Foreword to *Colleges and the Urban Poor: The Role of Public Higher Education in Community Service*, by Doris B. Holleb, pp. xiii–xiv. Lexington, Mass.: Lexington Books, D. C. Heath, 1972.

"More Effective Education for the Professions." In *Human Resources and Economic Welfare: Essays in Honor of Eli Ginzberg*, edited by Ivar Berg, pp. 229–40. New York: Columbia University Press, 1972.

"Summary of Conference." In *Proceedings of the National Conference an Cooperative Education*, pp. 45–47. Sponsored by the U.S. Office of Education, Manpower Institute, National Council of Northeastern University and National Commission for Cooperative Education. Newton, Massachusetts, April 20–21, 1972. Boston: Center for Cooperative Education, Northeastern University, 1972.

1973

"The Autonomous Teacher." In *Facts and Feelings in the Classroom*, edited by Louis J. Rubin, pp. 33–59. New York: Walker, 1973; reissued, New York: Viking, 1973.

"Can a University Determine Its Future?" In *Proceedings of the Higher Education Colloquium*, pp. 24–40. Chicago, March 11, 1973. ED 132 920.

"Educational Evaluation in the Revolutionary Age." In *Educational Communication in a Revolutionary Age*, compiled by I. Keith Tyler and Catharine M. Williams, pp. 101–18. Papers presented at the Edgar Dale Communication Conference, Ohio State University, May 9, 1970. Worthington, Ohio: Charles A. Jones, 1973.

"E. F. Lindquist, Educational Pioneer." In *Frontiers of Educational Measurement and Information Systems: 1973*, edited by William E. Coffman, pp. 5–11. Proceedings of an invitational conference on the Occasion of the Dedication of the Lindquist Center for Measurement, University of Iowa, Iowa City, April 6–7, 1973. Boston: Houghton Mifflin, 1973.

"An Evaluation of Test Development Procedures Used and Implications for Curriculum Design." In *A Structure of Concept Attainment Abilities*, by Margaret L. Harris and Chester W. Harris, pp. 387–94. Madison: Wisconsin Research and Development Center for Cognitive Learning, University of Wisconsin, 1973.

The Future of the University: Stasis and Change. CDC Development Paper 9. Lexington: Center for Developmental Change, University of Kentucky, 1973. 21 pp.

"How to Improve Instruction on the Basis of Evaluation." In *Better Instruction through Better Evaluation*, pp. 3–8. Proceedings of the Twenty-fifth Annual State Conference on Educational Research. Conducted by the California Teachers Association for the California Advisory Council on Educational Research, Los Angeles, November 29–30, 1973. Burlingame: California Teachers Association, 1973.

"Hutchins, Robert Maynard." In *Encyclopaedia Britannica*, vol. 11, 1973, pp. 913–14.

"Keynote Address." In *Getting Research and Evaluation Underway at All Levels of Community Education*, edited by Edward V. Kelley and Lawrence R. Wilder, pp. 1–10; "Concluding Remarks," pp. 35–36. Flint, Mich.: National Community Education Association, 1973.

Research in Science Teaching in a Larger Context. Science Education Information Reports, Occasional Paper Series, Science Paper 9. Columbus: ERIC Information Analysis Center for Science, Mathematics, and Environmental Education, Ohio State University, 1973. 14 pp. ED 076 426.

"The Right Student, the Right Time, and the Right Place." In *College/Career Choice: Right Student, Right Time, Right Place,* edited by Kenneth J. McCaffrey and Elaine King, pp. 1–13. Proceedings of the 1972 ACT Invitational Conference, Iowa City, May 8–9, 1972. Monograph 9. Iowa City: American College Testing Program, 1973. ED 089 598.

"Schools for Young Children: The Recent American Past." In *Education in Anticipation of Tomorrow*, edited by Robert H. Anderson, pp. 7–25. Worthington, Ohio: Charles A. Jones, 1973.

Tyler, Ralph W., et al. "Evaluating the Effectiveness of a Foundation Grant." In *Sharpening the Focus of Philanthropy*, pp. 31–38. Proceedings of the Fifteenth National Conference of the National Council on Philanthropy, Atlanta, October 25–27, 1972. Cleveland, Ohio: National Council on Philanthropy, 1973.

1974

Educating Children of the Poor: 1975–1985. Invitational Conference on Educating Children of the Poor, Chicago, April 1974. 19 pp. ED 092 643.

"Education: An Optimistic View." In *Social Psychiatry*, vol. 1, edited by Jules H. Masserman, M.D., and John J. Schwab, M.D., pp. 33–41. Colloquium, Fourth International Congress on Social Psychiatry, Jerusalem, 1972. New York: Grune and Stratton, 1974.

Foreword to *New Roles for Youth in the School and the Community*, pp. vii–x. National Commission on Resources for Youth. New York: Citation, 1974.

Preface to *Learning and Growing through Tutoring: A Case Study of Youth Tutoring Youth*, by Bruce Dollar, pp. i–iii. New York: National Commission on Resources for Youth, 1974. ED 118 661.

"The Theoretical Phase of Psychoanalytic Education: Teaching and Learning." In *Conference on Psychoanalytic Education and Research, Commission 1: The Tripartite System of Psychoanalytic Education Position Paper*, pp. 88–101. New York: American Psychoanalytic Association, 1974.

"The Use of Concepts in Developing a Curriculum." In The *Concept Approach to Programming in Adult Education: With Special Application to Extension Education*, edited by Mary L. Collings, pp. 16–32. U.S. Department of Agriculture Extension Service. Springfield, Va.: National Technical Information Service, U.S. Department of Commerce, 1974.

Tyler, Ralph W., and Richard M. Wolf, eds. *Crucial Issues in Testing*. National Society for the Study of Education Series on Contemporary Educational Issues. Berkeley, Calif.: McCutchan, 1974. 170 pp.

Tyler, Ralph W., et al. *Proceedings of the National Advisory Panel* [on Career Education]. Palo Alto, Calif.: American Institutes for Research in the Behavioral Sciences, 1974. 205 pp.

1975

"Competency-Based Education: A Curriculum Point of View." In *Competency-Based Education: Theory, Practice, Evaluation*, edited by Paul M. Halverson, pp. 117–35. Papers presented at a Conference on Competency-Based Education, University of Georgia, May 16–17, 1975. Athens: College of Education, University of Georgia, 1975.

"Education of Children for Environmental and 'Social' Awareness." In *Environment and Society in Transition: World Priorities*, edited by Boris Pregel, Harold D. Lasswell, and John McHale, pp. 250–52. Annals of the New York Academy of Sciences, vol. 261. Second International Conference on Environment and Society in Transition, held under the joint auspices of the American Division of the World Academy of Art and Science and the New York Academy of Sciences, May 6–11, 1974. New York: New York Academy of Sciences, 1975.

Foreword to *Update on Education: A Digest of the National Assessment of Educational Progress*, by Simon S. Johnson, pp. xi–xii. Denver: Education Commission of the States, 1975. ED 113 381.

"Historical Efforts to Develop Learning on a Competency Base." In *A CBC Primer*, by William R. O'Connell, Jr., and W. Edmund Moomaw, pp. 55–64. Report of a Conference: Competency-Based Curricula in General Undergraduate Programs. Atlanta: Southern Regional Education Board, 1975. ED 104 297.

"Implications of the IEA [International Association for the Evaluation of Educational Achievement] Studies for Curriculum and Instruction: Commentary 2." In *Educational Policy and International Assessment: Implications of the IEA Surveys of Achievement*, edited by Alan C. Purves and Daniel U. Levine, pp. 89–92. National Society for the Study of Education Series on Contemporary Educational Issues. Berkeley, Calif.: McCutchan, 1975.

"Managing and Evaluating Innovative Programs." In *Improving Education through Project Management, Evaluation and Communication*, pp. 1–3. Ohio Department of Education Spring Conference, March 26–28, 1975. Columbus: Ohio Department of Education, n.d.

"Procedures for Implementing Curriculum Changes in Local Educational Agencies." In *Improving Vocational Curricula in Local Education Agencies*, compiled and edited by Daniel E. Koble, Jr., and James G. Bumstead, pp. 55–65. Seventh Annual National Leadership Development Seminar for State Directors of Vocational Education. Columbus: Center for Vocational Education, Ohio State University, 1975. ED 112 114.

"The School of the Future: Needed Research and Development." In *The Future of Education: Perspectives on Tomorrow's Schooling*, edited by Louis Rubin, pp. 165–80. Research for Better Schools. Boston: Allyn & Bacon, 1975.

"Social Change and School Responsiveness." In *School Reforms of the 1970's*, edited by Audrey J. Schwartz, pp. 1–26. Proceedings of the Third Annual Conference of the Sociology of Education Association, Asilomar, Pacific Grove, California, January 31–February 2, 1975. Berkeley: Sociology of Education Association, School of Education, University of California, 1975.

"Specific Approaches to Curriculum Development." In *Strategies for Curriculum Development*, edited by Jon Schaffarzick and David H. Hampson, pp. 17–33. Berkeley, Calif.: McCutchan, 1975.

1976

The American Schools Can Meet the New Demands They Are Facing. Distinguished Lecture, Annual Convention of the American Association of School Administrators, Atlantic City, February 20–23, 1976. 8 pp. ED 119 305.

"Assessing Needs and Determining Goals." In *Proceedings: Conference on the Community/Junior College*, pp. 19–26. University of Tennessee, April 25–26, 1974. Knoxville: University of Tennessee, 1976. ED 203 889.

"The Competencies of Youth." In *From School to Work: Improving the Transition*, pp. 89–115. A collection of policy papers prepared for the National Commission for Manpower Policy. Washington, D.C.: U.S. Government Printing Office, 1976. ED 138 724.

"Dialogue." In *The Student as Colleague: Medical Education Experience at Case Western Reserve*, edited by Thomas Hale Ham, M.D., p. 92. Published under the aegis of the Division of Research in Medical Education, School of Medicine, Case Western Reserve University. Ann Arbor, Mich.: University Microfilms International, 1976.

Facilitating Learning with Adults: What Ralph Tyler Says, edited by G. L. Carter, Jr. Madison: University of Wisconsin–Extension, 1976. 54 pp. ED 132 289.

Foreword to *Reason and Art in Teaching Secondary-School English*, by Morris Finder, pp. xvii–xix. Philadelphia: Temple University Press, 1976.

Introduction to *Facing the Future: Issues in Education and Schooling*, by John I. Goodlad, pp. xi–xiii. New York: McGraw-Hill, 1976.

"An Overview of Basic Principles of Curriculum and Instruction. "In *Planning Curricula in Physical Therapy,* edited by Jean S. Barr, pp. 3–23. Washington, D.C.: Section for Education, American Physical Therapy Association, 1976; reissued, Birmingham, Ala.: Pathway Press, 1982. (Based on material in *Building the Social Work Curriculum* [1961].)

Perspectives on American Education: Reflections on the Past:. Challenges for the Future, edited by Dorothy Neubauer. Chicago: Science Research Associates, 1976. 165 pp. (Includes revised versions of the Patten Lectures published in Viewpoints 51 [March 1975]: 1–106.)

Prospects for Research and Development in Education. Edited by National Society for the Study of Education Series on Contemporary Educational Issues. Berkeley, Calif.: McCutchan, 1976. 183 pp.

"Rebuilding the Total Educational System." In *Between Home and Community: Chronicle of the Francis W. Parker School, 1901–1976*, edited by Marie K. Stone, pp. 297–302. Chicago: Francis W. Parker School, 1976. (A version of the paper was also published in *Schooling and Society,* 1981.)

"Trends, Issues and New Directions in American Education." In *Addresses and Interactions: Project 2000 Forum for Agricultural Education in Iowa*, pp. 182–91; panel discussion, pp. 192–204. Ames: Department of Agricultural Education, Iowa State University of Science and Technology, 1976. ED 147 479. (An outline of the Tyler address is included in *Summary of Proceedings: Project 2000 Forum for Agricultural Education in Iowa.* ED 147 478.)

"Uses and Abuses of Testing." In *Policy Issues in Education*, edited by Allan C. Ornstein and Steven I. Miller, pp. 19–28. Lexington, Mass.: Lexington Books, D. C. Heath, 1976.

1977

"The Curricular Deliberation." In *From the Scholar to the Classroom: Translating Jewish Tradition into Curriculum*, edited by Seymour Fox and Geraldine Rosenfield, pp. 98–103. New York: Melton Research Center for Jewish Education, Jewish Theological Seminary of America, 1977.

"Desirable Content for a Curriculum Development Syllabus Today." In *Curriculum Theory*, edited by Alex Molnar and John A. Zahorik, pp. 36–44. Selected Papers from the Milwaukee Curriculum Theory Conference held at the University of Wisconsin–Milwaukee, November 11–14, 1976. Washington, D.C.: Association for Supervision and Curriculum Development, 1977. ED 158 426.

Foreword to *Curriculum Evaluation: Theory and Practice, with a Case Study from Nursing Education*, by Joan L. Green and James C. Stone, pp. vii–ix. New York: Springer, 1977.

Foreword to *A Theory of Education*, by Joseph D. Novak, pp. 7–8. Ithaca, N.Y.: Cornell University Press, 1977.

"Innovation and Productivity: Possibilities, Conflicts, and Resistance." In *Innovation and Productivity in Higher Education*, edited by David T. Tuma, pp. 10–22; "Discussion," pp. 23–32. Papers and summaries of discussion from a conference held at Carnegie-Mellon University, Pittsburgh, October 14–16, 1976, cosponsored by United States Steel Foundation and Westinghouse Educational Foundation. San Francisco: San Francisco Press, 1977.

Interview in *Curriculum Change Toward the 21st Century*, by Harold G. Shane, pp. 156–58. Curriculum Series. Washington, D.C.: National Education Association, 1977. ED 140 443.

"Planning, Development, and Coordination: Overview." In *International Encyclopedia of Higher Education*, edited by Asa S. Knowles, vol. 7, pp. 3259–65. San Francisco: Jossey-Bass, 1977.

"The Total Educational Environment." In *Education for Responsible Citizenship: The Report of the National Task Force on Citizenship Education*, pp. 15–25. Cosponsored by the Danforth Foundation and the Institute for Development of Educational Activities, Charles F. Kettering Foundation. New York: McGraw-Hill, 1977.

"What Have We Learned about Learning?" In *Learning: An Overview and Update*, edited by Kenneth H. Hansen, pp. 1–13. Report of the Chief State School Officers 1976 Summer Institute. Sponsored by the U.S. Office of Education in cooperation with the Council of Chief State School Officers and the Colorado Department of Education. San Diego, July 29–August 6, 1976. Washington, D.C.: Office of Education, U.S. Department of Health, Education, and Welfare, 1977. ED 137 211.

Tyler, Ralph W., et al. *Implications of American Democratic Civic Ethics for Schools.* Edited by Joan D. Wallace. A symposium discussion sponsored by the Edward W. Hazen Foundation and the U.S. Office of Education, Washington, D.C., June 16, 1977. Philadelphia: Research for Better Schools, 1977. 34 pp. ED 150 062.

1978

"Accountability and Teacher Performance: Self-Directed and External-Directed Professional Improvement." In *The In-Service Education of Teachers: Trends Processes, and Prescriptions*, edited by Louis Rubin, pp. 132–52. Boston: Allyn & Bacon, 1978.

"Comments." [Achievement test selection for program evaluation.] In *Achievement Testing of Disadvantaged and Minority Students for Educational Program Evaluation*, edited by Michael J. Wargo and Donald R. Green, pp. 324–29. Papers presented at a conference sponsored by the U.S. Office of Education, Reston, Virginia, May 1976. Monterey, Calif.: CTB/McGraw-Hill, 1978.

"Conserving Human Resources: The School Dropout." In *From Youth to Constructive Adult Life: The Role of the Public School*, edited by Ralph W. Tyler, pp. 122–25. National Society for the Study of Education Series on Contemporary Educational Issues. Berkeley, Calif.: McCutchan, 1978.

"Education: Past, Present, and Future." In *Educational Reform for a Changing Society: Anticipating Tomorrow's Schools*, edited by Louis Rubin, pp. 177–87. Research for Better Schools. Boston: Allyn & Bacon, 1978.

"Educational Values of Cooperative Education." In *Developing and Expanding Cooperative Education*, edited by James W. Wilson, pp. 65–73. New Directions for Experiential Learning Series 2, 1978. San Francisco: Jossey-Bass, 1978.

Foreword to *Curriculum for Better School: The Great Ideological Debate,* Michael Schiro, pp. vii–viii. Englewood Cliffs, N.J.: Educational Technology, 1978.

Foreword to *The State of Teacher Education,* 1977, by Lewin Associates, Inc., p. i. Sponsored Report Series [National Survey of the National Center for

Educational Statistics. Washington, D.C.: U.S. Department of Health, Education, and Welfare, 1978]. ED 164 487.

"The Future of American Education." In *Focus on the Future: Implications for Education*, edited by B. Dell Felder et al., pp. 7–23. Houston: College of Education, University of Houston, 1978.

"Historical Perspective on the Role of the Parents in Education." In *Whose Child Is This?* pp. 1–7. Illinois Advisory Committee on Non-Public Schools Conference, October 10–11, 1977, Center for Continuing Education of the University of Chicago. Chicago: Illinois Advisory Committee on Non-Public Schools, 1978. ED 186 114.

"How Schools Utilize Educational Research and Development." In *Research and Development and School Change*, edited by Robert Glaser, pp. 93–105. A symposium of the Learning Research and Development Center, University of Pittsburgh. Hillsdale, N.J.: Lawrence Erlbaum Associates, 1978.

"A New Kind of Curriculum for the New Times." In *Perspectives on Improving Education: Project Talent's Young Adults Look Back*, edited by John C. Flanagan, pp. 39–46. New York: Praeger, 1978.

"A Statement from the ACT Board of Trustees." In *The American College Testing Program Annual Report, 1978,* p. 1. Ralph W. Tyler, Chairperson. Iowa City: American College Testing Program, 1978.

"What the Curriculum Field Needs to Learn from Its History." In *What the Curriculum Field Needs to Learn from Its History*, edited by Daniel Tanner, pp. 4–10. Symposium sponsored by SIG [Special Interest Group]: Creation and Utilization of Curriculum Knowledge, American Educational Research Association Annual Meeting, Toronto, March 30, 1978. ED 170 217.

Tyler, Ralph W., et al. *The Florida Accountability Program: An Evaluation of Its Educational Soundness and Implementation.* A Report of the Independent Evaluation Panel under contract to the Florida Teaching Profession–NEA and the National Education Association, Ralph W. Tyler, Chairperson. Washington, D.C.: National Education Association; Tallahassee: Florida Teaching Profession–NEA, 1978. 24 pp. ED 161 954.

1979

"An Advanced Study Center for Vocational Education: Goals and Challenges." In *Advanced Study Center: Proceedings of the National Faculty Plenary Conference*, compiled and edited by Elise B. Jackson and Earl B. Russell, pp. 11–16. Columbus: National Center for Research in Vocational Education, Ohio State University, 1979. ED 189 379.

"Conclusions." In *China's Schools in Flux*, edited by Ronald N. Montaperto and Jay Henderson, pp. 163–72. Report by the State Education Leaders Delegation, National Committee on United States–China Relations. White Plains, N.Y.: M. E. Sharpe, 1979.

"Curriculum Planning in Vocational Education." In *Vocational Instruction*, edited by Aleene A. Cross, pp. 57–66. American Vocational Association 1980

Yearbook. Arlington, Va.: American Vocational Association, 1979. ED 181 333.

"Educating Children Democratically." In *Educating All Our Children: An Imperative for Democracy*, edited by Doxey A. Wilkerson, pp. 2–15. Westport, Conn.: Mediax, 1979.

"Educational Improvements Best Served by Curriculum Development." In *Value Conflicts and Curriculum Issues: Lessons from Research and Experience*, edited by Jon Schaffarzick and Gary Sykes, pp. 237–62. Published in cooperation with the Association for Supervision and Curriculum Development. Berkeley, Calif.: McCutchan, 1979.

"Educational Objectives and Educational Testing: Problems Now Faced." In *Testing, Teaching and Learning: Report of a Conference on Research on Testing*, pp. 36–47. Sponsored by the National Institute of Education, U.S. Department of Health, Education, and Welfare, August 17–26, 1978. Washington, D.C.: U.S. Government Printing Office, 1979. ED 181 080.

Foreword to *The Skills of Teaching: Teaching Delivery Systems*, by Sally R. Berenson, David H. Berenson, and Robert R. Carkhuff, pp. i–ii. Amherst, Mass.: Human Resource Development Press, 1979.

"A Message from the Board of Trustees." In *The American College Testing Program Annual Report, 1979*, p. 3. Ralph W. Tyler, Chairperson. Iowa City: American College Testing Program, 1979.

"Teacher Education and the Improvement of Instruction." In *Teacher Education and National Development: International Perspectives on the Role of Teacher Education in Nation Building*, edited by Howard B. Leavitt and Frank H. Klassen, assisted by Woo Hyun Chyung, pp. 38–45. Proceedings of the 26th ICET World Assembly, Seoul, Korea, August 6–10, 1979. Washington, D.C.: International Council on Education for Teaching, 1979. ED 185 033.

Tyler, Ralph W., and Sheldon H. White. "Chairmen's Preface" and "Chairmen's Report." In *Testing, Teaching and Learning: Report of a Conference on Research on Testing*, pp. v–vi, 1–28. Sponsored by the National Institute of Education, U.S. Department of Health, Education, and Welfare, August 17–26, 1978. Washington, D.C.: U.S. Government Printing Office, 1979. ED 181 080. (The "Chairmen's Report" was also published separately in pamphlet form: *Testing, Teaching and Learning: Chairmen's Report of a Conference on Research on Testing*. Washington, D.C.: U.S. Government Printing Office, 1979. 37 pp. ED 214 950.)

1980

"Achievement Testing and the Publisher." In *Proceedings, The Third National Conference on Testing: Uniting Testing and Teaching*, edited by Richard M. Bossone, pp. 107–16. New York: Center for Advanced Study in Education, the Graduate School and University Center of the City University of New York, 1980. ED 190 647.

Educational Evaluation: A Retrospective View. Paper presented at the Annual Meeting of the American Psychological Association, Montreal, September 1–5, 1980. 11 pp. ED 193 275.

"Educational Technology: Influence and Future." In *Educational Media Yearbook 1980*, edited by James W. Brown and Shirley N. Brown, pp. 17–19. Littleton, Colo.: Libraries Unlimited, 1980.

If Not I.Q., What? September 18, 1980. 23 pp. ED 235 883.

"The Management of Educational Decline." In *Critical Issues in Educational Policy: An Administrator's Overview*, edited by Louis Rubin, pp. 4–12. Boston: Allyn & Bacon, 1980.

"The Needs of Elementary and Secondary Education for the 1980's." In *Needs of Elementary and Secondary Education in the 1980's: A Compendium of Policy Papers*, pp. 75–89. Committee print, Subcommittee on Elementary, Secondary, and Vocational Education, Committee on Education and Labor, House of Representatives, 96th Congress, 2d sess., January 1980. Washington, D.C.: U.S. Government Printing Office, 1980. ED 185 660 and ED 194 480.

"Parental Involvement in Curriculum Decisionmaking: A Review and Critique." In *A Two-Way Street: Home School Cooperation in Curriculum Decisionmaking*, edited by Robert L. Sinclair, pp. 1–8. Boston: Institute for Responsive Education, 1980. (The Tyler paper was entered separately into the ERIC data base: ED 191 596.)

"Reactor's Comments and Concluding Remarks." In *The Role of Education in the Re-Industrialization of the United States*, pp. 53–57. Proceedings of a conference multisponsored by Office of Occupational Planning, Bureau of Occupational and Adult Education, U.S. Department of Education; Council for Occupational Education of the American Association of Community and Junior Colleges; and American Society for Training and Development. San Francisco, March 30, 1980. Washington, D.C.: U.S. Department of Education, 1980. ED 204 606.

The Role of Assessment Information in Improving Educational Programs. Paper presented at the American Educational Research Association Annual Meeting, Boston, April 7–9, 1980. 19 pp. ED 194 563.

"Three Major Movements: As Viewed from Three Perspectives." In *Measuring Achievement: Progress over a Decade*, edited by William B. Schrader, pp. 69–72. Proceedings of the 1979 ETS [Educational Testing Service] Invitational Conference. New Directions for Testing and Measurement 5, 1980. San Francisco: Jossey-Bass, 1980.

1981

"Challenges for Teaching." In *The Future of Education: Policy Issues and Challenges*, edited by Kathryn Cirincione-Coles, pp. 141–52. Beverly Hills, Calif.: Sage, 1981.

Foreword to *Testing in the States: Beyond Accountability*, edited by Dale Carlson, pp. ix–xi. New Directions for Testing and Measurement 10, 1981. San Francisco: Jossey-Bass, 1981.

An Interview with Ralph Tyler. Conducted by Jeri R. Nowakowski. Occasional
   Paper Series 13. Kalamazoo: Evaluation Center, College of Education,
   Western Michigan University, 1981. 44 pp. ED 222 507. (Adaptation
   published as "On Educational Evaluation: A Conversation with Ralph
   Tyler." *Educational Leadership* 40 [May 1983]: 24–29.)
"Rebuilding the Total Educational System." In *Schooling and Society*, pp. 29–
   36. Perry Dunlap Smith Memorial Lectures. Chicago: College of Educa-
   tion, Roosevelt University, 1981. (A version of the lecture was published
   in *Between Home and Community: Chronicle of the Francis W. Parker
   School*, 1976.)
"Remarks." [Communication and its role in the education and development of
   children.] In *The Parent Participation TV Workshop Project Manual*, Part
   2, pp. 1–9. Third National Parent Participation TV Workshop Conference,
   Chicago Public Library Cultural Center, October 10, 1980. New York:
   Teachers Guides to Television, 1981.
"Societal Expectations for the American School: A Long View." In *Education
   in the 80's: Curricular Challenges*, edited by Lois V. Edinger, Paul L.
   Houts, and Dorothy V. Meyer, pp. 13–22. Essays in Memory of Ole
   Sand. Washington, D.C.: National Education Association, 1981. ED 209
   157.
"Testimony of Ralph Tyler." In *Minimum Competency Testing Clarification
   Hearing, July 8, 1981* [Day 1], pp. 196–216. Sponsored by the National
   Institute of Education. Washington, D.C.: National Institute of Educa-
   tion, U.S. Department of Education, 1981. ED 215 000.
"The Values of Cooperative Education from a Pedagogical Perspective." In *A
   Strategy for the Development of Human and Economic Resources*, pp. 31–
   36. Proceedings of the Second World Conference on Cooperative Edu-
   cation. Sponsored by Northeastern University, Boston, April 23–24, 1981.
   Boston: Northeastern University, 1981. ED 212 833. (Published simultaneously in *Journal of Cooperative Education* 17 [Summer 1981]: 43–
   56.)
"What Is Affective Education and How Do We Bring It About?" In *Children
   and Our Future*, edited by Irving N. Berlin, M.D., pp. 31–33. International Year of the Child Conference. Albuquerque: Division of Child and
   Adolescent Psychiatry, University of New Mexico School of Medicine,
   1981.

1982

"Integrated Research, Development, Dissemination and Practice in Science
   Education." In *Proceedings: Project Directors Meeting*, pp. 1–13. Washington, D.C., February 5–7, 1981. Washington, D.C.: Division of Science
   Education Development and Research, National Science Foundation,
   1982. ED 199 071 and ED 216 875.

1983

"The Meaning of Community Education: An Historical Perspective." In *For Every School a Community: Expanding Environments for Learning*, edited by Robert L. Sinclair, pp. 1–8. Boston: Institute for Responsive Education, 1983. ED 240 037.

Preface to *Philosophy for Education*, edited by Seymour Fox, pp. ix–x. [Festschrift dedicated to Robert Maynard Hutchins.] Jerusalem: Van Leer Jerusalem Foundation, 1983; Atlantic Highlands, N.J.: Humanities.

"A Rationale for Program Evaluation." In *Evaluation Models: Viewpoints on Educational and Human Services Evaluation*, edited by George F. Madaus, Michael S. Scriven, and Daniel L. Stufflebeam, pp. 67–78. Boston: Kluwer-Nijhoff, 1983.

The Tasks of UCEA for the '80's. UCEA Occasional Paper 8302. Paper presented at a UCEA Conference on Educational Leadership in Honor of Jack Culbertson, University of Texas at Austin, May 1982. Tempe, Ariz.: University Council for Educational Administration, 1983. 10 pp. ED 239 385.

"Testing Writing: Procedures Vary with Purposes." In *Literacy for Life: The Demand for Reading and Writing*, edited by Richard W. Bailey and Robin M. Fosheim, pp. 197–206. New York: Modern Language Association of America, 1983.

Tyler, Ralph W., and Ronald S. Brandt. "Goals and Objectives." In *Fundamental Curriculum Decisions*, pp. 40–52. Prepared by the ASCD 1983 Yearbook Committee, Fenwick W. English, Chairperson and Editor. Alexandria, Va.: Association for Supervision and Curriculum Development, 1983. ED 225 948.

1984

[Comments on questions.] "How Do We Get What We Know into Common Practice?" and "How Do We Develop Skill and Artistry in Our Practice?" In *Using What We Know about Teaching*, pp. 6, 9–10. [ASCD 1984 Yearbook.] Philip L. Hosford, Chairperson and Editor. Alexandria, Va.: Association for Supervision and Curriculum Development, 1984. ED 240 088.

"Comparing the Use of Research in Other Professions with Research in Education: 'The Use of Research by Engineers' and 'Diffusion and Adoption in Educational Practice.'" In *Using What We Know about Teaching*, pp. 18–19, 19–23. [ASCD 1984 Yearbook.] Philip L. Hosford, Chairperson and Editor. Alexandria, Va.: Association for Supervision and Curriculum Development, 1984. ED 240 088.

"Curriculum Development and Research." In *Using What We Know about Teaching*, pp. 29–41. [ASCD 1984 Yearbook.] Philip L. Hosford, Chairperson and Editor. Alexandria, Va.: Association for Supervision and Curriculum Development, 1984. ED 240 088.

"Evaluation in Human Resource Development." In *Joint Ventures Between Business and Higher Education: Human Resource Evaluation*, pp. 10–12. Report of the Conference Hosted by Arthur Andersen and Northwestern University. St. Charles, Ill.: Arthur Andersen, 1984.

Introduction to *No Adversary Situations: Public School Education in California and Wilson C. Riles, Superintendent of Public Instruction, 1970–1982*, edited by Sarah Sharp, pp. ix–xii. Berkeley: Regional Oral History Office, Bancroft Library, University of California, 1984.

"System Development Foundation." In *Foundations*, edited by Harold M. Keele and Joseph C. Kiger, pp. 407–409. Greenwood Encyclopedia of American Institutions 8. Westport, Conn.: Greenwood, 1984.

"Using Research to Improve Teaching Effectiveness." In *Perspectives on Effective Teaching and the Cooperative Classroom*, edited by Judy Reinhartz, pp. 38–41. Washington, D.C.: National Education Association, 1984. ED 250 279.

1985

"Conditions for Effective Learning." In *Education in School and Nonschool Settings*, edited by Mario D. Fantini and Robert L. Sinclair, pp. 203–229. Eighty-fourth Yearbook of the National Society for the Study of Education, part 1. Chicago: University of Chicago Press, 1985.

"Curriculum Resources." In *The International Encyclopedia of Education: Research and Studies*, edited by Torsten Husen and T. Neville Postlethwaite, vol. 2, pp. 1263–65. Oxford: Pergamon, 1985.

"Education for the Twenty-first Century: The Professorate, Curricula, and Applied Technology." In *Thirty-ninth Annual Proceedings of the National Conference of Academic Deans*, compiled by Thomas A. Karman, pp. 1–9. Oklahoma State University, July 28–31, 1985. Stillwater: Oklahoma State University, 1985.

Foreword to *Adapting Instruction to Individual Differences*, by Margaret C. Wang and Herbert J. Walberg, pp. ix–xii. National Society for the Study of Education Series on Contemporary Educational Issues. Berkeley, Calif.: McCutchan, 1985.

"National Assessment of Educational Progress." In *The International Encyclopedia of Education: Research and Studies*, edited by Torsten Husen and T. Neville Postlethwaite, vol. 6, pp. 3478–80. Oxford: Pergamon, 1985.

——— et al. *Conversations: 20 Years in American Education*, edited by Joslyn Green. Denver: Education Commission of the States, 1985. 47 pp.

Publications about
Ralph W. Tyler, and a
Bibliography of Tyler's Works,
1985–2002

COMPILED BY LISA N. FINDER, SERIALS LIBRARIAN, HUNTER COLLEGE

SELECTED CONVERSATIONS WITH
RALPH W. TYLER IN *EDUCATING AMERICA*

Chall, Malca. (Excerpts) Interviews conducted in 1985, 1986, 1987. In *Ralph W. Tyler. An Interview Conducted by Malca Chall.* Berkeley: Regional Oral History Office, Bancroft Library, University of California, 1987.

Fishbein, Justin M. "The Father of Behavioral Objectives Criticizes them: An Interview with Ralph Tyler." *Phi Delta Kappan* 55 (September 1973): 55–57.

Mickler, Mary Louise. "Interviews with Ralph W. Tyler." *Educational Forum* 50 (1985): 23–46.

Nowakowski, Jeri R. *An Interview with Ralph Tyler.* Occasional Paper Series, no. 13. Kalamazoo: Evaluation Center, College of Education, Western Michigan University, 1981.

Ryan, Kevin, John Johnston, and Katherine Newman. "An Interview with Ralph Tyler." *Phi Delta Kappan* 58 (March 1977): 544–47.

Shane, June Grant, and Harold G. Shane. "Ralph Tyler Discusses Behavioral Objectives." *Today's Education* 62 (September–October 1973): 41–46.

Tyler, Ralph W. "A Talk with Ralph Tyler." *Phi Delta Kappan* 49 (October 1967): 75–77.

ARTICLES ABOUT RALPH W. TYLER

Bloom, Benjamin S. "Ralph Tyler and the University of Chicago Examination System." *Teaching Education* 2 (1988): 47–53.

Bramwell, R. D. "Beyond Survival: Curriculum Models for Senior Adult Education." *Educational Gerontology* 18 (1992): 433–46.

Cooley, William W. "Review of *Educational Evaluation*, by Ralph Tyler." *Educational Researcher* 19 (December 1990): 29–30.

Eakins, Beverly K. "Alter Ego." *National Review* 48 (1996): 48–50.

Evangelauf, Jean. "At 86, a Minister's Son Still Spreads the Gospel of Education Reform." *The Chronicle of Higher Education* 34 (July 20, 1988): A3.

Goodlad, John I. "Ralph Tyler: The Educators' Educator." *Educational Policy* 9 (1995): 75–81.

Guskey, Thomas R. "Defining the Differences between Outcome-Based Education and Mastery Learning." *School Administrator* 51, no. 8 (1994): 34–37.

Helsby, Gill, and Murray Saunders. "Taylorism, Tylerism, and Performance Indicators: Defending the Indefensible?" *Educational Studies* 19 (1993): 55–77.

Hiatt, Diana Buell. "No Limit to the Possibilities: An Interview with Ralph Tyler." *Phi Delta Kappan* 75 (1994): 786–89.

Hlebowitsh, Peter S. "Amid Behavioural and Behaviouristic Objectives: Reappraising Appraisals of the Tyler Rationale." *Journal of Curriculum Studies* 24 (1992): 533–47.

Horowitz, Rosalind. "A 75-Year Legacy on Assessment: Reflections from an Interview with Ralph W. Tyler." *Journal of Educational Research* 89 (1995): 68–75.

Hunkins, Francis P., and Patricia A. Hammill. "Beyond Tyler and Taba: Reconceptualizing the Curriculum Process." *Peabody Journal of Education* 69, no. 3 (1994): 4–18.

Jones, Lyle V. "The Assessment of Student Achievement: The Hundred Years War." Paper presented at the Annual Meeting of the American Educational Research Association, Montreal, Quebec, Canada, April 19–23, 1999. ED 430 009.

Kliebard, H. M. "The Tyler Rationale Revisited." *Journal of Curriculum Studies* 27 (1995): 81–88.

Kridel, Craig. "Basic Principles of Curriculum and Instruction." Review of *Basic Principles of Curriculum and Instruction* by Ralph W. Tyler. *Educational Leadership* 57, no. 8 (2000): 80.

Lyons, Richard D. "Ralph W. Tyler, 91; Researcher Devised Nationwide Testing." *New York Times* (February 23, 1994): A17.

McLean, James E. "Sixty Years of Research in the Schools: A Conversation with Ralph W. Tyler." *Research in the Schools* 1 (1994): 1–8.

Meek, Anne. "On Setting the Highest Standards: A Conversation with Ralph Tyler." *Educational Leadership* 50, no. 6 (1993): 83–86.

Mickler, Mary Louise. "Interviews with Ralph W. Tyler." *Educational Forum* 50 (1985): 23–46.

Miller, James Grier. "Obituary" [includes edited excerpts from interview conducted in 1979]. *Behavioral Science* 40 (1995): 7–14.

"Ralph Winfred Tyler." *Encyclopedia of World Biography*, 2nd ed. 17 vols. Reproduced in *Biography Resource Center*. Farmington Hills, Mich.: Gale Group, 2003. Available at www.galenet.com/servlet/BioRC.

"Ralph Winfred Tyler." *Contemporary Authors Online*. Reproduced in *Biography Resource Center*. Farmington Hills, Mich.: Gale Group, 2003. Available at www.galenet.com/servlet/BioRC.

Reid, W. A. "Does Schwab Improve on Tyler? A Response to Jackson." *Journal of Curriculum Studies* 25 (1993): 499–510.

_____. "Ralph Tyler Revisited" [four questions critical to curriculum alignment]. *EPIEgram Materials* 15, no. 5 (1987): 1–3.

Rubin, Louis J. "Obituary." *Educational Researcher* 23 (June/July 1994): 32–33.

_____. "Ralph W. Tyler: A Remembrance." *Phi Delta Kappan* 75 (1994): 784–85.

_____. "Ralph W. Tyler Remembered." *Educational Leadership* 51 (1994): 84–85.

Schubert, William H. [Untitled.] *Journal of Curriculum and Supervision* 6, no. 1 (1990): 85–86. Lists books and videotapes featuring Ralph W. Tyler.

Simpson, R. D. "Ralph Tyler on Curriculum: A Voice from the Past with a Message for the Future." *Innovative Higher Education* 24 (1999): 85–87.

Smith, Robert G. "Fashioning Effective Solutions: The Promise of School." *Equity & Excellence in Education* 29 (1996): 20–29.

Stone, James C. "Review of *Educational Evaluation*, by Ralph Tyler." *Educational Evaluation and Policy Analysis* 12 (1990): 102–6.

Townsend, L. F. "An interview with Ralph Tyler." *Curriculum Review* 27 (1988): 16–18.

Walsh, S. M. "Toward Curriculum Development and Implementation: How Can Classical Concepts of an Educational Theorist Be Translated into a Specific Curriculum for a Course in Writing 'For Business and the Professions'?" Paper presented at the Annual Spring Conference of the National Council of Teachers of English, Boston, March 20–23, 1996. ED 397 445.

Wolf, Richard M. "The National Assessment of Educational Progress: The Nation's Report Card." *NASSP Bulletin* 77, no. 556 (1993): 36–45.

ARTICLES BY RALPH W. TYLER

Lorge, Irving, J. P. Guilford, and Ralph W. Tyler.. "Developing Conceptions of Educational Evaluation." *Illinois School Research and Development* 28, no. 2 (1992): 2.

_____. "Developing Tests to Assist in the Improvement of Education." *Improving Inquiry in Social Science: A Volume in Honor of Lee J. Cronbach*, edited by Richard E. Snow and David E. Wiley, pp. 325–32. Hillsdale, N.J.: Lawrence Erlbaum Associates, 1991.

_____. "Measurement and Testing." *Educational Measurement: Origins, Theories, and Explications*. Vol. 1: *Basic Concepts and Theories*, edited by Annie W. Ward, Howard W. Stoker, and Mildred Murray-Ward, pp. 1–123. Lanham, Md.: University Press of America, 1996.

Tyler, Ralph W. "Charles Hubbard Judd: As I Came to Know Him." *Teaching Education* 1 (1987): 19–24.

———. "A Comment." *The Educational Forum* 53 (1989): 135–37.

———. "Curriculum and Aims." Review of *Curriculum and Aims*, by Decker F. Walker. *Teachers College Record* 88 (1987): 604–608.

———. "Education Reforms." *Phi Delta Kappan* 69 (1987): 277–80.

———. "Equity as a Priority for Education in a Democratic Society." *Equity & Excellence in Education* 29 (1996): 9–10.

———. "Examining the Current Demands for Curricular Reforms from a Historical Perspective." *National Forum: Phi Kappa Phi Journal* 67, no. 3 (1987): 12–16.

———. "The Five Most Significant Curriculum Events in the Twentieth Century." *Educational Leadership* 44, no. 4 (1986/1987): 36–38.

———. "Making Education Reform Work." *The Education Digest* 53 (1988): 14–16.

———. "Placing Teaching in the Proper Perspective." *Kappa Delta Pi Record* 33 (1997): 155.

———. "Progress in Dealing with Curriculum Problems." Eighty-seventh Yearbook of the National Society for the Study of Education, part 1, pp. 267–76. Chicago: University of Chicago Press, 1988.

———. "Psychologically Informed Education: Historical Foundations." *Learning and Education: Psychoanalytic perspectives*, edited by Kay Fields, Bertram J. Cohler, and Glorye Wool, pp. 127–42. Madison, Conn.: International Universities Press, 1989.

———. "Reflections on My Experiences in and Observations of Education." *Reflections: Personal Essays by 33 Distinguished Educators*. Ed. Derek L. Burleson. Bloomington, Ind.: Phi Delta Kappa Educational Foundation, 1991.

———. "Review of *Curriculum*, by William Henry Schubert and *Curriculum and Aims*, by Decker F. Walker." *Teachers College Record* 88 (1987): 604–8.

———. "Review of *Progressive Education for the 1990s*, Eds. Kathe Jervis and Carol Montag." *Educational Policy* 7 (1993): 225–26.

———. "The Role of the Principal in Promoting Student Learning." *Educational Planning* 7 (1989): 38–42.

DISSERTATIONS ABOUT RALPH W. TYLER

Antonelli, George A. *Ralph W. Tyler and the Curriculum Arena: A Historical Interpretation*. Dissertation, Southern Illinois University, 1972. Ann Arbor, Mich.: University of Michigan, 1987.

Brown, Lee Howard. *A Study of a Process of In-service Education for Teachers of English with Reference to Chicago School Criticism and the Tyler Curricular Rationale*. Dissertation, State University of New York at Albany, 1987. Ann Arbor, Mich.: University of Michigan, 1987.

Greenland, David W. *Examination of the Propositions of Tyler and Dewey: Toward Deriving Implications for Program Development*. Dissertation, Temple University, 2000. Unpublished.

Levy, Richard David, and Ralph Winfred Tyler. *A Study of Ralph W. Tyler's Statement, Development, and Later Modifications of his Rationale as Set Forth in Basic Principles of Curriculum and Instruction*. Disseration, Temple University, 1972. Ann Arbor, Mich.: University of Michigan, 1987.

Muhamad, Mazanah. *Ralph W. Tyler's Perspectives on Designing and Facilitating Adult Learning*. Disseration, North Carolina State University, 1988. Unpublished.

Nash, Timothy Gerard Joseph. *Business Curriculum Development: A Model for Assessing Outcomes in a University Business Curriculum Using the Tyler Curriculum Model Framework*. Disseration, Wayne State University, 2002. Unpublished.

Park, Sang-Jin. *A Curriculum Model of Christian Education for Faith as Knowing God: A Critique of the Tylerian Model and a Search for an Alternative on the Basis of New Epistemology*. Dissertation, Union Theological Seminary and Presbyterian School of Christian Education, 2001. Unpublished.

Parker, Linda Carol. *A Historical Study of the Use of Program Evaluation in Education*. Dissertation, University of Tulsa, 1994. Unpublished.

Prestamo, Felipe J. *Architectural Education in Postindustrial America: An Application of the Tyler Model to the Development of a Curriculum Framework*. Dissertation, University of Florida, 1990. Unpublished.

Rumjahn, Miriam Cassandra. *A Chronicle of the Professional Activities of Ralph W. Tyler: An Oral History*. Dissertation, Pepperdine University, 1984. Ann Arbor, Mich.: University of Michigan, 1987.

Tyrrell, Ronald W. *Ralph W. Tyler's Influence on the Field of Curriculum*. Dissertation, Case Western Reserve University, 1970. Ann Arbor, Mich.: University of Michigan, 1987.

Vernazza, Martha Elin. *The Evaluation Principles of Ralph W. Tyler: Criteria for Decision Makers and Program Evaluators*. Dissertation, University of California, Berkeley, 1982. Ann Arbor, Mich.: University of Michigan, 1987.

Wesolowski, Mildred. *An Investigation of Selected Baccalaureate Programs in Nursing through Application of the Tyler Rationale*. Dissertation, Temple University, 1982. Ann Arbor, Mich.: University of Michigan, 1987.

INTRODUCTORY REMARKS BY RALPH W. TYLER

Tyler, Ralph W. Foreword to *Cooperative Education in a New Era: Understanding and Strengthening the Links between College and the Workplace*, by Kenneth G. Ryder, James W. Wilson, et al., pp. xiii–xvi. San Francisco: Jossey-Bass, 1987.

———. Preface to *The Ramah Experience: Community and Commitment*, by Sylvia C. Ettenberg and Geraldine Rosenfield. New York: Jewish Theological Seminary of America in cooperation with the National Ramah Commission, 1989.

BOOKS BY RALPH W. TYLER

Kirst, Michael W., and Ralph W. Tyler. *Evaluating State Education Reforms: A Special Legislative Report*. Denver, Colo.: National Conference of State Legislatures, 1987.

Tyler, Ralph W. *Changing Concepts of Educational Evaluation*. Oxford, N.Y.: Pergamon, 1986.

_____. *Improving School Effectiveness*. Amherst, Mass.: National Coalition for Equality in Learning, School of Education, University of Massachusetts, 1992.

_____. *Perspective on the Purpose of American Education*. Williamsburg, Va.: College of William and Mary, 1988.

Tyler, Ralph W., George F. Madaus, and Daniel L. Stufflebeam. *Educational Evaluation: Classic Works of Ralph W. Tyler*. Boston: Kluwer Academic, 1989.

Tyler, Ralph W., Carl Tjerandsen, and Malca Chall. *Education: Curriculum Development and Evaluation*. Berkeley: Regional Oral History Office, Bancroft Library, University of California, 1987.

Tyler, Ralph W., and Lucy Townsend. *Ralph W. Tyler*. DeKalb, Ill.: Northern Illinois University, Department of Leadership and Educational Policy Studies, 1988.

VIDEOTAPES BY RALPH W. TYLER

Tyler, Ralph W. *The Odyssey in Teacher Education: President's Brunch*. San Diego: s.n., 1988.

_____. *Ralph Tyler Educating America*. Bloomington, Ind.: Agency for Instructional Technology, 1994.

CASSETTE TAPES BY RALPH W. TYLER

Tyler, Ralph W. *Education for the 21st Century*. St. Louis: Association of Teachers of English National Conference, 1989.

_____. *The Odyssey in Teacher Education*. St. Louis: Association of Teachers of English National Conference, 1988.

_____. *Where Have We Been and Where Are We Going?* Alexandria, Va.: Association for Supervision and Curriculum Development, 1990.

Tyler, Ralph W., Gerald W. Bracey, Robert J. Sternberg, et al. *Issues in Testing and Assessment*. 3 audiotapes. Bloomington, Ind.: Agency for Instructional Technology, 1996.

Tyler, Ralph W., Graham Down, Maxine Greene, Walter Parker, and Barak Rosenshine. *Rethinking the Curriculum for the Next Decade*. 6 audiotapes.

Alexandria, Va.: Association for Supervision and Curriculum Development, 1990.

Tyler, Ralph W., Louis Rubin, and Harry Broudy. *Restructuring Schools: The Good, True, and Beautiful.* Alexandria, Va.: Association for Supervision and Curriculum Development, 1990–1991.

BOOKS ABOUT RALPH W. TYLER, 1986–

(Not including published dissertations, listed above.)

Chall, Malca. *Ralph Tyler. An Interview Conducted by Malca Chall.* Berkeley: Regional Oral History Office, Bancroft Library, University of California, 1987.

Kolodziey, Helen M., compiler. *Ralph W. Tyler: A Bibliography, 1929–1986.* Washington, D.C.: Ralph W. Tyler Project, National Foundation for the Improvement of Education, 1986.

Lackey, George H., Jr., and Michael D. Rowls. *Wisdom in Education: The Views of Ralph Tyler.* Columbia, S.C.: College of Education, University of South Carolina, 1989.

Lagemann, Ellen Condliffe. *An Elusive Science: The Troubling History of Education Research.* Chicago: University of Chicago Press, 2000.

Index

About the Author

MORRIS FINDER is Professor Emeritus of English Education, School of Education, the State University of New York, Albany. He is the author of many professional articles and books. He received his Ph.D. in Education from the University of Chicago, where he met Ralph W. Tyler. He has taught in universities in the United States and abroad.